Praise for
Free to Believe

"Religious freedom is one of the most important civil rights issues of our time, and Luke Goodrich is at the forefront of the battle. If you want to understand religious freedom and how to protect it, you need this book."

—ERIC METAXAS, *New York Times* number one best-selling author
of *Bonhoeffer, Martin Luther,* and *If You Can Keep It*

"Religious liberty is too important to be just another culture war skirmish. If the soul is not free, every other freedom is in jeopardy. We live in a time when religious freedom is rarely discussed without either alarmism or dismissal. Luke Goodrich is one of the nation's most respected thought leaders in the arena of liberty of conscience. In this book he reframes our context, connecting us with generations past and prognosticating on the challenges of the future. I hope many people, both religious and secular, will read this volume and recommit to a society where all consciences are free to believe, to worship, to serve, and to live."

—RUSSELL MOORE, president of the Ethics and Religious Liberty
Commission of the Southern Baptist Convention

"With the religious freedoms that Americans have long taken for granted now under fierce attack, Luke Goodrich not only sounds an alarm about the challenges ahead but also offers practical guidance on how to confront them. This wise, faith-filled, and eminently readable book should be in the hands of everyone who values religious liberty."

—MARY ANN GLENDON, Learned Hand Professor of Law at Harvard
University and author of *A World Made New*

"Today more than ever, thoughtful citizens need a clear, credible, and intelligible text that makes the case for preserving the precious gift of religious liberty. In *Free to Believe* Luke Goodrich provides this much-needed narrative."

—Most Reverend Joseph E. Kurtz, DD, archbishop of Louisville and former president of the United States Conference of Catholic Bishops

"The first time I heard Luke Goodrich speak about religious freedom, I realized he was inviting me into a conversation I had never had before. Luke's teachings on religious freedom are based not on fear, tradition, or partisanship but on Jesus. He has opened my eyes, as a pastor, to the reality that religious liberty is not something invented by our US Constitution but is deeply embedded in the Bible, the gospel of Jesus, and the heart of God. Pastors, this book is a gift to us! It's a remarkable tool that helps us reimagine for ourselves and our congregations what it means to respond to the religious liberty conversation through the lens of the gospel."

—Kyle Costello, lead pastor of Mariners Church Huntington Beach

"As a journalist who writes about religious liberty issues, I often despair over how little Christians know about dire looming threats to our most fundamental freedom. Luke Goodrich's book is the smart, plainspoken, biblically literate, and legally sound guide that churches, Christian schools, and business-owning believers desperately need to read as the conflicts between the faith and its enemies intensify. Buy this book and read it closely: the institution you save may be your own."

—Rod Dreher, author of *The Benedict Option*

"Today religious liberty is more likely to be carelessly disregarded as a special interest than faithfully upheld as a fundamental human right. People who love freedom need compelling arguments to offer in response—the kind of arguments that Luke Goodrich makes in *Free to Believe*. In addition to offering biblical and theological reasons that all people (not just Christians) should have freedom of religious conscience, Goodrich uses his experience as a lawyer with a winning record before the Supreme Court to address the most challenging religious liberty issues that our culture faces today."

—Philip Ryken, president of Wheaton College

"*Free to Believe* is a book for Christians struggling to understand biblical principles of freedom of religion—a freedom that extends to all faiths and even to unbelief. Authors who truly understand the principles of our First Amendment are rare, and those among them who know and love the Scripture are rarer still. Luke Goodrich, one of America's top litigators in religious freedom cases and a devoted servant of Christ, is both, and his book offers insight, faith, passion, and above all clarity."

—Michael McConnell, director of the Constitutional Law Center at Stanford Law School and former circuit judge on the United States Court of Appeals for the Tenth Circuit

"Religious freedom is the quintessential firewall against totalitarianism. In his new book Luke Goodrich equips us with this truth: freedom to believe stands as the facilitative womb from which all other freedoms flow. This book will not only inform you but also inspire you to stand as an advocate for religious freedom, not just for our generation but for generations to come."

—Samuel Rodriguez, lead pastor of New Season, president of the National Hispanic Christian Leadership Conference, author of *You Are Next,* and executive producer of the movie *Breakthrough*

"Goodrich's defense of religious liberty is compelling for four reasons: it's comprehensive about today's challenges to our First Amendment; it's filled with both an unvarnished realism and hope grounded in deep faith; it's shaped by the author's keen legal intellect and rich experience with the law; and it's wonderfully readable. The United States is a republic founded on the commonsense and fundamental rights of everyday citizens. This is a vitally important book for all of us who value those rights and the best ideals of our nation."

—Most Reverend Charles J. Chaput, OFM Cap., archbishop
of Philadelphia

"As a top attorney with Becket, our nation's premier religious liberty appellate advocacy law firm, Luke Goodrich has been on the front lines in the battle to protect the rights of people of every faith and shade of belief. With the basic human—and constitutional—right to religious freedom under assault from many different quarters, it is a difficult and ongoing struggle. As Goodrich recounts in his marvelous new book, there have of late been some important and exciting victories in the Supreme Court and other federal and state tribunals. But enormous challenges lie ahead. In meeting these challenges, having an informed and engaged citizenry is critical. That's why *Free to Believe* is such a blessing."

—Robert P. George, McCormick Professor of Jurisprudence
at Princeton University

"Should Christians defend the religious liberty of non-Christians? And if so, why and how? These are but some of the crucial questions on which Luke Goodrich focuses his formidable intellect in his important new book, *Free to Believe.* Goodrich brings to bear his experience as one of the country's premier religious liberty litigators and his lifelong love of the Scriptures. The result is a book that no one, on any side of these questions, can ignore. And it's a great read besides."

—Kevin J. "Seamus" Hasson, founder and president emeritus
of the Becket Fund for Religious Liberty and author of *The Right to Be Wrong*

FREE
TO
BELIEVE

FREE
TO
BELIEVE

The Battle over Religious
Liberty in America

LUKE
GOODRICH

MULTNOMAH

FREE TO BELIEVE

Hardcover ISBN 978-0-525-65290-8
eBook ISBN 978-0-525-65291-5

Published in the United States by Multnomah, an imprint of Random House, a division of Penguin Random House LLC.

MULTNOMAH® and its mountain colophon are registered trademarks of Penguin Random House LLC.

Library of Congress Cataloging-in-Publication Data
Names: Goodrich, Luke W., author.
Title: Free to believe : the battle over religious liberty in America / Luke W Goodrich.
Description: First Edition. | Colorado Springs : Multnomah, 2019. | Includes bibliographical references.
Identifiers: LCCN 2018055238 | ISBN 9780525652908 (hardcover) | ISBN 9780525652915 (electronic)
Subjects: LCSH: Freedom of religion—United States
Classification: LCC BV741 .G65 2019 | DDC 323.44/20973—dc23
LC record available at https://lccn.loc.gov/2018055238

Printed in the United States of America
2019—First Edition

10 9 8 7 6 5 4 3 2 1

SPECIAL SALES
Most Multnomah books are available at special quantity discounts when purchased in bulk by corporations, organizations, and special-interest groups. Custom imprinting or excerpting can also be done to fit special needs. For information, please email specialmarketscms@penguinrandomhouse.com.

For the church.

Not by might, nor by power, but by my Spirit,
says the LORD of hosts.
—Zechariah 4:6

Contents

Introduction

No one told me the lawyers' table in the Supreme Court is so close to the justices. I could almost reach across the massive mahogany bench and touch them. I sat just feet from Justice Breyer, studying his face and listening intently—when suddenly he suggested my client should lose.

My heart dropped into my stomach.

Had we come so far only to lose at the last moment? Our team had spent months preparing our legal arguments. The *Wall Street Journal* called it one of the "most important religious liberty cases in a half century."[1] Now we were finally in front of the justices, and no one knew how the case would end.

But I knew how it began—with a simple disagreement that could happen at any church.

This time it was Hosanna-Tabor Evangelical Lutheran Church in Redford, Michigan. The church had 150 members and a small grade school with seven teachers. The fourth-grade teacher, Cheryl Perich, fell ill and missed the first half of the school year. To keep the doors open, the school initially combined three grades in one classroom. But when parents complained, the school hired a replacement teacher and asked Perich to consider taking the rest of the semester off and returning to work the following school year.

Perich wasn't happy. She presented a doctor's note saying she was cleared for work, showed up at school, and demanded her job back. When the school explained that it couldn't just fire the replacement teacher, Perich threatened to sue the church.

This behavior was deeply troubling to the church. Perich had a long-standing relationship with the church, and she knew they had no lawyer and no money. More importantly, she knew they were a *church*—a group of Christians who are supposed to love one another, not sue one another.

Unable to reconcile with Perich, the school board met with church leadership. Together they met with the congregation and Perich. After much prayer and discussion, the congregation voted to remove Perich from her teaching position.

It was a hard decision, with hurt feelings on both sides. But it wasn't an unusual decision. Churches have to make hard decisions like this all the time. Most of the time, people move on and life returns to normal. But this time life didn't return to normal: Perich sued the church.

Perich claimed the church had discriminated against her by not letting her return to work immediately and by firing her when she threatened to sue. She demanded her job back, along with hundreds of thousands of dollars in damages and attorneys' fees.

In response, the church said Perich was no longer qualified to be a teacher because she had threatened to sue the church in violation of 1 Corinthians 6:1–8, which instructs Christians not to sue one another in secular court. It also argued it would be unconstitutional for a court to force the church to employ a teacher who had violated church teaching.

By the time the case reached the Supreme Court, the stakes couldn't have been higher. The case was no longer about a small Lutheran church in Michigan; it was about the freedom of *all* churches to choose their leaders in accordance with their beliefs. Could a church be sued for discrimination if it hired only male pastors? Could a Christian school be sued for discrimination if it dismissed a teacher for having an extramarital affair?

These are the kinds of questions the justices debated as we sat among the massive marble pillars of the Supreme Court.

FOOD FOR THOUGHT

Before I tell you the outcome, I'd like you to consider a few questions:

First, have you heard of this case before? It was decided in 2012 and is one of the most important religious freedom cases in a generation. Yet most Christians haven't heard of it. Why do you think that is?

Second, how do you think the case *should* turn out? And, more importantly, how would you explain your answer to a skeptical friend?

As for the first question, most Christians haven't heard of the case because they're busy with other important things—family, work, school, church, and so forth—and don't have time to follow every new religious freedom case. What they know about religious freedom comes mostly from what they hear in the news, see on social media, or learn from family and friends. Religious freedom is not their top priority.

As for the second question—how *should* the case turn out and why?—many Christians would struggle to give a confident answer. Some instinctively side with the teacher because she lost her job and claims to be a victim of discrimination—and we all know discrimination is bad. Others tend to side with the church because, well, it's the church. Most have a hard time explaining who should win and why it matters.

These responses are neither surprising nor unreasonable. Religious freedom is only one of many important issues affecting our lives, and we can't be experts on everything.

But this also means most Christians are very poorly informed about religious freedom. We may have been told that the Supreme Court removed prayer from public schools or that there is yet another lawsuit challenging a nativity scene at Christmas. We may have heard that a county clerk got in trouble for refusing to issue same-sex marriage licenses or that a baker was sued for refusing to bake a cake for a same-sex wedding. But most of this information comes to us as mere background noise. We have a vague sense that religious freedom conflicts are increasingly common and that maybe we should start paying more attention. But we don't know where to start.

As long as life keeps humming along normally and we never face a violation of our religious freedom, our inattention won't be a problem. But if things change—if our culture shifts and we start facing violations of our religious freedom—we'll be caught unprepared.

AMONG CHRISTIAN LEADERS

This point hit home when I attended a gathering of Christian leaders who were concerned about religious freedom—pastors, theologians, university presidents, and ministry CEOs, many of them prominent leaders in the Christian world. We gathered as courts across the country were starting to legalize same-sex marriage.

The fear in the room was palpable. These leaders were *not* apathetic about religious freedom; they were on full alert. They had a deep sense of responsibility for the organizations they led and the people they served. They also had a deep sense of concern that our culture is changing and that the climate for religious freedom is deteriorating. Some of these leaders had already been confronted with religious freedom conflicts of their own: their organizations had been kicked off university campuses, penalized by local governments, or pilloried in the media.

Although these leaders were on high alert, they were also unprepared— and they knew it. They asked basic, sometimes misguided questions. Few had solid answers. Most didn't know what legal risks they faced or how to prepare for them. Even among the pastors, many seemed to lack a theological understanding of religious freedom or the tools needed to equip their congregations for the challenges ahead.

I don't mean this as a criticism. It is simply a description of fact. When religious freedom is secure, we don't give it much thought—just like when I had no children, I didn't give parenting much thought. But when I found out my wife was pregnant, I realized I'd better start learning! Otherwise I'd be unprepared.

Many Christians are now in the same position. We've long lived in a country where religious freedom was secure, and we didn't need to give it much thought. Now we're realizing the country is changing and we might not enjoy the same degree of religious freedom forever. If we don't start thinking about it now, we'll be unprepared.

GETTING PREPARED

That's why I've written this book. Our culture is changing. Religious freedom is not as secure as it once was. And the church is unprepared.

What can we do about it?

As I spoke with the gathering of Christian leaders, I realized the pastors, theologians, university presidents, and ministry CEOs in the room felt ill equipped to help the church prepare. They were just waking up to the issue themselves.

This reminded me of what C. S. Lewis once said about church leadership on social issues. He wrote that people often want the church to take the lead: "But, of course, when they ask for a lead from the Church most people mean they want the clergy to put out a political programme. That is silly. . . . We are asking them to do a quite different job for which they have not been trained."[2]

Instead, Lewis said, "the job is really on us, on the laymen. The application of Christian principles, say, to trade unionism and education, must come from Christian trade unionists and Christian schoolmasters; just as Christian literature comes from Christian novelists and dramatists—not from the bench of bishops getting together and trying to write plays and novels in their spare time."[3]

The same is true of religious freedom. The clergy has a crucial role to play in equipping the faithful and walking with them through difficult times. Yet to understand religious freedom at a deep level and to help prepare the church for the challenges ahead, we also need Christians who are steeped in the field of religious freedom.

I've been steeped in nothing but religious freedom for over a decade, serving as an attorney at the Becket Fund for Religious Liberty, the nation's only law firm dedicated to protecting religious freedom for people of all faiths. During that time, I've helped win four Supreme Court cases and many more lower court cases. I've taught and debated religious freedom at universities and on television. I've published articles about religious freedom in academic journals and newspapers. Most importantly, I've walked with faithful, courageous Christians and people of other faiths through some of the most difficult trials of their lives.

My hope is that this experience can be used to help the church understand religious freedom at a deeper level and prepare for the challenges ahead.

A Plan

Based on many conversations with Christians over the years, I believe we have three primary needs that must be met before we're fully prepared.

First, we need a theology of religious freedom. Too often we begin thinking about religious freedom as a legal, cultural, or political problem without first recognizing that it is a theological problem. Our thinking about religious freedom must be grounded first in the truth of God as revealed in Scripture. You might be surprised at how much Scripture has to say about religious freedom. So part 1 of this book offers a theological understanding of religious freedom, drawing on the doctrine of God, the doctrine of man, and examples of religious freedom conflicts in Scripture.

Second, we need to understand the unique religious freedom challenges of our current culture. Our challenges today are different from the religious freedom challenges of fifteen years ago and different from those in other countries. We can't be prepared for our challenges if we don't understand what they are. Thus, part 2 applies our theology of religious freedom to the five most pressing religious freedom challenges in modern culture: (1) religious discrimination, (2) abortion rights, (3) gay rights, (4) Islam, and (5) the public square. As a lawyer on the front lines in these conflicts, I'll explain what the key legal problems are, how they can be resolved, and what Christians can expect from our legal system in the coming years.

Finally, we need to take action. Our faith is not a set of abstract principles; it's a calling covering every aspect of our lives. How should we, as Christians, live our daily lives when religious freedom is under threat? What can we do about it?

American Christians haven't faced serious violations of their religious freedom for a long time, but much of Scripture was written to Christians who were facing just that. To live our faith in modern culture, we need to reclaim and reacquaint ourselves with what Scripture says to the persecuted church. Thus, part 3 is practical. Drawing on Scripture's message to the persecuted church, it addresses how Christians should live when religious freedom is under threat.

A FINAL WORD

Before we begin, I should tell you how the Supreme Court case involving the teacher and the church turned out.

We won—unanimously. The court ruled that churches must be free to choose "who will preach their beliefs, teach their faith, and carry out their mission."⁴ The decision stands as one of the greatest religious freedom victories in the last fifty years.

In that spirit, I want to begin with a word of hope.

When I met with that gathering of Christian leaders, they were burdened by fear. They felt the culture changing around them, and they were worried about the serious religious freedom challenges ahead. Even now you can find any number of Christian books and blogs that play on these fears, warning that our culture is lost and that our rights will soon vanish.

But that is not this book. This is a book of hope, not fear.

Why?

As Americans, we can be tempted to place our hope in human institutions. Compared with the rest of the world, we have a stable legal system with broad constitutional guarantees of religious freedom. We have laws that protect our freedom to worship, to evangelize, to found Christian ministries, and to run businesses in accordance with our faith. Our Supreme Court has repeatedly ruled in favor of religious freedom. We think if we can just preserve those institutions . . . win the next election . . . get the right Supreme Court justices appointed . . . then we have hope.

But that kind of hope is hollow. As soon as we lose an election or lose a big case, that hope is replaced by fear.

And what about Christians elsewhere? As I write this, Christians in China face harassment, arrest, and imprisonment for worshipping in the underground church. Christians in Egypt risk death at the hands of suicide bombers who target their churches. Christians from Iraq and Syria are fleeing genocide at the hands of Islamic militants. Christians throughout history have suffered terrible persecution. Yet Scripture calls *all* of us to "rejoice in hope" (Romans 5:2), whether we live in North America or North Africa. Where does that hope come from?

That hope is not rooted in any human institution. It is not rooted in fair laws, favorable election results, or friendly Supreme Court justices. It is rooted in a person: Jesus Christ. He has already conquered every enemy we'll ever face, and He has promised us an imperishable inheritance in heaven. So even when we're "grieved by various trials," we still "rejoice with joy that is inexpressible" (1 Peter 1:6–8).

This doesn't mean we become Pollyannas, pretending everything is good when it isn't. Nor do we become Nero, fiddling indifferently while the world around us burns. Instead, we fully acknowledge the evil in the world even as we hope in the Savior of the world and join in His work in the world.

That is the spirit in which I offer this book.

We worship a Savior who is a realist. He told us, "In this world you will have trouble" (John 16:33, NIV). And when it comes to religious freedom, we *will* have trouble.

But that is not cause for alarm, because we worship a Savior who is also triumphant. The One who said "In this world you will have trouble" also said "Take heart! I have overcome the world" (verse 33, NIV).

That is the message we must remember as we consider the religious freedom challenges ahead: "Take heart! I have overcome the world."

Part 1

What Is Religious Freedom?

How Christians Get It Wrong

Why does religious freedom matter? Ask three Christians, and you might get four answers. Some will say religious freedom allows Christianity to flourish. Others will say it's a founding principle of our nation. Still others may question whether religious freedom matters at all, given that the church flourishes under persecution.

This is because we all approach the question of religious freedom with different assumptions about what religious freedom is and why it matters. These assumptions are not always clearly articulated or well grounded in Scripture, so before we explore what Scripture says about religious freedom, we must examine our own assumptions.

At the risk of overgeneralizing, I would say most evangelical Christians (and many nonevangelicals too) fall into one of three "camps" when it comes to religious freedom. These are not well-defined schools of thought, nor does every Christian necessarily fall into one of them. Still, they describe common tendencies in our thinking, and they're each mistaken in different ways. I call them the "Pilgrims," the "Martyrs," and the "Beginners."

PILGRIMS

Pilgrims believe religious freedom is a founding principle of our nation. In their view, our nation was founded by Christians from Europe who were fleeing persecution. They came to America to be free to worship God as He commanded. And although they experienced some bumps along the road, they ultimately succeeded: religious freedom was enshrined as the "First Freedom" in our Constitution, and America has enjoyed a level of religious freedom unseen anywhere else in the world.

Some Pilgrims go further, arguing that America is a chosen nation, a city on a hill, and a unique instrument of God to bring freedom and blessing to the world—perhaps even the modern equivalent of Israel in the Old Testament. Others, more modestly, say America is at least a Judeo-Christian nation—that most of the Founding Fathers had a Judeo-Christian worldview and that America has reaped tremendous blessings from its Judeo-Christian heritage.

All Pilgrims would say Christianity is right and true and it's wrong for the government to restrict it. Some think it might even be good for the government to promote it, at least in mild ways. For example, the government should be free to acknowledge that Christ is the reason for Christmas by displaying a nativity scene in the public square; it should be free to honor the religious foundation of our laws by displaying the Ten Commandments in prominent places; it should be free to foster religion by initiating prayer in public schools. At a minimum, they say, these practices are important acknowledgments of our Judeo-Christian heritage, and they shouldn't be stamped out.

For Pilgrims, the bottom line is that Christianity deserves a special place in our society because it's true and because we're a Judeo-Christian nation. Religious freedom is important because it allows Christianity to flourish and preserves the blessings of our Judeo-Christian heritage.

PILGRIMS' PROBLEMS

I love the Pilgrims. I was raised a Pilgrim, and the Pilgrim view contains some important truths. But it also has significant problems.

The first problem is biblical. The Pilgrim view tells us Christians deserve a privileged place in society—that we should expect the government will protect us and the rest of society will accept us. But Scripture teaches just the opposite. It says we should expect to be persecuted; we should expect to be scorned; we should expect the lowest place. Jesus said, "If they persecuted me, they will also persecute you" (John 15:20). And Paul wrote that "*all* who desire to live a godly life in Christ Jesus *will* be persecuted" (2 Timothy 3:12). This doesn't mean we should desire persecution or be indifferent to it. But it does mean we shouldn't be surprised by it or expect a privileged place in society simply because we're Christians.

Second, the Pilgrim view has historical problems. Historically, Christianity hasn't been dominant, at least in most of the world; it has been persecuted. Even in America, the Founding Fathers weren't exclusively Christian, and in many cases they weren't particularly devout.

Nor does America have an unblemished record of protecting religious freedom. Take just a few examples:

- The Puritans—our heroic forebears who fled to America from persecution in Europe—brutally persecuted the Quakers. They threw Quakers in prison, whipped them, mutilated them, and publicly hanged four of them at Boston Common.[1]
- American Protestants have a long history of persecuting Catholics. They barred Catholics from voting or holding office in the early colonies and sometimes banned them altogether. They expelled Catholic children from public schools in the mid-1800s for refusing to read from the Protestant Bible or recite Protestant prayers. And anti-Catholic rioters attacked and burned Catholic churches.[2]
- Similarly, the early colonies banned Jews from voting or holding public office. The first religious freedom case after ratification of the Constitution held that Jews could be fined substantial sums if they refused to testify in court on the Sabbath.[3]

This doesn't mean our nation isn't special. It means our nation isn't perfect. The idea that we've enjoyed over two hundred years of unbroken religious freedom is a myth, just as the idea that religious freedom will continue indefinitely is a myth.

Third, Pilgrims need to be careful what they wish for. A government that promotes Christianity sounds good in theory but typically works out badly in practice. When the state supports the church—by giving it a privileged legal position and exclusive financial support—it inevitably tries to control the church. The church becomes accountable to the state, and the church gets lazy. This was true of the government-supported churches in the early colonies, and it is true of many government-supported churches in Europe today.

In fact, at the time of the founding, the most vocal advocates of state-supported churches were the Enlightenment rationalists, who were deeply suspicious of faith. They wanted the state to support religion precisely to *tame* it—or, as David Hume put it, "to bribe [its] indolence."[4] That is why one of the first acts of the French revolutionaries was to pay clergy as employees of the republic.[5] By contrast, the most vocal advocates of church-state separation were fervent evangelicals who were fresh off the Great Awakening. They believed getting the government out of religion would allow religion to flourish. Today's Pilgrims sometimes seem to believe the opposite.

Finally, the Pilgrim view can have some unfortunate practical effects—both on those who hold it and on the rest of society. First, it often produces fear. Many Pilgrims see society changing around them; they see Christianity losing its favored place, and they're afraid. They're afraid that they or their children may soon face persecution and that our society will descend into decadence and chaos.

The Pilgrim view can also produce anger. If Christianity deserves a special place in society, then the loss of that place can feel like a personal attack on Pilgrims and on what they hold dear. When someone attacks you, it's natural to feel angry.

It's also natural to want to fight back. So the Pilgrim view can also tend to make Christians belligerent. As Christianity loses its privileged place, it feels like a loss of valuable rights. That makes Christians want to fight back, fueling the culture war.

Last, because of the anger and belligerence it can produce, the Pilgrim view can alienate nonbelievers from Christianity and from the idea of religious freedom generally. Rightly or wrongly, nonbelievers see Christians as more interested in fighting for their rights than in laying down their lives. And they see religious liberty as just a thin disguise for trying to maintain Christian dominance.

In sum, the Pilgrim view tends to turn religious freedom into a means of maintaining a privileged place in society for Christianity. That is not a sound view biblically or historically, and it is not good for religious freedom or for Christianity.

MARTYRS

Martyrs are in some ways the opposite of Pilgrims and, in some cases, a direct reaction against them. Martyrs say Christians shouldn't expect or seek a position of cultural dominance. That's contrary to the way of Jesus. Instead, the church should be countercultural. Jesus and the early church were persecuted; we should expect the same. In fact, when we're persecuted, we're blessed.

Martyrs reject the idea that America is a uniquely chosen nation. (My wife, acting on her Martyr tendencies, once spray-painted her car to read "God bless *South* America"—her way of saying God doesn't love the United States more than the rest of the world.) Even if America is a Judeo-Christian nation, it's not a very good example of one. Our nation brutally massacred thousands of Native Americans, systematically denied women equal treatment, and forcibly enslaved millions of human beings. Just because our Founding Fathers valued something—whether religious freedom or the Three-Fifths Compromise—doesn't make it right.

Martyrs are also quick to quote Tertullian, the early church father who famously wrote that the blood of the martyrs is the seed of the church.[6] They note that the gospel first spread beyond Jerusalem because of persecution. The first-century church grew explosively under persecution. And other churches, such as the Chinese church, have seen rapid growth under persecution. The American church, by contrast, is arrogant, overfed, and unconcerned. Perhaps a little persecution would wake us up.

Martyrs are also tired of the culture wars. They see that Jesus said a lot about caring for the poor and downcast, turning the other cheek, and identifying with the broken; He said much less about gay rights or Ten Commandments monuments. Martyrs don't want to preserve a special place for Christianity in American culture; they want to be *counter*cultural.

So when you ask a Martyr, "Why does religious freedom matter?" the Martyr might reply, "Yeah—why *does* religious freedom matter?" They suspect that religious freedom is just an excuse for trying to maintain a position of cultural dominance, and just one more front in the culture war. They're tired of fighting those battles.

MARTYRS' MALAISE

I love Martyrs too. Some of my good friends are Martyrs. (Not literally.) The Martyr view reflects important truths. But it also contains significant errors.

First, it distorts the teaching of Scripture. To be sure, Scripture teaches that we should expect persecution and rejoice when it comes. Paul said, "Everyone who wants to live a godly life in Christ Jesus *will be persecuted*" (2 Timothy 3:12, NIV). Jesus said, "Blessed are you when others revile you and persecute you. . . . Rejoice and be glad, for your reward is great in heaven" (Matthew 5:11–12).

But Scripture does *not* teach that persecution is a good thing. It's an evil thing that God can use for His purposes, and it's an injustice that God will rectify. We see this most vividly in Revelation 6:9–11:

When he opened the fifth seal, I saw under the altar the souls of
those who had been slain for the word of God and for the witness
they had borne. They cried out with a loud voice, "O Sovereign
Lord, holy and true, how long before you will judge and avenge our
blood on those who dwell on the earth?" Then they were each given
a white robe and told to rest a little longer, until the number of their
fellow servants and their brothers should be complete, who were to
be killed as they themselves had been.

The saints in heaven aren't rejoicing at having been killed; they're crying out with a loud voice for God to avenge their blood. And later in Revelation, God does just that.

Second, the Martyr view breaks with centuries of Christian tradition.
The early church didn't view persecution as a good thing. Although the
apostles rejoiced after they had been beaten for preaching about Jesus (Acts
5:41), they also "made great lamentation" when Stephen was killed (8:2)
and prayed fervently for Peter to be released (12:5). The famous line about
the blood of the martyrs being the seed of the church comes from a docu-
ment in which Tertullian demanded that the Roman governors *stop* persecuting the church. And it simply isn't true that the church always flourishes
under persecution. Persecution in the Soviet Union, Eastern Europe, and
the Middle East has often decimated the church.

Third, the Martyr view can negatively affect those who hold it.
Some Martyrs judge Pilgrims rather harshly, writing them off as more
loud than loving and more Republican than righteous. (Some Pilgrims,
of course, judge Martyrs too.) Martyrs can also tend toward cynicism—
disparaging the voices of those who are concerned about religious freedom and downplaying the stories of those who have suffered a violation
of it. Or they can become apathetic, caring little about an important
form of injustice.

In short, while Martyrs rightly reject the idea that religious freedom
should be valued as a means of maintaining Christian cultural dominance,

they can go too far in the opposite direction, viewing religious freedom as a luxury that can be abandoned lightly.

BEGINNERS

Many Christians don't find themselves in either the Pilgrim or the Martyr camp. They're unsure what to think about religious freedom or simply haven't given it much thought. But they're beginning to take an interest in it. These I call the Beginners.

Beginners tend to think religious freedom is important, but they may struggle to articulate why. They agree that persecution is bad. They know that religious freedom is in the Constitution. They might even say that religious freedom gives us more opportunities to spread the gospel. But ask them whether a county clerk should have the right to refuse a same-sex marriage license or whether a Muslim congregation should have the right to build a mosque on Main Street, and they're not sure how to answer.

This uncertainty can lead to fear. Beginners may hear about restrictions on religious freedom and may be afraid of what will happen in the coming years. Or their uncertainty can lead to disinterest. Conflicts over religious freedom can seem like distant events that are irrelevant to everyday life.

The Beginner view may be fine when religious freedom is fully protected and there's no need to think about it. But when times change—as they're changing now—the Beginner view isn't enough. Religious freedom is an important issue on which Scripture has much to say. It also has important implications for how we live our everyday lives. Thus, we need to move beyond the Beginner mind-set.

A BETTER WAY

This book is written for Pilgrims, Martyrs, Beginners, and everyone in between. The question of why religious freedom matters is vital, and as society changes around us, we need a solid answer.

My answer is simply stated.

Religious freedom is not, as Pilgrims would have it, a tool for maintaining Christian cultural dominance.

It is not, as Martyrs would have it, a luxury that can be abandoned lightly.

It is not, as Beginners might treat it, a pretty good idea that we don't need to think much about.

Rather, religious freedom is a basic issue of biblical justice, rooted in the nature of God and the nature of man.

What do I mean by that? Simply put, human beings are created for relationship with God, and God desires relationship with us. But a relationship with God can never be coerced. It must be entered into freely. So God Himself has given human beings freedom to embrace or reject Him.

That is where religious freedom comes from. If God Himself doesn't coerce us into relationship with Him, then how much less should the government? In fact, that is the very definition of a violation of religious freedom: when the government uses its coercive power to interfere in the relationship between God and man. When the government does that, it's violating the created order and perpetrating an injustice.

This understanding of religious freedom has profound implications for Christians—theologically, culturally, and practically. That is what the rest of this book is about.

I hope this book will accomplish three things. First, I hope it will help ground Christians in the deep scriptural and theological underpinnings of religious freedom. I hope Pilgrims will realize religious freedom isn't about maintaining Christian cultural dominance, Martyrs will realize religious freedom isn't just a culture-war issue, and Beginners will realize religious freedom isn't something they can ignore. Instead, I hope the church will unite behind the truth that religious freedom is a basic issue of biblical justice.

Second, I hope this book will help the church understand the most important legal and cultural threats to religious freedom in the coming years. The sky is not falling. America is not about to become Communist China. But real and significant threats do exist—and they might not be quite what you think.

Finally, I hope this book will help equip the church—practically—to live out our faith within a changing culture. Much of Scripture was written to the persecuted church, and we need to reacquaint ourselves with that message. It is a message that teaches us to seek neither cultural dominance nor martyrdom but to entrust ourselves to God and seek the common good.

We'll begin with a simple but crucial question: Where does religious freedom come from?

How to Get It Right

As the Roman soldiers prepared Paul for a beating, he appealed to Roman law: "Is it lawful for you to flog a man who is a Roman citizen and uncondemned?" (Acts 22:25).

As American Christians prepare for potential violations of religious freedom, we often appeal to American law: Is it lawful to take away religious freedom when it is enshrined in the Constitution?

But religious freedom isn't rooted in Roman law or the American Constitution. It goes much deeper than that. It's rooted in God's original design for humanity—in the way God created us (for relationship with Him) and in the way God relates to us (giving us freedom to embrace or reject Him).

These truths are taught throughout Scripture. But they're easy to overlook, particularly if we've fallen out of the habit of thinking about the issue. So the goal of this chapter is to examine what Scripture says about God's design for humanity and how that gives rise to religious freedom. Along the way, I'll also answer several common theological objections to religious freedom.

MADE FOR RELATIONSHIP WITH GOD

We first encounter mankind in Genesis 1:26. God had created day and night, heaven and earth, the seas and plants. He had filled the heavens and the earth with the moon and stars, sea creatures, birds, and all kinds of land animals. Then He created mankind: "God said, 'Let us make man in our image, after our likeness. . . .' So God created man in his own image, in the image of God he created him; male and female he created them" (verses 26–27).

This is the first mention of mankind in Scripture, and we immediately see a crucial point: we are made in God's image. What does this mean, and why does it matter?

Being made in God's image means, among other things, that we reflect what God is like. We do this in many ways—through our creativity, capacity for reason, sense of moral responsibility, and ability to make choices. But we also reflect God in another important way: through our capacity for relationships with Him and with one another. God Himself is a relational being. He has existed from all eternity in a loving union of Father, Son, and Holy Spirit. Being made in God's image, then, means we're created with a unique capacity to enter loving relationships with one another and with God Himself.

God Pursues Us

Unfortunately, we know how the relationship between God and mankind turned out: Adam and Eve disobeyed God, eating the forbidden fruit and rupturing their relationship with Him. Genesis describes the broken relationship so poignantly: "They heard the sound of the LORD God walking in the garden in the cool of the day, and the man and his wife hid themselves from the presence of the LORD God among the trees of the garden" (3:8). The image bearer now hides from the image maker. The relationship between God and mankind is shattered.

Thankfully, it doesn't end there. Rather, the rest of Scripture tells the amazing story of how God seeks to restore us to right relationship with Him. It began right there in the garden, as Adam and Eve were hiding, with God's simple question: "Where are you?" (verse 9). God didn't ask this question because He couldn't find Adam and Eve; He asked it because He wanted to reach them. In this beautiful question we see the dynamic that unfolds throughout the rest of Scripture: even as we turn away from God, He seeks loving relationship with us.

We see this again and again. As mankind spiraled into corruption, God rescued Noah from the Flood and entered a covenant with him—a mutual relationship based on a generous promise from God (Genesis 6–9). God called Abraham and entered a covenant with him (12; 15). God extended that covenant to Isaac and Jacob (26; 28). God rescued His people from slavery in Egypt and entered a covenant with them at Mount Sinai (Exodus 19–24). Over and over, God declared His desire for covenant relationship with Israel: "You shall be my treasured possession" (19:5); "I will take you to be my people, and I will be your God" (6:7; see also Leviticus 26:12; Deuteronomy 7:6; Jeremiah 11:4; Ezekiel 36:28). Even as Israel rejected Him, God sent the prophets to call His people back to faithful relationship with Him.

All these efforts culminated in the incarnation of Jesus Christ. God Himself became flesh. He didn't wait for us to come to Him; He came to us. He suffered for our sins on the cross. He rose again, and because of that, we're finally restored to right relationship with God. As Paul said, we who were once "alienated and hostile in mind" are now "reconciled" to God (Colossians 1:21–22).

The book of Revelation portrays this reconciled relationship between Christ and the church as a great wedding feast at the end of time:

Let us rejoice and exult
   and give him the glory,
for the marriage of the Lamb has come,
   and his Bride has made herself ready. . . .

Blessed are those who are invited to the marriage supper of the Lamb. (19:7, 9)

In short, time and again, Scripture teaches that God desires a relationship with us. He created us for relationship with Him. Even when we reject Him, He continues to pursue us. And He will ultimately restore us to right relationship with Him at the great marriage supper of the Lamb.

THIRSTING FOR GOD

Not only does God desire relationship with us, but we also desire relationship with Him. My favorite description of this is in Psalm 63, which David wrote from the bone-dry wilderness of Judah:

> O God, you are my God; earnestly I seek you;
>> my soul thirsts for you;
> my flesh faints for you,
>> as in a dry and weary land where there is no water. (verse 1)

I used to read this psalm exclusively as a description of David's *feelings:* David loves God so much that his feelings are like an insatiable thirst. If I'm honest, though, I must admit I rarely have such strong feelings for God. So I used to take this psalm as simply one more example of how I don't measure up to the heroes of the faith.

But that isn't the whole story. This psalm is not merely a description of David's feelings. *It is a declaration of truth about the human soul,* written for all Christians at all times. The truth is that even if we don't feel like it, our souls have an insatiable thirst for God. We can medicate it with money. We can dampen it with drugs. We can bury it with busyness. But deep down, our flesh faints for God in a dry and weary land where there is no water. Our souls will never be satisfied except with God Himself.

The author of Ecclesiastes said God has "put eternity into man's heart" (3:11). Deep down, we know there is something more to life than what we can see. And we want it. We're made for it. We're made, as Paul said, "so that [we] would seek him and perhaps reach out for him and find him, though he is not far from any one of us" (Acts 17:27, NIV). Or as Augustine put it, "You made us for yourself and our hearts find no peace until they rest in you."[1]

FREE TO EMBRACE OR REJECT GOD

God longs for us, and we long for Him. That should be the end of the story, right? We should all live happily ever after in loving relationship with God.

But that isn't how the story turns out—at least not yet. Instead, we see almost every kind of sin and broken relationship imaginable. Why?

The answer is simple: even though God wants relationship with us and we're made for relationship with Him, He doesn't force anyone to be in relationship with Him. Instead, He allows us to either embrace Him or reject Him.

We see this throughout Scripture. God created Adam and Eve in His image and gave them dominion over the earth, but they ate the forbidden fruit and hid themselves from Him. God rescued Israel from slavery and made them His special people, but Israel rejected Him and turned to idolatry.

We see it most clearly, again, in Jesus. He is God in the flesh, who came to reestablish relationship with His people, yet "he came to his own, and his own people did not receive him" (John 1:11). "He was despised and rejected by men" (Isaiah 53:3). In one poignant scene, after a hard teaching, "many of his disciples turned back and no longer walked with him" (John 6:66). But Jesus never forced anyone to return. Even with the twelve disciples, He merely asked: "You do not want to leave too, do you?" (verse 67, NIV). In the end, of course, one of them did leave Him; Judas betrayed Him to death.

Why did God create us with this capacity to reject Him? The answer isn't complicated: He did it because He wants a loving relationship with us. A loving relationship with God can never be coerced. If it is coerced, it is no longer love. If I plop my child in a chair, grab her hand, and force her to draw me a picture, I might have a pretty picture, but it won't come from her act of love.

In the same way, a loving relationship with God is possible only when it is a voluntary relationship. If it is coerced, it is not love.

This, ultimately, is where religious freedom comes from. It is written into the created order. We were created in the image of God for relationship with Him, but we can't have an authentic relationship with Him unless we also have the freedom to embrace or reject Him. And if God Himself doesn't coerce us in our relationship with Him, how much less should the government? When the government tries to do so—when it prevents us from freely relating to God—it is elevating itself above God and violating the created order.

An Issue of Justice

In that sense, religious freedom not only is written into the created order but also is an issue of justice. How so? To answer that question, we need an understanding of biblical justice.

The biblical concept of justice is rich and multilayered, extending to every facet of human relationships. It includes a personal calling to live in right relationship with those around us—being people of integrity, loving our neighbors, and caring for the poor. But it also includes a public calling to give people what they are due—punishment for those who do wrong and protection for those who are vulnerable. In short, biblical justice is both personal and public.[2]

The public aspect of justice places important limits on civil government. Scripture describes government as a "servant of God," "sent by him to punish those who do evil and to praise those who do good" (Romans

13:4; 1 Peter 2:14). It demands fair laws (Isaiah 10:1) and impartial judges (Deuteronomy 16:19). It condemns rulers who abuse their power, such as David, who committed adultery with Bathsheba and killed her husband (2 Samuel 11–12), and Ahab, who killed Naboth and seized his vineyard (1 Kings 21). It also condemns rulers who elevate themselves to godlike status, such as Pharaoh, who lost his firstborn son after killing the infant sons of Israel (Exodus 1:22; 12:29); Nebuchadnezzar, who went insane after praising his own glory (Daniel 4:28–33); and Herod, who was eaten by worms after refusing to glorify God (Acts 12:21–23). It calls on government to let people "lead a peaceful and quiet life, godly and dignified in every way" (1 Timothy 2:2).

Jesus Himself underscored the limits of government when He was asked about paying taxes to Caesar. After calling for a Roman coin, He pointed to Caesar's likeness and inscription and said, "Render to Caesar the things that are Caesar's, and to God the things that are God's" (Matthew 22:21). This means we should pay our taxes (Romans 13:7), but it also means Caesar's authority has limits. Some things don't belong to Caesar, and for Caesar to demand those things is a form of injustice.

AN EXAMPLE OF INJUSTICE

That brings us back to religious freedom. To understand why a violation of religious freedom is a form of injustice, consider a famous example: Daniel and the lions' den (Daniel 6). Daniel was a faithful Israelite who prayed to God three times a day. But several government officials wanted to find fault with Daniel, so they convinced King Darius to pass a law making it illegal to pray to anyone but the king for thirty days. Out of obedience to God, Daniel broke the law and suffered the consequence—being thrown into a den of lions.

This punishment was unjust in two ways. First, it's an example of Caesar (i.e., Darius) demanding what belongs to God. Daniel owed God his faithful obedience through prayer. But Darius made that obedience illegal. So Daniel faced a choice: Should he obey God or Darius? Like the apostles centuries later, Daniel decided that he "must obey God rather than men" (Acts 5:29)—and he was punished.

This was unjust because the government was attempting to exercise authority that didn't belong to it. It is as if the father of one family were punishing the child of another family without that family's permission. Even if the child might deserve it, meting out punishment is not that father's job. He is invading the other family's authority. In Daniel's case, Darius was acting unjustly because he was invading a realm over which only God has authority.

The lions' den was also unjust in another sense: it deprived Daniel of what he deserved. Daniel was made in the image of God, which includes the capacity to enter relationship with God. So when Darius punished Daniel for the way he related to God, Darius was taking away something Daniel deserved—namely, the opportunity to embrace or reject relationship with God, free from coercion by human authority. To use our previous analogy, not only is the father of one family punishing the child of another, but he is also now punishing the child when the child doesn't deserve it.

In that sense, the denial of religious freedom is similar to other forms of injustice. Take, for example, government oppression of the poor. The poor are made in the image of God, and as such, they are entitled to dignity and respect. But when the government denies them dignity and respect—when it oppresses them for being poor—it commits an injustice. Just as imprisoning someone for being poor is a form of injustice, so, too, is imprisoning someone for following her conscience.

In sum, the denial of religious freedom is a form of injustice in two respects: it is an attempt by the government to invade a realm that belongs only to God, and it is a denial of something that every human being deserves—the opportunity to freely embrace or reject relationship with God.

WHAT ABOUT ISRAEL?

Now that we've sketched a theological basis for religious freedom, we'll consider three potential objections. The first is theological: What about Old Testament laws that deprive people of religious freedom? Are those laws unjust? Do they suggest that religious freedom is not part of God's design?

Deuteronomy 17:3–5, for example, says that if a man or woman "has gone and served other gods and worshiped them . . . then you shall bring out to your gates that man or woman who has done this evil thing, and you shall stone that man or woman to death with stones." Similarly, Leviticus 24:16 says, "Whoever blasphemes the name of the LORD shall surely be put to death. All the congregation shall stone him."

If God is so keen on religious freedom, why did He command Israel to execute anyone who committed blasphemy or idolatry?

The answer to this question is rooted in Israel's unique place in God's plan for the world. Israel was not simply a nation-state with a good set of laws. Israel was God's chosen people. God entered a unique covenant with Israel, saying, "You are a people holy to the LORD your God, and the LORD has chosen you to be a people for his treasured possession, out of all the peoples who are on the face of the earth" (Deuteronomy 14:2).

As part of the covenant, God gave Israel the Law, or Torah, which governed virtually every aspect of human life—from religious worship, to personal relationships, to civil government.

But the Torah wasn't a blueprint for running an ordinary civil government. It was a blueprint (and much more than a blueprint) for a one-of-a-kind covenant people—"a kingdom of priests and a holy nation" (Exodus 19:6). Most importantly, the ruler of that nation was not to be a man or woman but God Himself.

We see this when Moses blessed Israel before his death. He didn't call himself Israel's ruler. Instead, he said that when the covenant was established at Mount Sinai, "the LORD became king in [Israel]" (Deuteronomy 33:5).

We see the same thing when Israel rejected Samuel's sons and asked Samuel to appoint a king. The Lord told Samuel, "They have not rejected you, but they have rejected me from being king over them" (1 Samuel 8:7; see also 12:12). The bottom line is that the king of Israel was God Himself.

If God was Israel's king, that changes things. Most importantly, there was no division between what belonged to God and what belonged to Caesar. God *was* Caesar. Caesar was God. So when the Torah commanded punishment for blasphemy or idolatry, it was not imposing a civil punishment that can just as easily be meted out by modern civil governments. It was imposing a divine judgment that pointed ahead to the final judgment. Indeed, sometimes this divine judgment was carried out directly by God Himself, as when fire consumed Nadab and Abihu after they offered incense that God had not commanded (Leviticus 10:1–3) and when the ground opened and swallowed Korah and his followers after they rebelled against God (Numbers 16:1–34).

In other words, when God is king, a law prohibiting blasphemy or idolatry is not a case of Caesar demanding what belongs to God; it is a case of *God* demanding what belongs to God. It is not a case of government exceeding its limited authority; it is a case of God exercising His divine authority. And it is not a case of injustice; it is a case of divine judgment. Thus, the Torah doesn't teach us that religious freedom is undesirable. It teaches us that it is temporary and that there will be a final judgment when "every knee [will] bow . . . and every tongue [will] confess that Jesus Christ is Lord" (Philippians 2:10–11; see also Romans 14:11).

The objection based on Old Testament laws also tends to equate the government of ancient Israel with the government of modern America—as if America is now God's chosen people. But that's a mistake. The modern equivalent of Israel is not America but the church, which is a "chosen people, a royal priesthood, a holy nation, God's special possession" (1 Peter 2:9, NIV). Like Israel, the church has authority to address blasphemy and idolatry among its members. But unlike Israel, Caesar and God are now separate (Matthew 22:21). The church doesn't wield civil power (which belongs to Caesar), and Caesar doesn't enforce divine law (which belongs to God).

What About Heretics?

That brings us to a second objection. It's easy enough to see that religious freedom is an issue of justice when a person is pursuing a *right* relationship with God. For example, we can easily conclude it was unjust to throw Daniel in the lions' den for faithfully praying to God. We also can easily conclude it was unjust to beat the apostles for "obey[ing] God rather than men" (Acts 5:29). But what about people who *reject* a right relationship with God? Is it unjust for the government to punish them? If God will judge those people at the end of time, why can't the government judge them now?

It can't for several reasons. First, as just explained, God created us for a loving relationship with Him, which can't be coerced. So when the government punishes someone for rejecting God, it doesn't bring that person any closer to Him. At best it produces feigned agreement. At worst it drives that person away from God and interferes with the opportunity to freely respond to Him.

Second, when the government punishes someone for rejecting God, it is usurping God's authority. The one who "convict[s] the world concerning sin and righteousness and judgment" is the Holy Spirit, not the government (John 16:8). When the government tries to take over that role— when it tries to dictate how human beings relate to God—it is demanding authority that belongs only to God.

Third, as a practical matter, governments are bad judges of divine truth. They're often wrong about who God is and what He commands. So if they're empowered to punish those who are "wrong" about God, they'll often punish the wrong people.

In short, the government shouldn't punish people who preach against Jesus any more than it should punish people who preach for Him. This isn't because we're relativists; it's just the opposite. It's because we believe the fundamental truth that God created people for relationship with Himself and that God Himself gives people the opportunity to freely embrace or reject Him.

WHAT ABOUT LIMITS?

That brings us to our third objection: If the government can't punish people who are wrong about God, does that mean religious freedom has no limits? Some people, for example, might believe God commands child sacrifice (2 Kings 3:27; 21:6; 2 Chronicles 28:3). Others might believe God wants them to use illicit drugs, cheat on their taxes, or commit acts of terrorism. Can people do whatever they want in the name of religious freedom?

Of course not. Every right has limits. The right of free speech, for example, doesn't mean businesses can deceive customers with false advertising. The right to bear arms doesn't mean citizens can bring guns onto airplanes. And the right of religious freedom doesn't mean parents can engage in child sacrifice.

But where do the limits on these rights come from? Well, let's start with where they *don't* come from. The limits on rights don't come from our opinion of the people exercising those rights. That is, we don't apply one set of false advertising rules to businesses we like and another to businesses we dislike. We don't apply one set of gun control rules to Republicans and another to Democrats, and we don't apply one set of religious freedom rules to Christians and another to Jews. The limits of religious freedom aren't based on a person's opinion about God. They're based on something else.

But what?

This is one of the most difficult questions in this book, and the answer will unfold throughout the coming chapters. But for now, we can start with a preliminary answer: the limits of religious freedom are based on the government's duty to protect *other* rights. In other words, protecting religious freedom is not the government's only job. The government must balance many competing rights. All people are created in the image of God. All are entitled to justice. So if one person's religion involves depriving another person of justice, the government can place limits on religious freedom.

Take an easy example: Suppose a man believes that God wants him to kill his neighbor. There are two competing rights—the man's right to religious freedom and the neighbor's right to life. In this case, the right to life obviously limits the right of religious freedom.

Or suppose a woman believes that God wants her to tear down her neighbor's house and build a temple in its place. The right of religious freedom conflicts with the neighbor's right to property, and the right to property will win.

These, of course, are easy cases. The task becomes much harder as the situations become more complex and the rights become less clear. For example, suppose parents want to withhold a certain medical treatment from their child and rely exclusively on prayer, but doctors believe the treatment may be the best way to improve the child's health. Or suppose a church wants to build a ten-thousand-seat sanctuary on a quiet residential street, but the local zoning board believes the massive sanctuary would disrupt the neighborhood and destroy local property values.

These are harder cases, and we'll explore many such cases throughout this book. But for now, the point is that religious freedom has limits, and those limits generally arise from the government's duty to uphold justice for all people.

Discerning the limits of religious freedom is also difficult because Scripture doesn't speak to the issue in much detail. Scripture clearly says we're created for relationship with God and have an opportunity to embrace or reject Him. It clearly says government is a servant of God to maintain justice for all people. But it doesn't clearly say when the government's duty to up-hold justice for all people allows it to restrict religious practices for some.

To answer that question, we'll start with Scripture. But we also need reason. We need to think. We need to study. We need to pray. We need a solid understanding of law and government. Even more, we need humility.

When Scripture doesn't speak clearly to an issue, Christians of good-will have room to disagree. At the same time, it's worthwhile to seek an-swers informed by Scripture, reason, and good judgment.

But what about people who don't care about Scripture? What about our skeptical neighbors, coworkers, or friends who may not even be con-vinced that religious freedom is a good thing? What can we say to them? Our theology of religious freedom is incomplete if we aren't ready to give an answer they can understand and accept.

The next chapter equips us to do just that.

How to Persuade Others

I once argued a case against my home state of Florida, and my parents came to watch. If you've ever watched a real courtroom argument—especially an appeal to a higher court—you know it's nothing like what we see on television. There is no jury. There are no passionate speeches. Instead, three judges grill the lawyers about complex legal issues.

My client was an Orthodox Jewish prisoner who wanted to keep a kosher diet in prison, just as Daniel and his friends wanted to keep a kosher diet in Babylonian captivity (Daniel 1). Most prison systems in our country allow this (as did Babylon), but Florida refused, saying it was too expensive.

What kind of arguments do you think I made? Do you think I appealed to the book of Daniel? "Your Honor, when Daniel was in captivity, he ate only vegetables for ten days and was healthier than the king's other young men. So my client should be allowed to eat kosher too."

Of course not. I relied on federal law. I talked about a federal statute called RLUIPA and legal concepts like strict scrutiny and voluntary cessation. To my parents, the legal jargon sounded like a foreign language. But the judges understood it, and we won the case.

We face a similar situation when discussing religious freedom with our skeptical neighbors and friends. If they don't believe in the Bible, they won't be persuaded by biblical arguments. We have to use arguments they can understand and accept. We have to speak their language.

The apostle Paul knew this. When he addressed Jews, he relied on

Jewish Scripture (Acts 13:33–41), but when he addressed Greeks, he quoted Greek poets (17:28).

So how do we discuss religious freedom with "Greeks"—our skeptical neighbors and friends? How can we persuade them that religious freedom matters, even if they don't believe the Bible?

There's no foolproof argument that persuades everyone every time. But I've found three arguments that resonate with many people who don't believe in the Bible:

1. **Religious freedom benefits society.** It promotes good works, protects the right of dissent, and reduces social tension.

2. **Religious freedom protects our other rights.** It establishes limits on what the government can do, which is the foundation for all other rights.

3. **Religious freedom is a fundamental human right.** It is rooted in human nature and, like other human rights, is worth protecting for its own sake.

The rest of this chapter equips Christians to make these arguments for our skeptical neighbors and friends.

Fixing a Common Misconception

Before making these arguments, however, we must correct a common misconception about religious freedom: the idea that religious freedom means religious people get to do whatever they want and the government can't do anything about it. If that's what skeptics think you mean by religious freedom, they won't listen to anything else you say. So as lawyerly as it may seem, you often need to start by defining what you mean by religious freedom.

I have a simple definition: *religious freedom means the government, within reasonable limits, leaves religion alone as much as possible.*

This definition avoids two extreme views of religious freedom. The first is the misconception described above—that religious freedom means religious people have free rein. That definition is obviously far too broad.

Religious freedom doesn't give you a right to kill someone or commit acts of terrorism in the name of your religion. There must be limits.

The other extreme view is that religious freedom simply means that the government can't intentionally *persecute* people because of their religion. That is, the government can't single out Jews for punishment because they're Jews, or Christians because they're Christians. But that view of religious freedom is too narrow. Religious freedom certainly *includes* the idea that government can't intentionally persecute people, but it also means more than that.

Many cases fall somewhere in between the two extremes: A Jewish boy wants to wear a yarmulke to school, but the school has a rule against hats. Or a church feels called to feed the homeless in a nearby park, but the city denies it a permit to do so. These are cases where religious people aren't wreaking havoc on society, and the government isn't intentionally persecuting them, but there is still a conflict between religious practices and the government's rules.

In these cases, religious freedom means the government should try to leave religion alone as much as possible—to make room for people to exercise their religion as freely as possible. That means letting the Jewish boy wear his yarmulke to school even if other children aren't allowed to wear hats. It also means allowing the church to feed the homeless even if neighbors don't want homeless people in the park.

(It also means the government doesn't use its power to *promote* religion, which is the subject of chapter 10.)

So that's a simple definition of religious freedom: the government, within reasonable limits, leaves religion alone as much as possible.

How Religious Freedom Benefits Society

Why should the government try to leave religion alone? That brings us to our first argument for why religious freedom matters: religious freedom benefits society. It does this in several ways.

Producing Moral Virtue

First, religious freedom allows religion to flourish, which produces the moral virtue necessary for democratic self-government.

This is an old-school argument you rarely hear anymore, but it was a major concern at the time of our nation's founding. The Founding Fathers were starting an unprecedented experiment in self-government. Instead of being governed by a king, the people would govern themselves. But the founders also knew that people are sinful and selfish, which creates a dilemma: How can sinful, selfish people govern themselves?

The answer, according to the founders, was that they *can't*. Self-government requires morally virtuous people. As George Washington put it, "Virtue or morality is a necessary spring of popular government."[1]

Where, then, would the moral virtue come from? The founders believed that it would come from religion—and that religious freedom would allow religion to flourish. As Washington said, "Whatever may be conceded to the influence of refined education . . . reason and experience both forbid us to expect, that national morality can prevail in exclusion of religious principle."[2] And as James Madison argued, reducing government control over religion would increase "the purity and efficacy of Religion."[3]

With over two hundred years of experience, we can now ask ourselves whether the founders were right.

The answer is a resounding yes. Compared with the widespread tyranny and oppression experienced throughout much of human history, the experiment in self-government has been a remarkable success, and religion and religious freedom have played a major role in that success by cultivating the moral virtue and good works that make self-government possible.

We see this throughout American history. Religious fervor fueled calls to abolish slavery and energized the subsequent civil rights movement. As the Reverend Martin Luther King Jr. put it, "The church must be reminded that it is not the master or the servant of the state, but rather the conscience of the state. It must be the guide and the critic of the state, and never its tool."[4] Despite its many imperfections, the church has repeatedly played this role.[5] The church has also supported a vast network of charitable works throughout the country, including schools, hospitals, nursing homes, orphanages, soup kitchens, food pantries, halfway houses, and many more.

The positive effect of religion on society is also confirmed by empirical data. After conducting multiple studies, Harvard political scientist Robert Putnam found there is one factor, more than any other, that predicts how generous, altruistic, and civically involved a person will be, measured by how much they give of their money and time, how often they help other people, and how much they are involved in civic and community life. That factor is *not* education, income, age, race, gender, or political persuasion. It is regular involvement in a religious community.[6] Similarly, a study from Georgetown University estimates that religion contributes over $1 trillion per year to US society through education, health care, local congregational activities, charities, media, food, and other social services.[7] That's more than the annual revenue of Google, Amazon, Apple, and the rest of the top ten tech companies in this country combined.[8]

I've seen this firsthand in my own cases. Among others, I've represented shelters that feed the homeless, hospitals that mend the broken, churches that convert gang members, and nuns who care for the elderly poor. I've seen how crucial religious freedom is for their ministries.

One example is the Boise Rescue Mission, a homeless shelter that provides over 350,000 meals and over 120,000 nights of shelter to needy individuals every year. One of the mission's most successful programs is a two-year-long drug and alcohol addiction recovery program, which has helped over two hundred men and women overcome their addictions. The backbone of the program is Christian discipleship, and it accepts no government funds.

Unfortunately, an ex-member of the program grew disenchanted with its Christian emphasis and sued the mission under the Fair Housing Act. She alleged that the program engaged in religious discrimination by requiring members to attend church services and participate in Bible study to remain in the program. She argued that because the mission was offering housing, it should be held to the same standard as everyone else: if a landlord down the street can't require his tenants to participate in Christian activities, neither can the mission.

This was not a frivolous lawsuit. It was brought by a government-funded organization that wins many cases under the Fair Housing Act—a law that does, in fact, prohibit religious discrimination. Thus, the lawsuit threatened the mission with a serious choice: either it could abandon the religious aspects of its program—the whole reason for its existence—or it could shut down. Merely defending the lawsuit in court could cost the mission over $100,000—money better spent serving the homeless. And the precedent set by the lawsuit would apply to hundreds of rescue missions across the country.

I had the privilege of defending the mission in court free of charge. We won the case because the Fair Housing Act has a commonsense religious exemption: if a religious organization is offering housing for a nonprofit purpose, it can give preference to persons of the same religion. In other words, a Christian recovery program can require its residents to engage in Christian activities.

This is a simple example of how protecting religious freedom allows good works to flourish. Absent religious freedom, the mission would have to either abandon the heart of its program or shut down. But because our law protects religious freedom, the mission is free to keep rescuing people from addiction.

Protecting Dissent and Diversity

Another way religious freedom benefits society is that it protects the right of dissent.

John Stuart Mill, the famous British philosopher, said dissent is valuable for two reasons. First, if the majority is wrong, dissent gives them "the opportunity of exchanging error for truth."[9] Second, even if the majority is right, dissent gives them a "clearer perception and livelier impression of truth, produced by its collision with error."[10] Either way, protecting dissent helps society toward truth.

Protecting dissent also ensures that vulnerable minority communities can live differently from the majority—thus protecting diversity. I've seen this in many of my cases, representing Jewish prisoners who wanted to keep a kosher diet, a Santeria priest who wanted to conduct animal sacrifices, Native Americans who wanted to worship on ancestral lands, Amish families who wanted to use traditional building methods, Muslims who wanted to build a new mosque, Hutterites who wanted to hold all their possessions in common, and inner-city pastors who wanted to serve the poor, among many others. If our society values diversity—as it claims to—it must also protect religious freedom.

Reducing Social Conflict

Finally, religious freedom benefits society by reducing social conflict.

The founders, of course, were familiar with the religious wars in Europe in the seventeenth century: "Torrents of blood," James Madison wrote, "have been spilt in the old world, by vain attempts of the secular arm to extinguish Religious discord, by proscribing all difference in Religious opinions."[11] In other words, the founders knew that attempts by the government to control religion often resulted in violence.

We've seen this in our own country too. In the 1600s, Massachusetts Bay Colony banned Quakers from preaching. But the Quakers just kept following their conscience and kept on preaching. They were imprisoned; they were flogged; three of them had their right ears cut off. Four were hanged at Boston Common.[12]

Quakers were also persecuted for refusing to swear oaths or provide military service. They were fined. Their property was confiscated. They were imprisoned. This went on for years, until the social conflict became too much to bear. Eventually, colony after colony enacted protections for conscientious objectors.[13]

What does this history teach us? It reveals that religion makes ultimate demands on people. Sometimes people will follow their conscience no matter what penalties the government might impose. And if the government won't accommodate their conscience, the result will be painful, long-term social conflict. Religious freedom reduces these conflicts by protecting conscientious objectors as much as possible.

This principle has huge implications for modern conflicts over abortion rights and gay rights, which are the subjects of chapters 6 and 7. But for now, the point is that religious freedom benefits society in multiple ways: it produces moral virtue and good works necessary for self-government, it protects dissent and diversity, and it reduces social conflict.

How Religious Freedom Protects Our Other Rights

That brings us to our second argument for why religious freedom matters: religious freedom imposes an essential boundary on the power of government, which ultimately protects all our other rights.

By its very nature, religious freedom carves out an area of human life that the government can't touch. As James Madison put it, because religion is "the duty which we owe to our Creator," it "can be directed only by reason and conviction, not by force or violence."[14]

So religious freedom starts from the premise that there is an internal realm of conscience that the government can't control through force or violence. That is because our conscience is responding to something higher than the government—the Creator.

This idea—that something is higher than the government—was a truly revolutionary concept at the time of our nation's founding. And it has profound implications.

If something is higher than the government, then the government is not the ultimate authority. This means our rights come from something higher than the government. As John F. Kennedy put it in his inaugural address, "The rights of man come not from the generosity of the state but from the hand of God."[15] And if our rights don't come from the state, the state has no authority to take them away.

This principle serves as the foundation for all other rights—like the rights of free speech, freedom of association, freedom of assembly, freedom from unreasonable search and seizure, and freedom from cruel and unusual punishment. If these rights are simply a gift of the state, then the state can take them away. But if they come from a higher power, the state cannot take them away.

Thus, we've seen around the world that religious freedom is like a canary in the coal mine for all other rights. When a government begins to take away religious freedom—as has been done in Soviet Russia and Communist China—watch out! Other rights will soon follow.

This principle, too, has arisen in my own cases. But it arose from an unlikely source: the Pledge of Allegiance to the US flag.

As you know, the Pledge of Allegiance says we are "one nation under God."[16] Several lawsuits challenged the words *under God,* arguing that those words promote religion and are therefore unconstitutional. One prominent court (the Ninth Circuit) even agreed with this argument and struck down the words *under God* as unconstitutional.

That's when my organization, Becket, stepped in. We realized something was missing. The government's lawyers were defending the pledge in a very odd fashion. They were claiming that the words *under God* were harmless because they were just a symbolic relic from the past. The words had been around so long and repeated so often that they had lost their religious meaning. In other words, the government was trying to save the pledge by arguing it was essentially meaningless.

That is not only bad strategy but also untrue. The words *under God* aren't meaningless. They hearken back to Abraham Lincoln, whose Gettysburg Address resolved that "this nation, *under God,* shall have a new birth of freedom."[17] They hearken back even further to the Revolutionary War, when the founders fought and died for the claim that all men "are endowed *by their Creator* with certain unalienable Rights."[18]

Far from being meaningless, the words *under God* are a profound statement of the political philosophy on which our nation was founded—that our rights don't come from the state but from something higher than the state. And because of that, the state can't take them away.

Happily, the Ninth Circuit eventually rejected the government's argument that *under God* was meaningless and adopted our argument instead.[19] The victory reminds us of an important truth: religious freedom matters because it imposes a clear limit on government power, thus providing a foundation for all other rights.

WHY RELIGIOUS FREEDOM IS A FUNDAMENTAL HUMAN RIGHT

That brings us to our last argument for why religious freedom matters: religious freedom is a fundamental human right.[20]

Note that our first two arguments—that religious freedom benefits society and protects our other rights—treat religious freedom as a *means to an end.* Those arguments say we should protect religious freedom because we want something else: self-government, good works, social peace, or other rights.

But our third argument treats religious freedom as an end in itself. That argument says religious liberty should be protected simply because it is a fundamental right rooted in our common humanity—full stop.

Let's unpack that. What does it mean to say that religious freedom is a fundamental human right?

Human rights, as the name suggests, are rooted in who we are as human beings. They don't come from the government. They don't come from a constitution or a declaration of rights. They arise out of the nature of our common humanity. Several features of our common humanity give rise to religious freedom.

The first is that we all desire truth, goodness, and beauty. That desire is written into human nature. We see this throughout history, as human beings have pursued truth, goodness, and beauty through philosophy, morality, and art. If someone desires only falsehood, evil, and ugliness, she has a diagnosable mental illness.

But human beings don't just flit randomly from one good to another without rhyme or reason. Instead, we also have the capacity to *choose*—to prioritize among competing goods, using our mind and reason and will. That's a fundamental part of what it means to be human: we're constantly on the lookout for good things, and we use our reason and will to choose among them.

Beyond that, while we're on the lookout for good things and using our reason and will to choose among them, we find something else within us, something that informs and governs our choices—an interior voice insisting that we choose the good and reject the evil. That's our *conscience.*

Conscience is both an inner capacity to judge and an insistent urge to obey those judgments. And conscience demands action. It demands that we embrace the truth and goodness we have found and live our lives accordingly. Conscience is universally recognized as a quintessentially human trait.

Finally, when all these faculties combine—when we're seeking the true, the good, and the beautiful, when we're making choices by our reason and will, and when our conscience is urging us to choose rightly and live accordingly—we find that *we're still not completely satisfied.* We still long for something more. We long for transcendent truth, for ultimate good, and for eternal beauty.

In other words, we long for God.

This thirst for something transcendent, this religious impulse, is a fundamental aspect of what it means to be a human being.

But there is something interesting about this religious impulse. By its very nature we can't act on it under coercion. We can't be coerced into embracing transcendent truth. We can seek and embrace truth authentically only when we do so freely.

In that sense, it's sort of like love. You can't coerce someone to love you.

If you try, you might get something that looks like love, but it isn't true love. In the same way, you can try to coerce someone to embrace transcendent truth. But unless a person embraces that truth willingly, he has not embraced it authentically.

So what does this mean for religious freedom?

It means that when the government tries to coerce us into embracing its version of truth—or forbids us from embracing our own—it is going against our very nature as human beings. It is treating us as less than fully human. It is, in short, violating a human right.

That's why religious freedom matters: it is a fundamental part of what it means to be a human being. And when the government violates religious freedom, it is doing something intrinsically wrong.

This principle is illustrated by many of my cases, but one case stands out. I once defended a nationally renowned Native American feather dancer named Robert Soto. Eagle feathers are a core part of Soto's religious practices. He believes that eagles are sacred and that by dancing with eagle feathers, he is sending prayers to the Creator.

The federal government, however, passed a law making it illegal for anyone to possess eagle feathers without a permit. According to the government, this was necessary to reduce unauthorized poaching of eagles.

The government made exceptions to the law, allowing farmers, ranchers, airports, and power companies to kill hundreds of eagles every year for commercial reasons. It also made exceptions for members of certain favored Native American tribes to possess feathers.

But Soto's tribe was not on the government's favored list, so Soto was banned from possessing even a single feather. To enforce this law, the government sent an undercover agent to Soto's powwow, who disrupted his sacred ceremony, confiscated his feathers, fined him, and threatened him with jail time.

That is an assault on human dignity. It's like telling Soto, "We don't care who you are; we don't care what your religion demands. We don't view you as fully human." But religious freedom demands that Soto be respected as fully human. It demands that he be allowed to live according to his deepest religious beliefs.

Soto's case is an easy one. What about harder cases?

Some of my hardest cases involve religious freedom for prisoners. In one of those cases, *Holt v. Hobbs,* I represented a Muslim prisoner named Abdul Maalik Muhammad. While he was in prison, Muhammad decided he wanted to get right with God, and he believed getting right with God included growing a beard. The prison didn't allow beards. But Muhammad asked for permission to grow a half-inch beard in accordance with his religious beliefs.

Why should it matter if Muhammad is forbidden to grow a beard? Many people say if he committed a crime, he should do the time. If he wanted so badly to be right with God, he shouldn't have committed a crime in the first place. Plus, he's a Muslim, and some people don't think Muslims should have religious freedom. So why should Muhammad be allowed to grow a beard?

We could invoke our first argument for religious freedom; we could say that letting Muhammad grow a beard is good for society. Some studies suggest that when prisoners practice their religion in prison, they are less likely to be violent in prison and less likely to commit crimes upon their release.[21] But while that might be true generally, can we really say that about Muhammad's beard specifically? We don't know whether growing a beard will improve his behavior in prison or after release.

We could invoke our second reason for protecting religious freedom— that it imposes limits on government that help protect our other rights. But this argument seems to be at its weakest in prison. Prisoners already lose many of their rights when they enter prison; that's the whole point. And we've long taken away rights from prisoners without taking away rights from the rest of society.

So the best reason for protecting Muhammad's beard is the third reason: we should protect Muhammad's beard because Muhammad is a human being. Even though personally we might think he's wrong, he is sincerely seeking transcendent truth and trying to live out the truth as he understands it. That is a quintessentially human endeavor. So if there is any way the government can allow Muhammad to grow a beard without undermining prison security, it should. That's what it means to treat him as a human being. Just as we don't subject prisoners to torture, starvation, or forced medical experimentation—as the Nazis did to Jews because they deemed them subhuman—we don't arbitrarily deprive prisoners of their fundamental human right to religious freedom.

We won Muhammad's case 9–0 at the Supreme Court. The court decided the prison could let Muhammad grow a beard without compromising prison security, so the prison was legally required to do so. This ensures that Muhammad is treated as a human being.

WHY IT MATTERS

This view of religious freedom as a human right has several important implications. First, it means religious freedom is an issue of justice—just as we saw in chapter 2. When the government pressures someone to go against her conscience, it is treating her as less than fully human and is committing an injustice. Just as imprisoning someone without cause is unjust, forcing someone to violate her conscience without cause is unjust. Not surprisingly, Scripture and reason bring us to the same conclusion.

Second, religious freedom matters regardless of whether it produces all the instrumental benefits we've discussed—morality, good works, social peace, or other rights. Those are good by-products of religious freedom, but they aren't the ultimate justification for it.

Finally, it means that religious freedom is for people of all faiths. Because religious freedom is an issue of justice, Christians should be concerned about religious freedom for Jews, Jews for Muslims, Muslims for Buddhists, and so forth. This isn't because we're relativists. It's because we're human beings. It's because we're all born with a thirst for transcendent truth. And it's because protecting conscience is the right thing to do.

SUMMING UP

These arguments show that you don't have to care about the Bible to care about religious freedom. Religious freedom is worth protecting because it benefits society, protects our other rights, and is a fundamental human right. These arguments may not persuade every skeptic, but they provide a sound basis for defending religious freedom regardless of one's religious views.

Now comes the hard part. It's easy to talk about religious freedom in the abstract because religious freedom is as American as apple pie. But what about when religious freedom collides with other hot-button issues— like abortion rights, gay rights, and Islam? What about when religious freedom becomes controversial?

These hot-button issues are the subject of part 2.

Part 2

What Are the Most Serious Threats?

Are Christians Under Attack?

I n 1990, the Supreme Court issued one of its worst religious freedom decisions ever—*Employment Division v. Smith*. The plaintiff was Al Smith, a devout Native American. As part of his religion, Smith consumed peyote—a small cactus that can be chewed or used for tea and has psychedelic effects. Native Americans have used peyote in religious ceremonies for thousands of years.

Although federal law permitted Native Americans to use peyote in religious ceremonies, the state of Oregon passed a law making it a crime to possess peyote, and it refused to make an exception for Native Americans. So Smith was fired from his job, denied unemployment benefits, and treated like a criminal—all because of his religion.

Smith's argument was simple: Oregon had criminalized a central tenet of his religion, a sacrament that Native Americans had practiced for thousands of years and that wasn't harming anyone. Surely that was a violation of the free exercise of religion.

Smith also had precedent on his side. The Supreme Court had long said the Constitution's Free Exercise Clause forbids the government from imposing a "substantial burden" on a religious practice except in rare cases. So, for example, the court had stopped the government from penalizing Amish parents who refused to send their children to school,[1] and a Seventh-day Adventist who refused to work on the Sabbath.[2] Surely it would also stop the government from penalizing Al Smith.

But Smith was in for a rude awakening—and so was every religious group in the country. The Supreme Court not only ruled against Smith but also threw out decades of religious freedom precedent. The court said it would no longer apply the substantial-burden test, which required the government to prove that each law burdening a religious practice was truly necessary. Instead, the court would ask whether a law *specifically targeted* a religious practice *because* it was religious. If so, it would be unconstitutional; if not, it would be upheld—even if it had a devastating effect on religious practices.

What did this mean? First, it meant Al Smith lost his case. Oregon wasn't intentionally targeting Native American religious practices; it was banning peyote for *everyone*. Therefore, the ban on peyote was constitutional even if it meant Native Americans were imprisoned for practicing their faith.

But the Supreme Court's ruling also posed a threat to every other religious group. Although the government couldn't target Orthodox Jews by banning yarmulkes in public schools, it could accomplish the same result by banning all hats. And although the government couldn't target Catholic pharmacists by requiring them to dispense abortion-causing drugs, it could accomplish the same result by requiring all pharmacists to dispense those drugs.

The response to this ruling was swift, strong, and bipartisan. Senator Ted Kennedy, the famous Massachusetts liberal, teamed up with Senator Orrin Hatch, the staunch Utah Republican, to sponsor the Religious Freedom Restoration Act (RFRA)—a law designed to restore the substantial-burden test the Supreme Court had rejected. RFRA (pronounced RIFF-ruh) passed the House unanimously, passed the Senate by a vote of 97–3, and was signed into law by President Bill Clinton.

RFRA was supported by a huge coalition of liberal and conservative groups—from the ACLU to Concerned Women for America and from Americans United for Separation of Church and State to the National

Association of Evangelicals. RFRA laws were also passed (or effectively imposed by court rulings) in over thirty states, from deep blue Connecticut and Illinois to deep red South Carolina and Texas.

What does this history teach us?

It teaches us that religious freedom was once a unifying force in national life. Conservatives and liberals, religious and nonreligious, all agreed that religious freedom should be protected. All agreed that RFRA was a great idea.

That was in 1993.

Now fast-forward twenty-two years to 2015.

The Supreme Court was about to hear oral argument in *Obergefell v. Hodges,* the big same-sex marriage case. Conservatives in Indiana were worried that legalizing same-sex marriage would threaten religious freedom, so they enacted a state-law version of RFRA, which was signed into law by then governor Mike Pence.

The Indiana RFRA was virtually identical to the federal RFRA, which had been signed by Bill Clinton and supported by the ACLU, and was virtually identical to RFRA laws in thirty other states. But this time, instead of widespread support, RFRA provoked a national firestorm. The ACLU blasted RFRA as discriminatory—claiming it would let businesses deny service to LGBT customers (even though federal and state RFRAs had never allowed this before). CEOs of major companies threatened to pull out of Indiana. Sports leagues like the NCAA, NBA, and NFL threatened to cancel future events. The governor of Connecticut banned all state-funded travel to Indiana—even though Connecticut had enacted a nearly identical RFRA twenty-two years earlier.

Stunned by the opposition, the Indiana legislature quickly amended its RFRA so it wouldn't apply to certain cases involving sexual orientation and gender identity. No RFRA in the nation's history had ever been amended in that way, but it was enough to mute the criticism and let the state's politicians move on to other matters.

Times Have Changed

The lesson here is that times have changed—dramatically. A religious freedom law that unified the country twenty-five years ago provokes a national firestorm today.

Why?

It would be easy to blame same-sex marriage, which was barely on the horizon in the mid-1990s but fueled both sides of the debate in Indiana. But same-sex marriage is only part of the issue. We face a variety of religious freedom threats that would have been unthinkable twenty-five years ago—from laws requiring religious groups to pay for abortions, to laws requiring doctors to help with assisted suicide, to restrictions on free speech on college campuses, to the elimination of long-standing tax exemptions for churches. Same-sex marriage doesn't explain all of these.

Something bigger has happened.

We're a Threat

This is not the first time our country has faced religious freedom controversies—not by a long shot. In the 1600s, Massachusetts brutally persecuted Quakers as heretics. In the 1700s, Virginia imprisoned dozens of Baptist preachers for preaching without a license. In the early 1800s, Missouri authorized the extermination of Mormons as enemies of the state. In the late 1800s, prominent politicians condemned Catholics as a threat to the republic. And in the 1900s, states expelled Jehovah's Witnesses from public schools for refusing to salute the flag.

In each of these examples, a religious minority was viewed as a threat to the prevailing culture. Quakers were a threat to the dominant Puritan culture. Baptists were a threat to the dominant Anglican culture. Mormons, Catholics, and Jehovah's Witnesses were a threat to the dominant Protestant culture.

Today's religious freedom threats come from a shift in our prevailing culture. For much of American history, common Christian beliefs (or at least Protestant beliefs) were largely compatible with the prevailing culture. There was nothing remarkable about believing that Christianity is true, that all other religions are false, that abortion is wrong, or that marriage is to be only between a man and a woman. Not everyone agreed with those beliefs, but they didn't provoke hostility. They weren't viewed as a threat to the dominant culture.

Now our culture has changed. For the first time in American history, common Christian beliefs are viewed as incompatible with the prevailing culture. Like other religious minorities before us, we're viewed as a threat. So religious freedom for Christians is under pressure like never before. To understand this new dynamic, we need to understand five key changes to our culture.

There Is No Absolute Truth

First, our culture has grown hostile to claims of absolute truth. We're all familiar with this dynamic; it's the fruit of postmodernism. Christianity may be "true for you," but don't try to impose it on anyone else. Everyone needs to find his own truth.

If we claim Christianity is true in the absolute sense, then we're also claiming other belief systems are false. That's "intolerant." We're "judging" other people, which is one of the only sins recognized by modern culture.

By making absolute truth claims, we're also "discriminating." We're saying someone else's view is false or someone else's conduct is wrong—which excludes and demeans that person.

We can see this cultural dynamic at work in many religious freedom conflicts, but one of the most important was a Supreme Court case called *Christian Legal Society v. Martinez*.[3] A group of Christian law students had formed a club at the University of California to conduct Bible studies and connect Christian students with one another. The club welcomed everyone at its events, but it required its leaders to be Christians.

The university, however, said this was illegal discrimination. It refused to recognize the club unless it allowed "any student" to "seek leadership positions, regardless of [her] status or beliefs."[4] The club argued that it couldn't maintain its distinctive Christian identity unless it could require its leaders to be Christians. But the university wouldn't budge. It said the club had to allow non-Christians to lead the group or else it couldn't be an official student group.

It's easy to criticize the university's (il)logic. Would the university require the student Democrats to have Republican leaders? Would it require sororities to have male leaders? Of course not. Every club discriminates in some sense. Otherwise it would be just a random collection of individuals.

Nevertheless, the Supreme Court ruled in favor of the university. The Christian student group had to follow the university's nondiscrimination policy, which meant it had to allow non-Christians to lead the group.

This ruling reflects an important shift in our culture. By simply believing in absolute truth and living accordingly, Christians are "discriminating." And our "discrimination" poses a threat to the dominant culture.

Abortion Must Be Accepted

We see the same dynamic at work in the second major area of cultural transformation: abortion. In *Roe v. Wade* and *Planned Parenthood v. Casey*, the Supreme Court decided there is a constitutional right to abortion.[5] According to the court, the choice to have an abortion is so "intimate" and "personal" and "central to personal dignity and autonomy" that the government can't interfere with that choice.[6]

Roe and *Casey* have rightly been criticized as unjust, illegitimate, and poorly reasoned.[7] But their underlying logic, taken at face value, has interesting implications for religious freedom. Specifically, in *Casey*, the court said that abortion has "profound moral and spiritual implications" on which "men and women of good conscience can disagree."[8] Because of that, the decision about the morality of abortion, according to the court, must remain *private*. That is, the government can't choose one side of the moral debate and impose that view by force of law.

That means the government can't tell a pregnant woman that abortion is immoral and stop her from having one. But it also means the government can't tell a doctor, nurse, or hospital that abortion is *moral* and force them to participate in one. In other words, "freedom of choice" goes both ways.

Thus, even while recognizing a "right" to abortion, our country has long protected the right of conscientious objection to abortion. Immediately after *Roe,* federal laws protected doctors and hospitals nationwide from being forced to participate in abortions. Virtually every state also passed similar protections. That principle has now been settled for almost fifty years: no one can be forced to participate in an abortion.

In recent years, however, that settled principle has come under attack. Groups like Planned Parenthood and NARAL Pro-Choice America now criticize conscientious objection to abortion as a "dangerous" form of "discrimination."[9] According to NARAL Pro-Choice America, if a doctor declines to perform abortions, he is "deny[ing] women access to all of their health-care options."[10] And if a religious employer declines to pay for abortions in a health-insurance plan, it is "discriminat[ing] against women's reproductive choices."[11] As Planned Parenthood put it, "religion" can't be used "as an excuse to discriminate against patients and deny people health care."[12]

For these groups, it is no longer enough to eliminate *government* restrictions on abortion; they must eliminate *private* opposition to abortion too. It is no longer enough to make abortion legal; it must be made acceptable. If religious people believe abortion is wrong and want to act accordingly, that is "discrimination" and must be eradicated. As the ACLU put it, "Discrimination is discrimination, no matter what the reasoning. And it's always illegal."[13]

This shift has produced a host of new religious freedom threats. The *Hobby Lobby* and *Little Sisters of the Poor* cases, which my firm handled in the Supreme Court in 2014 and 2016, are just the tip of the iceberg. Those cases involved a federal regulation requiring religious employers to provide insurance coverage for drugs like the morning-after and week-after pills, which can potentially cause abortions. It was the first time in history that the federal government ordered religious organizations to participate in what they viewed as abortion. Fortunately, the religious groups won.

But similar threats remain. California has issued a regulation requiring health-insurance plans to cover abortions—with no exemption even for churches.[14] Washington and Illinois have issued regulations requiring pharmacists to dispense drugs that can cause abortions.[15] The ACLU has sued Catholic hospitals for declining to perform abortions.[16] And cities across the country have passed laws requiring pro-life pregnancy centers to offer information about or refer clients for abortions.[17] These are just a few examples.

The bottom line is that conscientious objection to abortion used to be accepted as a common response to a controversial issue. Now it's increasingly viewed as a threat to the dominant culture and a form of discrimination that must be eradicated.

Sexual Autonomy Must Be Approved

The same dynamic is even more pronounced when it comes to sexual autonomy. The traditional Christian view is that human beings are created male or female, that sex is designed for marriage, and that marriage is meant to be permanent. Under that view, our bodies are not simply a means for pleasure and self-expression; they belong to God.

Although recent polls suggest Christians are increasingly divided over whether to accept same-sex relationships,[18] many Christians still hold this traditional view. And for most of American history, the culture agreed: sex was meant for a loving marriage between a man and a woman who were joined "until death do us part."

Not anymore. Our culture has changed. Sex is no longer reserved for marriage. Hookups abound. Cohabitation and divorce are expected. Same-sex marriage is celebrated. Even the basic idea that we are either male or female is now controversial.

But again, the problem is not simply that common Christian beliefs are out of step with the dominant culture; it is that those beliefs are viewed as a *threat* to that culture.

The dominant culture assumes we exist primarily for our own enjoyment and self-expression. To fully express ourselves, we must be free to have any consensual sexual relationship we want. We must be free to marry and divorce whomever we want. And we must be free to live as whatever gender we want. We must be free to "be who we really are."

But the culture wants still more. It's not enough to be *free* to be who we really are. We must also be *accepted* for who we really are. If someone refuses to accept me—if she tells me I'm wrong or condemns me because of whom I love—she is "judging" me and "discriminating" against me. That is a violation of my dignity and must be stopped.

That's why traditional Christian beliefs about human sexuality are viewed as a threat. If a Christian says that human beings are created male or female, that sex is designed for marriage, and that marriage is meant to be permanent, then he is necessarily claiming that other views of human sexuality are wrong. He is "judging" and "discriminating" against those who view their sexuality differently, which is an attack on their dignity.

Of course, the culture is also "judging" and "discriminating" against the traditional Christian view of human sexuality. But our culture isn't committed to universal tolerance. It is committed to tolerating everything except intolerance.

We see this in a variety of new religious freedom threats that were unthinkable just a few years ago. Wedding vendors—like photographers, florists, and bakers—have been punished for declining to help celebrate same-sex weddings.[19] Counselors have been punished for declining to counsel same-sex couples about their relationships.[20] Religious adoption agencies have been shut down for declining to place children with same-sex couples.[21] Religious schools have been sued for declining to hire teachers or other workers who enter same-sex marriages.[22] Religious hospitals have been sued for declining to perform gender transition surgeries.[23]

In every case, the cultural message is clear: full approval of sexual autonomy is not only a legal right but also a social duty. Anyone who refuses to approve of another person's sexual expression is discriminating and must be stopped.

Religion Is Less Important

The fourth major shift in our culture is that we've become less religious. From 2007 to 2014 the share of the American population that is religiously unaffiliated—including atheists, agnostics, and those who identify as "nothing in particular"—grew from 16 percent to 23 percent. The share of the population identifying as Christian fell by about the same amount. Thus, for possibly the first time in American history, the number of unaffiliated Americans is greater than the number of Catholics (21 percent) and mainline Protestants (15 percent) and almost as great as evangelicals (25 percent).[24]

It may be tempting to assume that the unaffiliated are spiritual but not religious—that is, they still care about religious things but simply reject organized religion. But that's not true. Instead, they are increasingly secular. An increasing share of the unaffiliated report that they don't believe in God, almost never pray, and rarely attend religious services.[25] More Americans identify as atheist or agnostic than ever before.[26]

Thus, religion is playing a reduced role in American life. Fewer people believe in God; fewer people regularly pray or attend religious services; and fewer people describe religion as important in their lives.[27]

This has a major impact on religious freedom. When people are religious, they tend to care more about religious freedom. At a minimum, they care about their own freedom as a matter of self-interest. But they also know what it's like to believe in God and feel bound to obey Him, so they tend to be sympathetic to religious freedom more generally.

When people aren't religious, they tend to be less sympathetic to religious freedom. Religious freedom doesn't benefit them directly, so there is no appeal to their self-interest. They may also view religion as harmful or misguided, so they're more likely to question why religious freedom should be protected at all—particularly when it conflicts with something they value, like abortion, gay rights, or the idea of nondiscrimination.[28]

So as the nation becomes less religious, it's no surprise that we would see more religious freedom threats. Fewer religious people means fewer people who need religious freedom.

Fewer religious people also means fewer people who want to see religion in the public square. Our nation has long treated religion as an important part of our history and culture—publicly honoring religious contributions to society, celebrating religious holidays, and erecting religious monuments. But as more people cut personal ties with religion, they have no reason to want religious references in the public square. They may even find such references offensive and want them eliminated. Thus, we see more conflicts over nativity scenes, Ten Commandments monuments, and religious content in the public schools. These conflicts are not new, but they're increasingly common—and increasingly intense—as our culture becomes less religious.

Religion Is More Diverse

The final major shift in our culture is that we've become more religiously diverse. Even as fewer people identify as Christian and more people identify with no religion at all, more people also identify with non-Christian faiths—like Hinduism, Buddhism, and Islam.[29] This creates several challenges.

First, more religious diversity means a wider variety of religious practices, which in turn creates the potential for more religious freedom conflicts. Take, for example, a typical workplace setting like a factory. If most of the employees are Christians, there are only so many potential religious freedom issues that may arise. Maybe some Christians will want Sundays off to observe the Sabbath. Maybe some will want a place in the break room where they can pray or read the Bible during breaks. But it's not too difficult to accommodate such desires.

Now assume the workplace also includes Orthodox Jews and Muslims. Orthodox Jews will require Saturdays off for their Sabbath. They will also require time off for the Jewish high holidays. Muslims will need Fridays off for their congregational prayer. They will also need to observe a different set of holidays and will need breaks for their five-times-a-day prayer. Now it's much harder to run the factory while still accommodating everyone's religious needs. So the factory owners might not want to accommodate anyone at all.

The government faces a similar dynamic. When the country is religiously homogenous, it has fewer religious practices to accommodate, making it easier for the government to accommodate them. When the country becomes religiously diverse, it has far more religious practices to accommodate, so it's harder to do so. The government may simply conclude it's too costly and difficult to protect religious freedom for everyone.

This was a key factor in the Supreme Court's notorious *Smith* decision, where it concluded that Oregon could punish Native Americans for using peyote. The court said, "We are a cosmopolitan nation made up of people of almost every conceivable religious preference," and because of that, trying to protect every religious practice would be "courting anarchy"—a "danger [that] increases in direct proportion to the society's diversity of religious beliefs."[30] In other words, more religious diversity means more chaos.

Religious diversity also presents us with an important test: Are Christians truly committed to religious freedom for all? Or do we invoke religious freedom primarily as a tool for maintaining a preferred status in society? As our country becomes less religious, many people suspect that Christians are invoking religious freedom only to protect Christianity. When they see Christians who are indifferent to religious freedom for Muslims, Hindus, or Jews—or even actively opposing them—they conclude Christians are hypocrites. They conclude we aren't interested in protecting religious freedom as a fundamental human right; we're just interested in protecting Christianity. That further erodes support for religious freedom.

What Now?

Our culture has changed. For the first time in American history, widespread Christian beliefs are viewed as a threat to the dominant culture. The belief in absolute truth is now viewed as a form of discrimination. The belief that abortion is wrong is now viewed as an assault on the health and dignity of women. The belief that God designed sex for marriage between a man and a woman is now viewed as an attack on the LGBT community.

Our nation is less religious than ever before, meaning fewer people need religious freedom. And our nation is more religiously diverse than ever before, meaning it is harder to protect religious freedom. This is a recipe for unprecedented attacks on religious freedom.

Does it mean Christians are under attack? Yes—in a sense. Not in the sense that Christians are under attack in Iraq, where Christians have faced murder, kidnapping, and forced migration at the hands of the Islamic State militants. Nor in the sense that Christians are under attack in North Korea, where they have been sent to labor camps or executed by the government. Most of us can't even comprehend that sort of attack.

Christians in the United States face something entirely different. It's far milder but still a form of attack. And it's something Christians in the United States haven't experienced before. Common Christian beliefs are now viewed as a threat to the dominant culture, and some parts of our society want to marginalize and punish Christians for holding and acting on those beliefs. This doesn't mean *most* of the country wants to do so, but a growing part of the country does. They have more influence than they've had before, and they're aided by a large portion of the country that is either indifferent or content to go along.

This doesn't mean our culture is hostile to religion generally. Rather, our culture draws a distinction between "good religion" and "bad religion." Good religion is *private;* it stays in the church or home and doesn't try to force its beliefs on others—especially in the marketplace or politics.

Good religion is *tolerant* and *relativistic;* it is accepting of other beliefs and doesn't tell other people they're wrong. And good religion is *nondiscriminatory;* it accepts people for who they are and doesn't condemn them for whom they love. Our culture likes good religion.

Bad religion is *public;* it makes demands on all human life, from the church to the home and from the marketplace to the capitol. Bad religion proclaims *absolute truth;* it says other belief systems are wrong and tries to persuade everyone it is right. And bad religion makes *moral claims* between right and wrong, particularly in the area of human sexuality; it says we're created male or female and sex is only for marriage between a male and a female. Bad religion is viewed by our culture as a threat.

Why do we need to understand this? First, it helps us understand the direction our country is headed and the nature of the threat we face. We can't understand what we're facing if we don't understand how our culture has changed. Second, it guides our response. We won't know how to respond if we don't know why we're under attack.

So what, exactly, are we facing? And how should we respond? That is what the following chapters are about.

We'll start with the crucial issue of discrimination. The culture says discrimination is evil and should be eradicated. But Christians discriminate all the time. Our ministries often hire only Christians, which is religious discrimination. Our churches often choose only male pastors or priests, which is sex discrimination. Our universities often forbid unmarried cohabitation, which is marital-status discrimination. Simply by believing in absolute truth we necessarily proclaim that other belief systems are false—which is yet another form of discrimination.

So what happens when the culture is fanatically committed to nondiscrimination but Christians can't play along? We get religious freedom conflicts. But what are the main conflicts? How should we respond?

How should Christians think about discrimination?

Is Discrimination Evil?

I live in Utah, the home of the Church of Jesus Christ of Latter-day Saints, also known as the Mormon church. Many years ago, the Mormon church built a gymnasium in downtown Salt Lake City for church-approved recreation. The gym was open to the public, but it was owned and subsidized by the church.

The church viewed the gym as part of its ministry. As with its other ministries, the church believed fellow Mormons would best carry out the goals of the ministry and reflect the church's values to the rest of the world. So the church decided all employees at the gym and in its other ministries should have a "temple recommend"—essentially a certificate of good standing in the Mormon church, showing that the person regularly attends church, tithes, and follows other religious requirements.

As the church reviewed its gymnasium employees, it discovered that one employee, Frank Mayson, didn't have a temple recommend. Mayson worked at the gym as a building engineer, where he maintained the facilities and supervised the custodians and parking lot attendants. The church offered Mayson an opportunity to obtain a temple recommend, but he declined. So the church let him go.

Mayson, represented by the ACLU, sued the Mormon church. He argued that the church had violated his religious freedom by discriminating against him based on his religion. The church, in response, argued that forcing it to hire non-Mormons would violate the religious freedom of the church.

The case went all the way to the Supreme Court. Who do you think won? More importantly, who *should* have won, and why?

THE COURT'S DECISION

Before answering these questions, we have to know a little bit about the law. The law at the heart of the case was called Title VII, which is part of the Civil Rights Act of 1964. Title VII prohibits employment discrimination based on race, color, sex, national origin, or religion. So, for example, an employer can't fire an employee because she is black or a woman or a Jew.

But when it comes to *religious* discrimination, Title VII also has a religious exemption: it says religious organizations have a right to hire "individuals of a particular religion" to carry out their work.[1] So Jewish organizations can hire only Jews, Mormon organizations can hire only Mormons, and so on. The Mormon church argued that it was protected by this exception. The ACLU argued that this exception was unconstitutional because it gave special privileges to religious organizations.

The Supreme Court sided with the Mormon church. It said Title VII's religious exception "alleviate[s] significant governmental interference with the ability of religious organizations to define and carry out their religious missions."[2] In other words, if the government could force a Mormon organization to hire non-Mormons, it wouldn't be a Mormon organization much longer.

So the Supreme Court ruled unanimously in favor of the Mormon church.[3]

NOT ALL DISCRIMINATION IS BAD

How should we think about this decision? Was the Supreme Court right? Should religious organizations have a right to hire only people of the same religion?

This isn't a trick question. Of course they should! But it's crucial to understand *why*. There are two main reasons: one based on common sense, and the other based on fundamental rights.

First, the common sense. Imagine the local grocery store says, "We won't hire Jews." Most people would agree that's morally wrong. But imagine the local Jewish school says, "We hire only Jewish teachers." Most people would agree that's permissible—or at least different.

The same can be said of other types of discrimination. Most people would agree that a business shouldn't refuse to hire women. But if the business is hiring male models to sell men's clothing, it's permissible. Most people would agree that movie producers shouldn't discriminate based on race. But if the studio is producing a film about Martin Luther King Jr., it can choose an African American actor for the lead role. Most people would agree that the government shouldn't refuse to hire someone based on age or disability. But if the government is choosing the members of a physically demanding SWAT team, it can.[4]

In each case, something that is normally a forbidden ground of discrimination—like age, race, sex, or religion—is important to the job. So discriminating based on that trait isn't morally wrong. It's permissible, and perhaps even necessary.[5]

That's the commonsense principle underlying the Supreme Court's Mormon gymnasium decision. Sometimes religious discrimination is wrong—like when the grocery store refuses to hire Jews. But other times it's not wrong at all—like when a Jewish school hires Jewish teachers.

For religious groups, religion is often an essential part of the job. In that case, discriminating based on religion isn't morally wrong. It might even be necessary for maintaining the religious mission of the group.

DISCRIMINATION VERSUS OTHER RIGHTS

But suppose some people are unconvinced by this commonsense argument. Can we offer any other argument?

That brings us to the second reason the Supreme Court's decision was correct: even when discrimination is arguably immoral, it's not necessarily illegal. Instead, we often recognize that *other* rights are even more important than the goal of eradicating discrimination.

Take, for example, freedom of speech. Most people would agree that it is morally wrong to stand in a public park and give a speech declaring that one race is superior to another. But such a speech is not illegal. It is protected by freedom of speech. The same is true of discriminatory books, newspapers, or websites: they're protected under freedom of the press. And the same is true of discriminatory personal relationships: the government doesn't punish people for choosing their spouses or friends based on racist criteria, because those relationships are protected by freedom of association.

In each of these cases, we've made a judgment that eradicating certain types of discrimination must take a back seat to protecting fundamental rights of speech, press, and association.

Of course, when a religious group discriminates by hiring coreligionists, it isn't doing anything nearly as invidious as engaging in hate speech, publishing racist literature, or forming discriminatory friendships. In many cases, it isn't doing anything wrong at all. But the point is that, even *assuming* religious discrimination is morally debatable, there is another important right on the other side of the scale: the right of *religious association*.

The right of religious association has been protected by US law for over two hundred years, and it simply means this: religious *individuals* have a right to practice their religion in religious *groups*.

But this right is often misunderstood, and it is now a significant battleground of modern religious freedom conflicts. So we have to understand what the right of religious association is and where it comes from.

THE RIGHT OF RELIGIOUS ASSOCIATION

Let's begin with where it comes from. In chapter 3, I explained that religious freedom is a fundamental human right rooted in who we are as human beings. We're all born with reason, conscience, and a thirst for transcendent truth. But we can't embrace truth authentically unless we embrace it freely. Therefore, to treat people as fully human, the government must, within reasonable limits, let people seek and embrace transcendent truth as they understand it. This right is inherent in every individual human being.

But human beings are not isolated individuals. We're also *social* beings. We're born and raised in families. We naturally seek relationships with other people. When we find transcendent truth, we naturally want to share that truth with others, inviting them to embrace and celebrate it with us. That's why every religion from the dawn of time has been expressed communally. It's also why every major human-rights declaration protects religious freedom not only as an individual right but also as a group right.[6] It's who we are as human beings.

We see this in Scripture too. God commanded Adam and Eve to "be fruitful and multiply" (Genesis 1:28). He promised to make Abraham into a great nation that would bless the entire world (12:2). And He ultimately fulfills that promise through Jesus Christ, who redeems the people of God and unites them into a community filled with the Holy Spirit—the church, which is the bride of Christ (Ephesians 2:11–22; 5:25–27). We're made to worship God in community with others.

That has profound implications for religious freedom. It means that to treat people as fully human, the government must let them seek truth not just individually but communally. It must respect their right to form religious groups and to practice their faith in religious groups. It must respect the right of religious association.

That's where the right of religious association comes from. But what does this right entail?

Historically, the right of religious association has meant three main things. First, it means religious groups have a right to *determine their religious beliefs and doctrine.*[7] The government might interfere with religious doctrine in many ways. Several of the early colonies had legally established churches with articles of faith that were dictated by the colonial legislatures. That's an extreme example. But the government can also interfere with doctrine in more subtle ways.

In the Mormon gymnasium case, for example, the ACLU argued that working for a gym was not a religious activity, but the Mormon church argued that, as a matter of Mormon doctrine, it was. If the court had ruled against the Mormon church on that question, it would have effectively decided a question of religious doctrine. As Justice Brennan put it, "determining whether an activity is religious or secular . . . results in considerable ongoing government entanglement in religious affairs" and "raises concern that a religious organization may be chilled in its free exercise activity."[8] In other words, religious groups must have freedom to decide religious questions.

Second, the right of religious association means religious groups have a right to *establish internal rules for governing themselves.* Some religious groups might organize themselves hierarchically, like the Roman Catholic Church. Others might organize themselves congregationally, like Baptist churches. Some might have formal ecclesiastical courts for deciding religious disputes. Others might resolve disputes by consensus. Some might have strict rules for excommunicating rebellious members. Others might have no formal membership at all.

The right of religious association means that the government, to the extent possible, leaves religious groups free to govern themselves. It doesn't dictate how they organize themselves or interfere in their religious disputes. It respects their right, as the Supreme Court has said, "to decide for themselves, free from state interference, matters of church government."[9]

Third, the right of religious association means religious groups have a right to *choose their members and leaders in accordance with their beliefs.* This means religious groups can exclude members who disagree with their religious beliefs or violate their religious principles. As the Supreme Court said in 1872, "We cannot decide who ought to be members of the church, nor whether the excommunicated have been regularly or irregularly cut off."[10] It also means religious groups can choose their leaders without government interference. As the court said in 2012, "The church must be free to choose those who will guide it on its way."[11]

This is not an exhaustive account of the right of religious association, but it gives us enough of a start that we can begin considering some of the key modern conflicts. Not surprisingly, those conflicts often come from the application—or misapplication—of antidiscrimination laws. We'll first consider the application of antidiscrimination laws to the selection of religious leaders; then we'll consider the application of those laws to the selection of lower-level employees.

CHOOSING RELIGIOUS LEADERS

The most important Supreme Court case on this topic is *Hosanna-Tabor*, which I discussed briefly in the introduction. To review, Hosanna-Tabor was a small Lutheran church in Michigan with 150 members and a small Christian school. In 2004, the fourth-grade teacher, Cheryl Perich, missed the first half of the school year with an illness, forcing the church to hire a replacement teacher for the remainder of the school year.

When Perich recovered, she demanded her job back, created a disturbance at the school, and threatened to sue the church if it didn't reinstate her immediately. The church had no money for a lawyer and couldn't just fire the replacement teacher. After meeting with Perich, the church decided to let her go, citing her "insubordination and disruptive behavior," as well as her "threatening to take legal action."[12]

Perich then sued the church under the Americans with Disabilities Act (ADA). The ADA prohibits employers from discriminating against qualified workers because of a disability. It also prohibits employers from retaliating against workers who threaten to assert their legal rights. According to Perich, the church had done just that: it had discriminated against her because of her illness and had retaliated against her for threatening to sue. Her lawsuit demanded her job back plus hundreds of thousands of dollars in damages and attorneys' fees.

The church, in response, said Perich had disqualified herself from the ministry by refusing to cooperate with church leadership, creating upheaval at the school, and threatening to sue the church. It specifically invoked 1 Corinthians 6:1–8, which instructs Christians not to sue one another in secular court. And it argued that it would violate the church's religious freedom to force the church to hire Perich after she had disregarded the church's leadership and violated church teaching.

Thus, on one hand was Perich, who claimed a right to be free from discrimination because of her disability. On the other hand was the church, which claimed a right to choose its teachers without government interference. Which claim should win: nondiscrimination or religious freedom?

As you may recall from the introduction, I represented the church in the Supreme Court, and we won the case 9–0. The Supreme Court ruled it would violate the church's religious freedom to punish it for firing Perich. To understand why we won—and why the decision is correct—it's helpful to consider an alternative scenario.

Imagine the elders of a local church decide to fire the church's pastor. The pastor didn't preach heresy or commit adultery. The elders simply decided he wasn't very effective; his sermons were mediocre and his leadership was uninspired. But the pastor believes he was a victim of discrimination. He was a sixty-three-year-old African American and was replaced by a thirty-five-year-old Caucasian. So he sues the church for discrimination based on his age and race.

This case presents the same sort of conflict *Hosanna-Tabor* did. On one hand is the pastor, who claims a right to be free from discrimination. On the other hand is the church, which claims a right to choose its pastor without government interference. Which claim should win: nondiscrimination or religious freedom?

If the pastor's lawsuit went forward, it would create serious problems. As a legal matter, the key question in the case would be a factual one: What was the *real* reason the elders fired the pastor? Was it because he was an ineffective pastor? Or was it because of his age or race?

To prove his case, the pastor would try to offer evidence of a discriminatory motive, such as racist or ageist comments by the elders. He would also offer evidence that he really *was* an effective pastor, such as testimony by church members who were inspired by his sermons.

The elders, on their part, would offer evidence that he was an ineffective pastor. They'd give examples of poor preaching or mediocre leadership.

A jury would then decide whose testimony was most credible. The court and jury, in effect, would decide whether the pastor was effective or not. And if the pastor won his case, the court would issue an order reinstating him to his job—meaning the elders would have to hire him as their pastor again or else face fines and imprisonment for contempt of court. In short, by enforcing its antidiscrimination laws, the government would choose the church's pastor. This would be a serious violation of religious freedom.

That is just one example. If antidiscrimination laws always trumped religious freedom, they would also prohibit churches from having an all-male clergy (which is sex discrimination). They would prohibit Orthodox synagogues from requiring their rabbis to be ethnically Jewish (which is ethnicity discrimination). And they would prohibit the Catholic Church from requiring priests to be celibate (which is marital-status discrimination).

Because of this, ever since Congress enacted antidiscrimination laws, the courts have also recognized what they call the "ministerial exception." Rooted in the First Amendment, the ministerial exception says the government can't enforce antidiscrimination laws in a way that would interfere with a religious group's choice of its religious leaders. So even if a religious leader may have been a victim of discrimination, the courts won't interfere because they can't decide who is qualified to lead a religious organization, much less impose an unwanted leader on a church.

That may sound easy enough, but who counts as a *religious leader*? Pastors, priests, and rabbis obviously count. Secretaries and janitors don't. What about everyone in between?

That was the key question in *Hosanna-Tabor*. Perich was not a pastor or a janitor; she was a schoolteacher. Should she be treated like a religious leader or not?

The question of how to define a religious leader is a delicate one, and our legal team spent hours contemplating the best way to draw the line, as did the Supreme Court. Ultimately, the court decided to avoid any "rigid formula" for defining religious leaders. Instead, it said Perich was a religious leader based on "all the circumstances of her employment."[13] These included the fact that the church had given her the formal title of "commissioned minister"; her title reflected a significant amount of religious training and a formal process of "commissioning" by a majority vote of the church congregation; she held herself out as a minister by speaking of her "teaching ministry"; and, most importantly, her job played "a role in conveying the Church's message and carrying out its mission"—specifically, by teaching her students a religion class four days a week, leading them in prayer three times a day, and leading the school-wide chapel service twice a year. In short, Perich "performed an important role in transmitting the Lutheran faith to the next generation."[14] So her lawsuit had to be dismissed.

The decision in *Hosanna-Tabor* has huge implications for religious freedom. For one thing, it means that when there's a conflict between anti-discrimination laws and religious freedom, religious freedom often wins. Sometimes this is because the alleged discrimination simply isn't wrong— like when a Christian group hires Christians to carry out its ministry. Other times, even if the alleged discrimination is arguably wrong, there's an even more important value on the other side—the right of religious association. So as a society and a legal system, we decide the government can't intrude on that right.

Practically speaking, this means religious groups don't have to worry about antidiscrimination lawsuits when they choose their religious leaders. That's a good thing. If the church in *Hosanna-Tabor* had lost, or if the Supreme Court had eliminated the ministerial exception altogether, religious groups could face lawsuits anytime they replaced their leaders. Many of those lawsuits would be baseless, but even baseless lawsuits impose significant costs in terms of emotional energy, time, and legal fees. And the risk of costly lawsuits would inevitably influence the selection of religious leaders. Rather than simply choosing the best person for the job, religious groups would also have to consider the risk of litigation.

Hosanna-Tabor doesn't answer every question a religious group might have about who qualifies as a religious leader. Pastors obviously qualify. So do schoolteachers like Perich, who have a religious title and help teach the faith to the next generation. Other courts have extended the ministerial exception to the principal of a religious school,[15] the chaplain at a Methodist hospital,[16] the communications director for a Catholic diocese,[17] the kosher food supervisor at a Jewish nursing home,[18] and the music director at a Catholic elementary school[19] or church.[20] There will always be positions closer to the line that involve some risk and require good legal counsel. But by and large, *Hosanna-Tabor* has given religious groups broad freedom to select their leaders. And that freedom is relatively durable, because the decision in *Hosanna-Tabor* was unanimous—meaning it is less likely to be eroded by the changing composition of the Supreme Court.

This means that some of the pressure on religious freedom has shifted away from the selection of religious leaders and toward the selection of lower-level religious workers. For lower-level workers, the law is less clear, meaning religious freedom conflicts are more likely. To those conflicts we now turn.

Choosing Religious Workers

Recall the Mormon gymnasium case that began this chapter. The Supreme Court based its decision on a federal statute, Title VII, which says *religious organizations* have a right to hire *persons of a particular religion.* So Mormon organizations can hire only Mormons, Catholic organizations can hire only Catholics, and so forth. This right is not limited to the hiring of religious *leaders.* It applies to *all* workers, from the pastor to the janitor.

But there are two big questions about this legal right: First, what counts as a religious organization? And second, what does it mean to hire persons of a particular religion?

Consider the "religious organization" question first. Can Walmart declare itself to be a religious organization and begin hiring only Christians? Of course not. Some organizations are obviously religious (like a church) and some aren't (like Walmart). Others fall somewhere in between—like a hospital that began as religious but has lost most of its religious identity. So courts sometimes must decide whether an organization is religious.

To do so, courts typically look at a variety of factors, such as whether the organization holds itself out to the public as religious, whether it is affiliated with a church or denomination, whether it is organized as a nonprofit, and whether it offers its services for free or at below-market rates. Based on these factors, courts have decided that World Vision (a Christian humanitarian aid organization),[21] a Jewish community center,[22] and a Mormon gymnasium are "religious organizations."[23] But a business that manufactures mining equipment,[24] a Methodist children's home,[25] and a private school that was nominally Protestant are not.[26] If this sounds like a mishmash, that's because it is. Courts have been inconsistent. They've also tended to focus too much on whether an organization is formally affiliated with a church and not enough on whether an organization holds itself out to the public as religious. But it hasn't mattered too much because religious groups aren't often sued for religious discrimination.[27]

The second (and far more important) question about the right to hire religious workers is, What does it mean to hire persons of a particular religion? It obviously means that a Catholic school can hire only Catholics— rejecting Protestants, Jews, Muslims, and atheists. But can a Catholic school also require its workers to *live* as faithful Catholics? What if the school's secretary gets pregnant out of wedlock or has an abortion? What if the basketball coach moves in with his girlfriend, starts living as the opposite gender, or publicly enters into a same-sex marriage? Can the school say, "We don't want workers who merely *claim* to be Catholic; we want workers who *model* the Catholic faith to the next generation"? Or if the school fires those workers, can it be sued for pregnancy discrimination, marital-status discrimination, gender-identity discrimination, or sexual-orientation discrimination?

This is going to be one of the most significant religious freedom questions of the next decade: Can religious groups require their workers to follow religious standards of conduct?

This question arises in two different kinds of cases. One is where a worker claims that a religious group is using religious standards of conduct as a *pretext* for illegal discrimination. The other is where a worker claims that the religious standards of conduct are *themselves* a form of illegal discrimination.

CLAIMS OF PRETEXT

Consider pretext claims first. Imagine, for example, that a Catholic school dismisses a teacher after she marries a divorced man in violation of Catholic teaching. The teacher, however, claims this wasn't the *real* reason she was dismissed; it was a *pretext*. The real reason, she says, was her age: she was over fifty years old and was the highest-paid teacher, and she was replaced by a younger, lower-paid teacher.[28]

What happens next? In the typical employment-discrimination case, both sides offer evidence and the jury ultimately decides who was telling the truth. But when the case involves a violation of religious teaching, this becomes tricky. The Catholic school in our example will offer testimony that divorce and remarriage in violation of Catholic teaching is a grave sin. The teacher will offer contrary evidence—such as testimony that the pope has softened the church's stance on the issue, that many Catholics ignore this teaching, or that the school has failed to discipline teachers for similar offenses. Ultimately, the jury will have to decide a deeply religious question: How serious was this religious offense? Was it serious enough that it must have been the motivation for the firing? Or was it minor enough that it was probably just a pretext for age discrimination?

A jury is not competent to decide this question. Many jurors will be unfamiliar with church teaching. Some may be hostile to Catholics (or other faiths). Even if they try to put aside their biases and understand unfamiliar church teachings, they might still misjudge the credibility of witnesses or the weight of evidence, meaning that erroneous judgments are inevitable. We might accept the risk of these sorts of errors when the defendant is a secular employer and the only cost is to the employer's pocketbook. But when the defendant is a religious group, these errors impose a heavy cost on the right of religious association: they penalize a church for making a legitimate, nondiscriminatory decision based on church teaching—sometimes at a cost of hundreds of thousands of dollars.

Unfortunately, the law on religious pretext claims is inconsistent. Although some courts have blocked these types of claims,[29] others have allowed them to go forward, saying that courts can determine a religious group's true motive without "calling into question the value or truthfulness of religious doctrine."[30] There is no sign that this will change anytime soon. If anything, as the culture becomes more hostile to "discrimination," we can expect more religious groups to face these sorts of claims.

Because of this, until the law improves, religious groups should consider adopting a few simple practices to reduce their risk. First, they should have clear, written standards of conduct that are communicated to all employees. If the standards are written and communicated in advance, a jury is much less likely to dismiss them as a pretext later.

Second, religious groups should have clear procedures for enforcing standards of conduct and should follow those procedures consistently. Procedural irregularities or inconsistencies can be taken as evidence of pretext.

Third, in all interactions with employees, religious groups should be gentle, gracious, and humble—not harsh, vindictive, or self-righteous. The goal should be reconciliation, not revenge (Romans 12:18–19). And if reconciliation is impossible, the relationship should end with as much grace as possible. Juries can tell when an employer has been harsh or unkind and will punish accordingly. More importantly, humility, gentleness, and grace are the way of Jesus.

Finally, before disciplining a worker for violating standards of conduct, religious groups should get legal advice, which can help avoid unnecessary legal conflicts.

CLAIMS THAT RELIGIOUS STANDARDS ARE ILLEGAL

Even more troubling than claims of pretext are claims that religious standards of conduct are *themselves* a form of illegal discrimination. Take, for example, abortion. Federal law prohibits employers from discriminating against workers because they've had an abortion.[31] But many religious groups view having an abortion as a serious violation of religious teaching. What happens, then, if a Catholic school fires a teacher for having an abortion and the teacher sues for discrimination?

Note how this is different from a pretext case. In a pretext case, the teacher says, "You fired me because of my age" (or race or disability or sex). The school says, "No, we didn't. We fired you because you violated church teaching." The dispute is over what the *real* reason was for the firing.

But in the abortion example, the teacher says, "You fired me because I had an abortion." The school says, "Yes, we did, because abortion is a serious violation of religious teaching." There is no dispute over the reason for the firing. The dispute is over whether the school can legally act on its religious beliefs.

This sort of dispute is not limited to abortion. It can arise in a variety of contexts. For example, a religious group might dismiss a worker for unmarried cohabitation or for divorce without cause and then get sued for marital-status discrimination.[32] A group might dismiss a worker for getting pregnant out of wedlock or for using in vitro fertilization and then get sued for pregnancy discrimination.[33] Or a group might dismiss a worker for entering a same-sex marriage or attempting to live as the opposite gender and then get sued for sexual-orientation or gender-identity discrimination.[34] In these cases, there would be no dispute over the *real* reason for the firing. The dispute would be over whether the religious group can act on its religious beliefs.

It's easy to see why this is a serious religious freedom problem. It's one thing for the government to say, "You can act on your religious beliefs, but we don't think that's actually what you were doing in this case." That's a pretext case. But it's quite another thing for the government to say, "We know you were acting on your religious beliefs, but we don't care; we're going to punish you anyway." When the government does that, it makes certain religious beliefs illegal. It makes it impossible to form religious groups based on those beliefs. And it strikes at the core of religious freedom, which is not just the right to hold religious beliefs as an individual but also the right to act on religious beliefs in community.

Accordingly, some courts have rejected these kinds of claims. In one case a Christian preschool dismissed a teacher for engaging in extramarital sex. When the teacher sued for pregnancy discrimination, the court rejected her claim, stating that the school's policy against extramarital sex was a "legitimate, non-discriminatory reason" for the dismissal.[35] In another case a Catholic school dismissed an English teacher for engaging in pro-abortion activism. When the teacher sued for sex discrimination, the court rejected her claim, emphasizing that religious groups have a right "to create and maintain communities composed solely of individuals faithful to their doctrinal practices."[36] In other words, religious groups have a right to both hire and dismiss people based on their religious conduct.[37]

Unfortunately, other courts have interpreted religious freedom more narrowly. These courts say religious groups can hire people who share their religious *beliefs* but can't enforce standards of *conduct* if those standards result in discrimination based on marital status, sexual orientation, or the like.

In one case, a Catholic school in Ohio dismissed an unmarried, lesbian teacher who became pregnant through artificial insemination in violation of Catholic teaching. The teacher sued for pregnancy discrimination, and the court allowed the case to go forward, resulting in a $171,000 jury verdict.[38] In another case, a Catholic school in Indiana dismissed a teacher who continued using in vitro fertilization after a priest explained that it violated church teaching and asked her to stop. The teacher sued for pregnancy discrimination, and the court sent the case to a jury, resulting in a $1.9 million verdict.[39]

Because the law in this area is unclear, and because common religious beliefs increasingly clash with cultural norms of nondiscrimination, we can expect more of these lawsuits in the future. Particularly in the area of human sexuality, religious groups need to be prepared for lawsuits claiming that their religious standards of conduct are discriminatory. Strong legal arguments for rejecting those claims exist. But courts have also shown a willingness to punish religious groups for acting on their standards of conduct, particularly if they seem to be acting harshly or inconsistently.[40]

Thus, until the law improves, religious groups should reduce their risk by clearly communicating their standards of conduct to employees in advance, establishing clear processes for enforcing those standards consistently with grace and humility, and consulting legal counsel before a conflict arises.

Summing Up

Where do all these cases and legal principles leave us? What is the main takeaway?

The main takeaway is that we live in a society that is zealously committed to the idea of nondiscrimination. But taken to an extreme, that zeal produces absurd results. It would make it illegal for the Catholic Church to have only male priests. It would require Christian churches to hire atheist leaders. Or, on the flip side, it would force gay-rights groups to hire Christians who oppose same-sex marriage.

The lesson of this chapter is that the concept of discrimination has limits. This is most obvious when it comes to "religious discrimination" by religious groups. When a Christian group hires fellow Christians, it isn't doing anything wrong. It's simply forming a *Christian* group.

This is not only common sense but also a fundamental aspect of religious freedom. Religious freedom is not just the right to hold beliefs as individuals; it is also the right to act on religious beliefs in religious groups. This right of *religious association* is rooted in who we are as human beings—people with a natural urge to seek and embrace transcendent truth in community with others. And the Supreme Court has recognized this right for decades. The court's 9–0 decision in *Hosanna-Tabor* (the Lutheran school case) recognizes the right of religious groups to select their religious leaders—a right that is virtually absolute. And the court's 9–0 decision in *Amos* (the Mormon gymnasium case) recognizes the right of religious groups to hire workers based on their religion.

There are some serious conflicts at the outer edges of this right, particularly when religious groups seek to hold lower-level employees to religious standards of conduct. But the core of the right of religious association is firmly established, and it teaches us that antidiscrimination laws simply can't touch some aspects of religious freedom.

That is a crucial lesson to keep in mind as we consider some of the more difficult conflicts between our society's commitment to nondiscrimination and its commitment to religious freedom—such as in the areas of abortion rights and gay rights.

To the issue of abortion we now turn—via a fascinating little detour about the stubbornness of the Quakers.

Will Abortion Have
to Be Accepted?

The year was 1658.[1] None of the American colonies had a standing army. Instead, they had local militias to defend themselves, and they required every able-bodied male to serve. If even a few men refused, it could mean the difference between life and death.

Enter the Quakers. They arrived from England in the mid-1600s, seeking freedom to practice their faith. They took Jesus's command to turn the other cheek literally (Matthew 5:39), so they refused to serve in the militia.

The colonial authorities were incensed. They punished Quakers with fines, threats of violence, and confiscation of their property. One Quaker was beaten by a local sheriff who "threatened to 'split [his] brains.'"[2] Another had much of his life savings confiscated. Many refused to pay their fines because "the money [went] to pay soldiers or buy weapons."[3] Instead, they "joyfully accepted the plundering of [their] property" (Hebrews 10:34).

The Quakers wouldn't budge. Punishing them was useless. So the government eventually gave in. In the late 1600s, Massachusetts and Rhode Island became the first colonies to exempt the Quakers from military service.[4] During the Revolutionary War, the Quakers received a major break when General Washington released several Virginia Quakers who had been drafted into his army and wrote that those "conscientiously scrupulous against [bearing arms] in every Case" should be excused.[5] After the war, multiple states enacted new protections for conscientious objectors.[6]

During the Civil War, the War Department issued instructions to accommodate conscientious objectors,[7] and the 1864 Draft Act extended exemptions to all "conscientious objectors who were members of religious denominations opposed to the bearing of arms."[8] Similar exemptions were adopted by Congress during World Wars I and II.[9] And during the Vietnam War, the Supreme Court extended the right of conscientious objection to protect not only religious objectors but also those who objected on moral or ethical grounds.[10]

Today, the right of conscientious objection to military service is widely accepted as a quintessential example of the right of religious freedom.

In short, the Quakers won.

The Quakers' Lesson

The Quakers' victory teaches us several important lessons. First, sometimes religious freedom is gained only through persistent suffering. When the Quakers arrived in America, no laws protecting conscientious objection existed. They were repeatedly fined and imprisoned as lawbreakers. They won their freedom only after decades of suffering showed that it was both pointless and unjust to keep punishing them.

Second, religious freedom is worth protecting even when it's costly. Protecting the right of conscientious objection deprives the country of able-bodied soldiers who could otherwise defend it. Sometimes it even requires other citizens to fight and die in a conscientious objector's place. Yet we place such a high value on freedom of conscience that we accept this cost.

Third, we accept this cost only for *conscientious* objection—not other types of objection. No one is excused from military service because he is afraid to die or because he voted against the president who authorized the war. He is excused only if his conscience forbids him from fighting. That's because forcing someone to go against conscience is fundamentally wrong in a way that forcing someone to go against his fears or political preferences is not.

Finally, religious freedom protects the right to live according to a different moral view—particularly when it comes to something as serious as taking human life. The Quakers believed it was wrong to take human life, even in war. Most of the rest of the country disagreed. Yet religious freedom meant the Quakers were allowed to live differently. The government couldn't force them to participate in the taking of human life.

That lesson has profound implications for modern religious freedom conflicts over abortion.

CONSCIENTIOUS OBJECTION TO ABORTION

In 1973, the Supreme Court decided *Roe v. Wade,* declaring that women have a constitutional right to obtain an abortion. This raised a new and troubling question: If women have a constitutional right to obtain abortions, do doctors and hospitals have an obligation to provide them?

Thankfully, the answer was swift and unanimous: no. On the same day it decided *Roe v. Wade,* the Supreme Court decided *Doe v. Bolton,* which involved a Georgia law allowing religious individuals and hospitals to refrain from participating in abortions. The court held that "these provisions obviously are in the statute in order to afford appropriate protection to the individual and to the denominational hospital."[11] In other words, women may have a constitutional right to abortion, which means the government can't stop them from having one. But doctors also have the right of religious freedom, which means the government can't force them to participate.

This principle is now firmly codified in laws across the country. Just weeks after *Roe,* Congress passed the Church Amendment, which prohibits the government from requiring individuals or institutions to assist in abortions in violation of conscience.[12] That law has been joined by many more, including similar laws in almost every state.[13] These laws protect not only doctors who object to performing abortions but also other health-care providers (like nurses) and institutions (like hospitals) who refuse to "'participate,' 'refer,' 'assist,' 'arrange for,' 'admit any patient for,' 'allow the use of hospital facilities for,' 'accommodate,' or 'advise' concerning abortion."[14]

In short, our legal system strongly protects the right of conscientious objection to abortion. Just as Quakers can't be forced to participate in war when they are conscientiously opposed, religious doctors, nurses, and hospitals can't be forced to participate in abortion.

The rationale for this rule is simple. Abortion, like war, is a deeply divisive moral issue. Some believe it is morally justified; others believe it is a grave moral evil. So if the government authorizes abortion (or a war), it must protect the rights of those who conscientiously disagree. It doesn't get to tell the Quakers, "This war is morally justified, so you must fight in it." And it doesn't get to tell a doctor, "Abortion is morally justified, so you must provide it." The government must leave conscientious objectors free to live according to their dissenting moral views.

Our society understands this when it comes to military service. But abortion is more controversial. Abortion-rights activists view conscientious objection as a threat. They fear losing the right to abortion, and they believe moral condemnation of abortion is discriminatory and harmful to women.[15] They want to punish conscientious objectors and normalize abortion to the point that it is treated like any common medical procedure.

Fortunately, the law on surgical abortions is clear: no health-care professional or facility can be forced to participate in one—at least for now. So abortion-rights activists have changed tactics, focusing on closely related issues like abortion-inducing drugs, abortion-related health insurance, abortion-related speech, and assisted suicide. In each area, pro-abortion activists try to use the power of law to punish conscientious objectors. And conscientious objectors seek the freedom to live according to their beliefs.

The rest of this chapter outlines where these fights are occurring, how they are playing out, and whether religious freedom will be preserved. We'll start with a little-known case about some courageous pharmacists.

THE COURAGEOUS PHARMACISTS

For four generations, the Stormans family owned a small grocery store and pharmacy in Olympia, Washington. One day the family received a phone call asking why their pharmacy didn't carry the morning-after pill, a controversial form of contraception that may cause early abortions. Upon researching the drug, the family learned it could prevent a newly formed human embryo from attaching to the wall of its mother's uterus, thus, in their view, destroying a human life.[16] Because the family was committed to caring for all human life, they decided they couldn't sell the drug. Instead, their employees would refer customers to nearby pharmacies that sold it.

That wasn't good enough for Planned Parenthood and local pro-abortion activists. They protested the store, yelling at customers and disrupting traffic. They filed complaints with the state. And they ultimately convinced the governor to pass a new regulation making it illegal for pharmacies to refer customers elsewhere for religious reasons—even though pharmacies could still refer customers for nonreligious reasons.

The Stormans family then faced a difficult choice: either sell the morning-after pill, which could destroy a human life, or close the pharmacy, which would destroy their livelihood. Because they didn't want to do either, they filed a federal lawsuit asking the courts to protect their religious freedom. I had the privilege of representing them.

Our lawsuit was based on the Free Exercise Clause of the Constitution. As you may recall from chapter 4, the Supreme Court adopted a narrow interpretation of the Free Exercise Clause in 1990 in the *Smith* case, which involved the religious use of peyote by Native Americans.

Before *Smith,* the court required the government to prove that *any* law burdening religious freedom was justified by powerful governmental interest. But in *Smith,* the court said this strict test applies only if a law *specifically targets* religion. Thus, to win their lawsuit, the Stormans family had to prove the state was targeting them because of their religion.

The state claimed it wasn't targeting the Stormans; it was simply trying to ensure that all citizens had access to medication. But at trial, this argument was exposed as a sham. Within a five-mile radius of the Stormanses' pharmacy, over *thirty* pharmacies sold the morning-after pill. It was also available at nearby physicians' offices, government health centers, hospital emergency rooms, and on the internet with overnight delivery. Despite years of litigation and a statewide recruiting effort by Planned Parenthood, the state was unable to find a single example of any patient in Washington who had ever been denied timely access to any drug due to reasons of conscience.

By contrast, the state's own documents showed that it was targeting pharmacists because of their religious beliefs. The governor urged her advisers to make sure the new regulation was "clean enough" for Planned Parenthood on "consci[ence]/moral issues." She appointed a new chairman of the pharmacy board, who stated that "I for one am never going to vote to allow religion as a valid reason for a [pharmacy] referral." The chairman said he viewed religious referrals as an "immoral" form of "sex discrimination" and would recommend prosecuting them "to the full extent of the law."[17] And the commission's own spokesperson admitted that the goal of the regulation was to prohibit referrals for religious reasons while allowing referrals for nonreligious reasons.

Based on the evidence, the trial court concluded there was "no problem of access to [the morning-after pill] or any other drug before, during, or after the rulemaking process."[18] Instead, the purpose of the regulation was to "bar pharmacists and pharmacies from conscientiously objecting" while "allowing pharmacies and pharmacists to refuse to dispense [drugs] for practically any other reason."[19] This, the court said, showed that the regulation targeted pharmacists because of their religion, rendering it unconstitutional. The Stormans family won.

I wish I could say that was the end of the story, but it wasn't. The state appealed the ruling to the Ninth Circuit. That court issued a ruling ignoring key facts, distorting the law, and rejecting the Stormanses' claims. We then appealed to the US Supreme Court. To get a hearing in the Supreme Court, we needed four justices to vote to hear our case. But just weeks after we filed our appeal, Justice Scalia died, leaving the court short one member. Our appeal received three votes—one shy of what we needed. We lost the case.

Justice Alito, joined by Chief Justice Roberts and Justice Thomas, wrote a strong dissent, saying, "This case is an ominous sign. . . . If this is a sign of how religious liberty claims will be treated in the years ahead, those who value religious freedom have cause for great concern."[20] To their credit, however, the Stormans family remains committed to following their conscience, no matter what it costs them.

The Pharmacists' Lesson

The *Stormans* case is indeed an ominous sign and a painful loss. But it also helpfully illustrates the three most common arguments against conscientious objection: (1) conscientious objection blocks access to health care; (2) conscientious objection is a form of discrimination; and (3) conscientious objectors should get another job.[21] Upon closer scrutiny, these arguments lack merit.

First, consider the argument that conscientious objection blocks access to health care. In *Stormans,* this argument was a sham. The morning-after pill was widely available from a host of locations, including over thirty pharmacies within a five-mile radius. Planned Parenthood and the state searched diligently for years to find any customer who had ever been denied access to a drug for reasons of conscience—and never found one. By contrast, the state found many customers who were denied access to drugs for common business reasons, but it left those business decisions entirely unregulated. This shows that the state's real concern wasn't ensuring access to medication but suppressing moral opposition to abortion.

Of course, the calculus would be different if conscientious objectors were interfering with customers seeking medication, such as by confiscating their prescriptions or misleading them about where they could find the drug. That would be as if the Quakers were not only refusing to serve in the military but also actively trying to sabotage the war effort. Conscientious objection allows people to step aside, not step in the way.[22] But that is not what the *Stormans* family—or any other pharmacist—was doing.

The access argument is also based on a misguided assumption: that most conscientious objectors are just bluffing. According to this assumption, if conscientious objectors face punishment, they will eventually cave in and dispense the drugs or perform the abortions. But that is not the case. Many conscientious objectors will resign rather than violate their consciences. Some already have.[23] Thus, pressuring pharmacists, nurses, or doctors to violate their consciences won't increase access to health care for anyone; it will instead drive qualified people from the profession, reducing access to health care for everyone.

Second, in addition to arguing about access, opponents of conscientious objection argue that it is a form of discrimination because "abortion is not an abstract thing; it is a thing that women do."[24] Thus, according to this argument, declining to perform an abortion is an "immoral" act of "sex discrimination."[25]

This is a gross abuse of the term *discrimination*. It's like accusing the Quakers of race discrimination because they wouldn't fight in the Civil War. The Quakers' refusal to fight wasn't based on discrimination against African Americans; indeed, they were some of the most ardent opponents of slavery. Their refusal to fight was based on their belief that it is morally wrong to fight in war. Likewise, conscientious objectors' refusal to perform abortions isn't based on discrimination against women; it is based on their belief that it is wrong to destroy unborn human life. Calling that "discrimination" is just an attempt to obscure the crucial moral disagreement at the heart of the debate.

Finally, opponents of conscientious objection argue that conscientious objectors should get another job. As a *New York Times* op-ed put it, "Any pharmacist who cannot dispense medicines lawfully prescribed by a doctor should find another line of work."[26] But this argument really is discriminatory: it would exclude an entire class of people from a profession solely because of their religious beliefs. We would never accept this sort of exclusion based on race, sex, or national origin. It is no more acceptable when it is based on religion.

The calculus would be different if a health-care professional wanted to specialize in an area where she objected to most of the work. But that has never been an issue in the health-care context. Doctors can do the vast majority of their work without participating in abortions, and pharmacists can do the vast majority of their work without dispensing abortion-causing drugs.

The get-another-job argument also ignores the fact that many health-care professionals entered their field long before abortion became part of their profession. Many doctors entered their profession while abortion was still illegal. And many pharmacists entered their profession long before abortion-causing drugs were approved. For example, two pharmacists who lost their jobs in *Stormans* had over sixty years of combined experience before the morning-after pill was approved. It is unjust to force these people out of their profession simply because new practices arise that conflict with their religious beliefs.

Additionally, the get-another-job argument conflicts with the access argument. Opponents of conscientious objection can't say there is a problem of access to health care while at the same time trying to drive qualified people from the profession. The two positions are irreconcilable—unless the goal is not actually to increase access to health care but to eliminate conscientious objection.

That, ultimately, is the lesson of the *Stormans* case. Abortion-rights activists aren't content with abortion being legal. They want it to be socially and morally accepted. The greatest impediment to that goal is the existence of conscientious objectors, so those people must be repressed. Nor is this a secret: a leading ACLU attorney has acknowledged that her goal is to establish a norm that declining to perform an abortion is an illegal act of sex discrimination.[27]

Given that goal, our legal system has two options. It can go along with the ACLU, punishing those who conscientiously object to abortion and seeking to suppress dissent; or it can create space for dissenters, allowing them to live according to a different moral view. That is what our country has done for the Quakers. And that is what it should do for those who conscientiously object to abortion.

Fortunately, the Ninth Circuit's ruling in *Stormans* was not the last word on this issue. A pair of landmark Supreme Court cases—one involving a chain of arts-and-crafts stores called Hobby Lobby and one involving Catholic nuns called the Little Sisters of the Poor—illustrates how our legal system can create space for dissenting moral views.

HOBBY LOBBY AND THE LITTLE SISTERS OF THE POOR

In 1970, David and Barbara Green founded a small arts-and-crafts store in their garage. That family business, called Hobby Lobby, has since grown to over eight hundred stores in forty-seven states. As devout Christians, the Greens seek to honor God in everything they do, including by "operating the company in a manner consistent with Biblical principles."[28] They close on Sundays, start their workers at over twice the minimum wage, and donate millions of dollars to charity.

The Little Sisters of the Poor are Catholic nuns devoted to caring for the elderly poor. They operate homes for the elderly poor in over thirty countries, including the United States. In every home, they care for the elderly poor as if caring for Christ Himself.

What the Greens and the Little Sisters have in common is that they both became the target of a government regulation that would have forced them to be complicit in abortion in violation of their faith. Both took their cases to the Supreme Court, and both won. I had the privilege of helping represent them.

The government regulation at issue was part of the Affordable Care Act (a.k.a. Obamacare), and it required the Greens and the Little Sisters to use their health-insurance plans to provide their employees with all forms of FDA-approved contraception—including drugs and devices that could cause an abortion. If they refused to comply, they would owe millions of dollars in fines to the IRS.

Because of their religious belief that life begins at conception, the Greens and the Little Sisters couldn't comply. So they asked the courts to protect them.

Our lawsuits were based on a federal law we've already discussed—the Religious Freedom Restoration Act (RFRA). As you may recall from chapter 4, RFRA was designed to fix the Supreme Court's bad decision in *Smith,* which rejected the religious use of peyote by Native Americans. RFRA says that if *any* law imposes a substantial burden on religion, the government must prove that the law is justified by a powerful governmental interest. (In other words, the Greens and the Little Sisters *didn't* have to prove targeting like the Stormans family did. More on that later.)

When we got to the Supreme Court, the government argued that it hadn't substantially burdened the Greens' or Little Sisters' religion because it wasn't *directly* requiring them to participate in an abortion; it was merely requiring them to provide health-insurance plans, which employees could then use to access abortion-causing drugs. The government also argued that free access to contraception was a powerful governmental interest that couldn't be accomplished without using the Greens' and Little Sisters' insurance plans.

In response, the Greens and the Little Sisters argued that using their insurance plans to provide abortion-causing drugs would still make them complicit in abortion in violation of their religious beliefs, and that forcing them to do so on pain of multimillion-dollar fines was a substantial burden on their religion. They also argued that the government had many other ways to provide access to contraception without using their health-insurance plans—such as by using the government's own health-insurance marketplaces or the government's own family-planning programs.

The Supreme Court agreed with the Greens and the Little Sisters. It said the government wasn't allowed to second-guess the Greens' and Little Sisters' religious beliefs about what would make them complicit in an abortion; rather, it said that was "a difficult and important question of religion and moral philosophy" for religious individuals to decide.[29] It also said the government could find other ways of providing access to contraception.[30] As Justice Kennedy wrote, religious freedom means "more than just freedom of belief. . . . It means, too, the right to express those beliefs . . . in the political, civic, and economic life of our larger community."[31]

After our victories in the Supreme Court, the government did find a way to increase access to contraception without forcing the Greens or the Little Sisters to violate their religious beliefs. It adopted rules protecting the Greens and the Little Sisters while allowing their employees to obtain free contraception from a government program called Title X.[32] Religious freedom and access to contraception didn't have to conflict.

The Supreme Court's Lesson

The *Hobby Lobby* and *Little Sisters* cases reveal several important lessons. First, they teach us that laws like RFRA matter. Without RFRA, the Greens and the Little Sisters would have had to prove that the government was intentionally targeting them because of their religious beliefs. That is often a tall order, as the case of the courageous pharmacists (*Stormans*) shows. But under RFRA, the burden of proof flips to the *government* to show that burdening people's religion is the only way to accomplish an extremely important governmental goal. That's a tall order for the government—and it's often the difference between winning and losing a case.

Given that difference, you might wonder why the courageous pharmacists didn't base their lawsuit on RFRA like the Greens and the Little Sisters did. The reason is that RFRA is a *federal* law that applies to actions only of the *federal* government.[33] The courageous pharmacists, however, were challenging a *state* regulation, so they couldn't rely on RFRA. And their state—Washington—hasn't adopted a state-level version of RFRA.

Second, these cases teach us that religious freedom extends beyond the four walls of our homes or churches and includes our ministries and businesses. In *Hobby Lobby*, the government argued that it wasn't infringing religious freedom because it was penalizing only a business (Hobby Lobby)—and businesses don't have a religion. But the Supreme Court rejected this argument because businesses are owned and operated by people—and people do have religion. So when the government punishes a business, it is punishing the people who own and operate that business.

Finally, these cases teach us that the law can and should create space for people to disagree. Some people have no moral objection to providing abortion-causing drugs. Others, like the Greens and the Little Sisters, do. Their conscience forbids them from participating in the destruction of human life. Forcing them to violate their conscience is wrong, just like forcing the Quakers to violate their conscience is wrong. It's wrong when the interests on the other side are weighty—like when the country is defending itself in time of war. And it's especially wrong when the interests on the other side are slight—like when the government can easily find other ways to provide contraception without forcing conscientious objectors to participate.

WHAT NOW?

I wish our victories in *Hobby Lobby* and *Little Sisters* were the final word on this issue, but they aren't. Pro-abortion activists continue to press the fight on four key battlegrounds.

First, pro-abortion activists are still trying to force conscientious objectors to include abortion in their health-insurance plans. Our victories in *Hobby Lobby* and *Little Sisters* were based on RFRA—a *federal* law that applies only to the federal government. It doesn't apply to the states. So pro-abortion activists are trying to accomplish the same goal using *state law*. Twenty-eight states have enacted contraception mandates similar to those at issue in *Hobby Lobby* and *Little Sisters,* requiring insurance plans to cover prescription contraceptives, often including drugs like the morning-after and week-after pills, which can cause abortions.[34] Four states—California, New York, Oregon, and Washington—have gone even further, requiring insurance plans to cover surgical abortions.[35] Some of these laws have religious exemptions, but some don't. All these laws are attempts to normalize abortion—to treat it like a common medical procedure and force conscientious objectors to accept it. And several of these states don't have laws like RFRA—meaning that conscientious objectors will have to fight against these laws one at a time and that victory is not assured.

Second, pro-abortion activists are filing lawsuits attempting to force Catholic hospitals to perform abortions and sterilizations in violation of Catholic teaching. In some cases, they argue that abortion is required as a form of emergency medical care.[36] In others, they argue that failing to perform an abortion or sterilization is a form of sex discrimination or medical negligence.[37] In still others, they try to block secular hospitals from merging with Catholic hospitals unless the newly merged hospital agrees to perform abortions and sterilizations.[38] So far these lawsuits have been unsuccessful. But pro-abortion activists will continue filing them until they find a receptive judge.

Third, pro-abortion activists are lobbying for laws that would restrict conscientious objectors' speech. Several jurisdictions have passed laws prohibiting peaceful conversations on public sidewalks within a certain distance of abortion clinics—so-called buffer zones. These laws are designed to stop pro-life counselors from speaking with women arriving at abortion clinics. In *McCullen v. Coakley,* a Supreme Court case argued by my

Becket colleague Mark Rienzi, the court struck down Boston's buffer-zone law and suggested that similar laws may be unconstitutional. But the Supreme Court has yet to overrule an earlier decision in *Hill v. Colorado,* which allows other buffer-zone laws to remain on the books.

In addition to passing buffer-zone laws, other localities have passed laws targeting the speech of crisis pregnancy centers, which are organizations that serve women facing unplanned pregnancies by giving them free pregnancy testing, ultrasounds, baby clothes, counseling, and other forms of support. Some laws have threatened crisis pregnancy centers with fines for "misleading" speech simply because they placed advertisements using the word *abortion.*[39] Other laws compel crisis pregnancy centers to issue disclaimers saying they don't provide abortions or to instruct clients on where they can get abortions for free.[40] The Supreme Court recently struck down one of the most intrusive disclaimer laws in *National Institute of Family and Life Advocates v. Becerra.*[41] But other similar laws remain on the books as a threat to pro-life speech.

Finally, an emerging battleground is the practice of assisted suicide, which is now legal in seven states and the District of Columbia.[42] None of these states currently require conscientiously objecting doctors or pharmacists to personally prescribe or deliver lethal drugs. But that is a goal for assisted-suicide activists. As a first step, they're arguing that "medical aid in dying" (i.e., assisted suicide) is a critical health-care service and that doctors shouldn't "restrict their patient's [*sic*] access to relevant treatment information."[43] In other words, doctors must present suicide as a valid option for their patients, and if they won't assist the suicide themselves, they must refer the patient to a doctor who will.

Understandably, many doctors believe that telling their patients they can kill themselves not only is bad medicine but also would make them complicit in the destruction of human life—and they conscientiously object to doing so. Nevertheless, assisted-suicide activists argue that "conscience protections of healthcare providers" cannot supersede "the rights of patients to access all of their own healthcare options and determine their medical treatment."[44] In other words, access to assisted suicide is just like access to abortion. Just as doctors must help patients kill their unborn children, now they must help patients kill themselves.

What Can Be Done?

What can we do about these emerging conflicts? A few things. First, as Christians, we must strive to be "a model of good works" (Titus 2:7). We must "show integrity, dignity, and sound speech that cannot be condemned, so that [our] opponent[s] may be put to shame, having nothing evil to say about us" (verses 7–8; see also 1 Peter 2:12; 3:8–17). This is not only a binding command of Scripture but also good practical advice. Opponents of conscientious objection are looking for bad examples. They want to find a pharmacist who belittles a customer, a business that mistreats its workers, or a religious leader full of hypocrisy. Bad examples enable them to enact bad laws and win bad cases.

But the Stormans family, the Green family, and the Little Sisters of the Poor are models of good works. Religious hospitals, crisis pregnancy centers, and end-of-life care doctors are models of good works. The Quakers are models of good works. They comfort the dying, contribute to their communities, and care for the most vulnerable members of society.

When conscientious objectors are full of good works, they show that nothing is gained by oppressing them—and much is lost. Their opponents may "revile [their] good behavior in Christ," but they will ultimately "be put to shame"—because the government doesn't typically like to suppress the source of good works (1 Peter 3:16). As Peter put it, "Who is there to harm you if you are zealous for what is good?" (verse 13).

Of course, good works are no guarantee of good treatment or good laws. Second, we must also be ready to "suffer for righteousness' sake" (verse 14), just like the Quakers and the early church. The Little Sisters of the Poor experienced this. They were facing multimillion-dollar fines starting on January 1, 2014, for refusing to provide abortion-causing drugs through their health insurance. On New Year's Eve, they still had no protection from any court. As a last-ditch effort—a legal Hail Mary—we filed an emergency appeal with the Supreme Court. The appeal fell to Justice Sotomayor, who was scheduled to drop the ball in Times Square that night. We had no reason to expect she would protect the Little Sisters. But as the minutes ticked by, the Little Sisters spent the night in prayer. Shortly before midnight, we called them with the good news—Justice Sotomayor had granted our request, staving off multimillion-dollar fines that would have started that morning. The Little Sisters were ecstatic. But they were also fully prepared to suffer for righteousness' sake.

Finally, we need to be able to make the case for religious freedom as a matter of both principle and pragmatism. As a matter of principle, it is simply wrong for the government to force conscientious objectors to participate in the destruction of human life, whether in war or abortion. Particularly on matters as fundamental as life and death, forcing someone to go against conscience violates the core of who we are as human beings.

But religious freedom is also valuable at a more practical level. Our country is deeply divided over the morality of abortion. Some believe it is morally permissible; others believe it is murder. Given the Supreme Court's decision to legalize abortion, the government has two options. It can double down on *Roe v. Wade*—picking one side of the moral debate and forcing everyone to conform by punishing conscientious objectors. Or it can preserve the freedom to live according to a different moral view by allowing conscientious objectors to live according to their beliefs. The former produces intense social conflict, as the Quakers can attest. They were beaten, fined, and imprisoned for decades for refusing military service. But the latter allows a truce: controversial practices like abortion may be allowed, but conscientious objectors are not forced to participate.

This sort of compromise is not entirely satisfying to either side of the moral debate, but it protects the fundamental right of conscientious objectors to live according to their dissenting moral views. It also enables citizens of opposing moral views to live together in relative peace.

This is what our country has been doing on the issue of abortion for the last forty years. The question now is this: Can we reach the same sort of compromise on gay rights? Or will the government force everyone to conform to a single moral view? To answer that question, we'll start with the story of a faithful couple from Iowa named Dick and Betty Odgaard.

Will Gay Rights Trump Religious Freedom? (The Problem)

In 2002, Betty and Dick Odgaard rescued an old Lutheran church that was going to be torn down and replaced with a gas station. They turned it into an art gallery, frame shop, and wedding venue.

They carefully preserved the sanctuary, where they displayed Betty's artwork, and they personally oversaw the details of each wedding. They met with each couple to help plan the schedule, flowers, decor, and food. And they attended each wedding to prepare the sanctuary and make sure every detail was just right.

In 2013, two men asked Betty and Dick to host their same-sex wedding. Betty and Dick had hired gay and lesbian employees and served gay and lesbian customers for many years. But their religious convictions wouldn't let them personally plan and host a same-sex wedding. They politely declined.

The next day, the men filed a discrimination complaint against Betty and Dick with the Iowa Civil Rights Commission. When the complaint hit the press, Betty and Dick became the target of a boycott, hate mail, and threatening messages. As one message put it, "You are mean, rude, selfish, mother f——er racist sons of b——es from hell . . . f——k your God f——k your religion. . . . Soon very bad things will happen to you. . . . You are finished[.] You are doomed[.] I warned you."[1]

My firm, Becket, represented Betty and Dick in court. During litigation, we discovered the men had already gotten married months before asking Betty and Dick to host their wedding, so the whole controversy appeared to be a setup. Nevertheless, facing years of emotionally draining legal proceedings, Betty and Dick decided to put the conflict behind them. They paid the couple $5,000 to settle the case and agreed to stop hosting weddings.[2] Without the income from weddings, they were forced to close the gallery a few months later.[3]

Betty and Dick were heartbroken to see over a decade of their life's work end this way. But they are convinced they did the right thing by following their conscience, and they remain committed to their faith. They eventually sold the church building to a local congregation, which now uses it as a house of worship.

How Big Is the Problem?

I wish Betty and Dick's story were rare. But it isn't. Since the Supreme Court legalized same-sex marriage in 2015, dozens of similar conflicts have erupted. Christians increasingly face difficult choices in their businesses, schools, congregations, and ministries.

Some Christians hear about these stories and fear the worst. They anticipate a slippery slope, where churches will eventually be forced to perform same-sex weddings and pastors will go to jail if they refuse. Other Christians dismiss these stories as fearmongering. They argue that Christians in other countries face much worse problems than we do, and they think American Christians are buying into a persecution complex that imagines problems where there are none.

Both views are mistaken. Pastors aren't going to jail anytime soon for refusing to perform same-sex weddings; our laws clearly protect against that. But conflicts between gay rights and religious freedom aren't going away anytime soon either. Acting on common Christian beliefs about marriage is increasingly viewed as a form of discrimination that should be punished. This will create a variety of significant legal conflicts, some of which will be costly and painful. Some will result in Christians being punished for following their consciences. The question is, first, how big is the problem? And second, what can we do about it?

Those questions are the subject of this chapter and the next. I'll start by diagnosing the size of the problem—explaining the key legal conflicts that have already arisen and the new conflicts that are coming soon. After that, in chapter 8, I'll offer some solutions.

Two Types of Conflicts

The collision of gay rights and religious freedom produces two different types of conflicts: (1) private lawsuits and (2) government penalties. Private lawsuits occur when one person sues another for allegedly violating the law—like when the gay couple filed a complaint against Betty and Dick Odgaard for declining to host their same-sex wedding. Private lawsuits are the type of conflict we're most familiar with. Because of their highly personal nature, they tend to generate the most emotion and grab the most headlines.

Government penalties occur when the government, on its own initiative, rather than in response to any private lawsuit, penalizes someone in some way—such as by denying a license, grant, tax exemption, or other government benefit. We'll consider both types of conflicts in turn, starting with private lawsuits.

Private Lawsuits

Private lawsuits involving gay rights and religious liberty are typically based on laws governing three key areas: (1) public accommodations, (2) employment, and (3) housing.

Public Accommodations

Public accommodations are businesses that provide goods or services to the public—like hotels, restaurants, or theaters. Various state and federal laws make it illegal for public accommodations to discriminate on specific grounds, such as race, color, religion, national origin, or sex. The most famous public accommodations law is Title II of the Civil Rights Act of 1964, which was enacted during the civil rights movement to combat pervasive discrimination against African Americans.[4]

Over time, the definition of *public accommodation* has expanded to include not just hotels, restaurants, and theaters but almost any entity (other than a church) that is open to the public—including nonprofit organizations like the Boy Scouts[5] or privately organized events like a parade.[6] The prohibited grounds of discrimination have also expanded to include not only race, religion, and sex but also age, disability, marital status, and—in some states and localities—sexual orientation and gender identity.[7]

The addition of sexual orientation and gender identity to public accommodations laws has created a number of conflicts for religious people. Most well-known are the conflicts involving wedding vendors—like florists, photographers, and bakers. In these cases, LGBT individuals have asked for wedding-related goods or services, and the religious business owner has declined as a matter of conscience—prompting a lawsuit. In addition to florists, photographers, and bakers, cases have been brought against wedding venues,[8] bed-and-breakfasts,[9] bridal shops,[10] caterers,[11] and others—sometimes resulting in tens of thousands of dollars in penalties.[12]

In 2018, in a case called *Masterpiece Cakeshop v. Colorado Civil Rights Commission,* the Supreme Court ruled in favor of a Christian baker who declined to bake a cake for a same-sex wedding.[13] But the Supreme Court left many issues unresolved, and the scope of its ruling is hotly contested. This means we can expect to see more of these lawsuits in the future.

Although cases involving wedding-related businesses have generated the most attention, they're only the tip of the iceberg. The definition of *public accommodation* also covers a variety of nonprofit services provided by religious groups, such as health care, education, meeting spaces, marriage counseling, family counseling, job training, childcare, gyms, day camps, life coaching, and adoption services. So if religious groups decline to provide these services to same-sex couples or transgender individuals, they will be subject to lawsuits. For example, a Catholic church has been sued for declining to rent its meeting space to LGBT groups.[14] Religious adoption agencies have been sued for declining to place children with same-sex couples.[15] And religious hospitals have been sued for declining to perform gender transition surgeries on transgender patients.[16] These are just a few examples of conflicts under public accommodations laws; many more will come.

Employment

Aside from public accommodations laws, the second major source of conflict is lawsuits alleging discrimination in employment. Many religious groups, like churches, schools, and other ministries, expect their employees to follow traditional Christian teachings on sexuality. If an employee is fired for rejecting those teachings—such as by entering a same-sex marriage—the employee may sue for employment discrimination.

Many lawsuits like this have already been threatened or filed against various religious schools and ministries.[17] As discussed in chapter 5, the law governing these conflicts is currently unclear: some courts say religious groups have a right to require their employees to live by their religious principles; other courts say this is a form of discrimination that can be punished. Currently, most states and the federal government don't prohibit employment discrimination based on sexual orientation, but gay-rights organizations are actively trying to change the law through litigation and legislation. If they succeed—as they already have in several jurisdictions—we can expect many more of these lawsuits to come.

Housing

A third source of conflict is lawsuits alleging discrimination in housing. These conflicts can arise when a private landlord has a religious objection to renting housing to a same-sex couple.[18] Or they can arise when a religious college or university limits married student housing to students in traditional marriages.[19] Although these lawsuits are less common, they still present another source of risk for religious individuals and institutions.

GOVERNMENT PENALTIES

The risk of private lawsuits, however, pales in comparison with the second type of conflict: the problem of government penalties. The federal, state, and local governments in this country play a pervasive role in everyday life. They issue permits and licenses that determine when and where people can live and work. They make decisions about what schools must teach and which schools can be accredited. They own vast amounts of property and resources. They hire tens of millions of people. They issue billions of dollars in grants, contracts, and loans. They collect trillions of dollars in taxes. This is not a lament about "big government"; it's simply a fact of modern life.

The problem comes when the government decides that traditional religious beliefs about sexuality are a form of discrimination that is against public policy. If the government adopts that view, it has an almost infinite array of penalties it can impose. Consider just five key areas where penalties have already begun to be imposed: (1) licenses and accreditation; (2) contracts, grants, and loans; (3) access to government facilities; (4) government jobs; and (5) taxes.

Licenses and Accreditation

Through licensing and accreditation, the government acts as the gatekeeper for a variety of endeavors. Adoption is a prime example. The government doesn't let just any organization place children for adoption. It requires an organization to have a license. To get a license, an organization must play by the government's rules. In Boston, Illinois, and the District of Columbia, the government decided that all adoption agencies must be willing to place children with same-sex couples. This meant that local branches of Catholic Charities, which had been placing children in adoptions for over one hundred years, would have to either violate Catholic teaching or lose their licenses. So these Catholic Charities offices were forced to end their ministries.[20]

Professional counselors face similar risks. In 2014, the American Counseling Association adopted new ethics rules requiring counselors to advise couples on their same-sex relationships, even when doing so would violate the counselors' religious beliefs.[21] The same ethics rules have been adopted in several states. Thus, counselors in these states can lose their license if they decline to counsel same-sex couples on their relationships. Two students who were studying to be counselors in Michigan and Georgia have already been expelled from their state university counseling programs for declining to counsel same-sex couples.[22] And a law in Tennessee protecting counselors from this sort of punishment has been heavily criticized by the American Counseling Association and gay-rights groups.[23]

Religious colleges and universities also face losing their accreditation because of their traditional beliefs about sexuality. In 2001, the American Psychological Association (APA), which has authority from the government to accredit psychology programs, considered adopting a policy that would deny accreditation to religious colleges and universities that have codes of conduct prohibiting sex outside traditional marriage.[24] Under pressure from the US Department of Education, the APA temporarily relented. But there is little to stop the APA from adopting the same policy today.[25]

In fact, in Canada, the British Columbia bar association refused to recognize a Christian university's law school solely because the university required students and faculty to refrain from sex outside traditional marriage. The Canadian Supreme Court upheld the denial, meaning the law school was unable to open.[26]

Closer to home, the experience of Gordon College in Massachusetts is instructive. In 2014, Gordon's president signed a bipartisan letter asking President Obama to protect religious freedom in an executive order.[27] This action, however, drew attention to Gordon's policy of requiring students and faculty to refrain from sex outside traditional marriage. Local governments in Massachusetts then retaliated. The city of Salem terminated a contract allowing Gordon to use the city's Old Town Hall, citing a city ordinance that prohibits contracting with organizations that "discriminate."[28] The city of Lynn banned Gordon students from serving as student teachers in its public schools, with one city official comparing Gordon to "the Ku Klux Klan."[29] And Gordon's accreditor threatened to revoke its accreditation.[30]

Although Gordon weathered the storm and remained accredited, the lesson from its experience is clear: state and local governments can impose a variety of penalties on religious groups that believe in traditional marriage.

Contracts, Grants, and Loans

Another source of penalties are the billions of dollars in contracts, grants, and loans that governments award every year. Take religious schools, which receive a variety of government-sponsored vouchers, tax credits, grants, and loans. Any of those could be revoked on the grounds that religious schools are guilty of discrimination.

In 1984, the Supreme Court held that Grove City College could be denied federal education funds because it declined to certify that it wouldn't discriminate based on sex.[31] The same logic can easily be extended to sexual orientation, and several jurisdictions have already begun to do so. The state of Maryland, for example, excludes religious schools from its voucher program if the schools require students to refrain from homosexual conduct.[32] And California recently considered legislation that would have barred the use of state scholarships at schools requiring students or faculty to refrain from sex outside traditional marriage.[33]

Nor is this sort of penalty limited to education. Social service providers—like hospitals, homeless shelters, substance-abuse programs, and adoption agencies—can also be denied grants and contracts if they are deemed to discriminate. A city in Maine, for example, passed a law cutting off housing and community development funds from Catholic Charities unless it agreed to provide spousal benefits to same-sex couples.[34] The city of Philadelphia canceled adoption contracts with Catholic Charities for declining to place children with same-sex couples.[35] The federal government issued a regulation denying funding to homeless shelters that "discriminate" based on gender identity.[36] And the federal government issued a regulation that would cut off billions in funding to religious hospitals if they declined to perform gender transition procedures.[37]

Government Facilities

Beyond contracts and grants, religious groups also face losing access to government programs and facilities. The experience of the Boy Scouts is illustrative. Because of the Boy Scouts' membership standards on homosexual conduct (which it later abandoned), the Boy Scouts were denied equal access to public after-school facilities,[38] participation in a state's charitable fund-raising program,[39] a lease for a government campground,[40] a berth at a city marina,[41] and a lease for a government building that had been their headquarters for seventy-nine years.[42] All this occurred even before the Supreme Court's 2015 decision legalizing same-sex marriage. Religious groups that remain committed to a traditional view of marriage can expect to face similar penalties in the future.

Government Jobs

Government workers also face penalties if they decline to affirm same-sex relationships. A small-town judge in Wyoming was publicly censured for saying she could not perform same-sex weddings.[43] A Kentucky judge was forced to resign after declining to hear adoption cases involving same-sex parents.[44] Government social workers in the United Kingdom have faced discipline for declining to facilitate adoptions by same-sex couples.[45] And other government workers have been fired merely for expressing traditional religious beliefs about sexuality on their personal time.[46]

Tax Exemptions

Finally, religious groups face loss of tax-exempt status if they decline to affirm same-sex relationships. In 1983, the Supreme Court held that the IRS could strip a religious university of its tax-exempt status because it opposed interracial marriage.[47] Gay-rights advocates now argue that the same logic applies to same-sex marriage.[48] Most famously, during oral argument in the Supreme Court's same-sex marriage cases, the US solicitor general said the tax-exempt status of these groups is "certainly going to be an issue."[49]

Although the IRS has not yet begun to press the issue, state and local governments have. In 2013, the California legislature considered a bill to strip the Boy Scouts of a state tax exemption valued at $250,000 because of its policy against having gay scout leaders.[50] The legislation passed the senate 27–9 but never reached a final vote in the assembly.[51]

In New Jersey, state and local authorities revoked a tax exemption for an ocean-side pavilion owned by a religious group after the group declined to host a same-sex wedding—and then imposed a $20,000 tax bill.[52] In the coming years other state and local governments will likely follow suit.

As one scholar who supports same-sex marriage has written, "Regardless of what happens with the IRS rule in the long-term, countless other laws and regulations . . . will reinforce a growing societal norm against sexual-orientation discrimination."[53] Under this "new norm," "beliefs condemning homosexual conduct will become very marginalized in our society by the time your children and grandchildren are adults. The process has already begun, and it will continue to accelerate."[54]

THE PROBLEM IS VERY BIG

So how big is the problem? Very big. The conflict between gay rights and religious freedom is the most significant threat to religious freedom in the United States today. If handled poorly, we can expect a variety of painful consequences. Religious business owners will suffer crippling fines. Religious counselors will lose their licenses. Religious universities will lose their accreditation. Religious hospitals, homeless shelters, adoption agencies, schools, and other ministries will be attacked by lawsuits and lose millions in funding and tax exemptions. Religious individuals will lose their jobs as judges, clerks, social workers, and military chaplains. This is to say nothing of purely private forms of social ostracism—like religious employees at private companies losing their jobs because they're labeled "bigots" or religious business owners facing boycotts because of their religious views.

To say that this problem is serious is not to discount the far more tragic suffering of Christians in countries like North Korea, Sudan, or Iraq. Compared with those countries, our problems are minuscule. But compared with what Christians in the United States are accustomed to and what we're ready for, the problem is massive. And regardless of the size of the problem, when religious adoption agencies are prohibited from placing children in loving homes, when religious counselors lose their licenses, and when religious schools are forced to close—all because their religious beliefs are branded as "bigotry"—that is unjust and should be opposed.

But the conflict between gay rights and religious freedom doesn't have to end in disaster. There are solutions. And there are a variety of possible outcomes. Let's imagine, for a moment, four possible ways the conflict might be resolved.

The Revival Scenario

First, Christians could persuade the culture that the traditional biblical view of sexuality is the most conducive to human flourishing and that unbounded sexual autonomy is a mistake. The culture would then embrace a biblical view of sexuality, and the conflict between gay rights and religious liberty would largely vanish, because the biblical view of sexuality would no longer be viewed as a threat.

Although we can hope and pray toward this end, widespread change like this takes time and seems unlikely in the near term.

The Race Scenario

Alternatively, the conflict between gay rights and religious freedom could be resolved like the conflict between racial equality and religious freedom. In the 1960s, our legal system comprehensively banned race discrimination. Some people resisted on religious grounds, claiming that their religious beliefs didn't allow them to participate in the integration of the races. But the courts rejected these religious freedom defenses.[55] Religious dissenters largely abandoned their racist views, and the conflict between racial equality and religious freedom disappeared.

Applied to the gay-rights context, this would mean that our laws would comprehensively ban discrimination based on sexual orientation or gender identity and reject religious freedom defenses. After some prominent losses, Christians would realize that the theology supporting their traditional views of sexuality is just as flawed as the theology that once supported racism, and they would abandon those views. The conflict between gay rights and religious liberty would largely vanish because almost no one would hold the traditional view of sexuality anymore.

Although this scenario will strike many Christians as implausible, it is the dominant view among legal scholars and the goal of many gay-rights advocates today.[56] They firmly believe that traditional Christian beliefs about sexuality will eventually vanish. The only question is how we get there—whether gradually, with light pressure and a mostly voluntary change of mind, or more quickly, with "those who cannot change their mind [being] sued, fined, forced to violate their conscience, and excluded from occupations if they refuse."[57]

I think these scholars are mistaken. The theology supporting the traditional view of sexuality is far more deeply rooted in Scripture and tradition than the theology that supported racism. And Christians in the United States are part of a broader community—the worldwide church—that is not nearly as influenced by American cultural trends. Some Christians will change their views, but many will not. Christians will not simply abandon en masse what the church has consistently taught for two thousand years.

The Widespread Conflict Scenario

That brings us to the third scenario—the widespread conflict scenario. In this scenario, the legal system turns up the heat on traditional religious beliefs about sexuality, but Christians don't change their views. They simply disobey and suffer the consequences. They are fined for discrimination. They are excluded from various professions. Their ministries are stripped of funding or shut down. The conflict between gay rights and religious liberty doesn't vanish—it intensifies.

Widespread conflicts like this are not common in American history, but some have occurred. Quakers in the early colonies faced severe punishment for preaching, refusing to take oaths, and conscientiously objecting to military service. Mormons in the late 1800s faced widespread imprisonment and confiscation of their property for practicing polygamy.[58] And Jehovah's Witnesses in the mid-1900s faced widespread punishment for their vigorous evangelism and refusal to pledge allegiance to the flag.[59]

But none of these conflicts were permanent. Our society and legal system aren't designed for permanent, widespread conflict. They tend to work toward a solution. Either the law is changed to protect religious dissenters, or religious dissenters change their views. The Quakers and Jehovah's Witnesses stood firm, and after significant suffering, the law was eventually changed to protect their right to preach and conscientiously object. The Mormons changed their views and eventually abandoned polygamy.

So the widespread conflict scenario has never been a final outcome; it has always been a temporary stage until a more lasting solution is reached. I think we're starting to see the beginnings of a widespread conflict. But the conflict will have to be resolved somehow—either by Christians abandoning their traditional views as in the race scenario or by the law protecting their dissenting views.[60]

The Abortion Scenario

That brings us to the fourth scenario—which I call the abortion scenario. As explained in chapter 6, our legal system recognizes a right to abortion, but it also recognizes that many people believe abortion is wrong. So it protects their right to live accordingly. This means religious health-care workers can't be forced to participate in abortions, and religious groups can expect their members to refrain from abortion.

Applied to the gay-rights context, this would mean the law would recognize same-sex marriages and would limit discrimination based on sexual orientation, but it would also recognize that many people believe sex is designed for marriage between a man and a woman and would protect their right to live accordingly. Religious people wouldn't be forced to participate in same-sex marriages, and religious groups could expect their members to refrain from sex outside traditional marriage.

The abortion scenario isn't a perfect fit in every respect. People who conscientiously object to same-sex marriage believe they're being asked to affirm an immoral relationship, while people who conscientiously object to abortion believe they're being asked to participate in murder. The objection to murder tends, in most people's minds, to carry greater moral weight. So it wouldn't be surprising if the law offered more protection to those who believe abortion is murder than to those who believe same-sex marriage is immoral. But the way the law protects conscientious objections to abortion points toward a solution for those who conscientiously object to affirming same-sex marriage.

WHAT NOW?

So where does that leave us? What scenario should we expect?

I think we're going to experience aspects of three of the scenarios I've described—widespread conflict, race, and abortion. We're currently entering a period of widespread conflict. It's not as intense as what the colonial Quakers or nineteenth-century Mormons experienced, but it's going to get worse before it gets better. It's also going to be far more intense than anything Christians in the United States have experienced in the last century.

From there, the question is how the conflict will resolve. Will it be more like the race scenario, where traditional views of sexuality are severely punished and Christians largely abandon them? Or will it be more like the abortion scenario, where Christians hold on to their traditional views and the law protects their right to live differently? I think we'll end up closer to the abortion scenario. But we won't get there entirely, and we'll experience elements of the race scenario too. And the outcome is far from guaranteed, because it depends on a variety of cultural, legal, and religious factors.

That's what the next chapter is all about. It explains why the abortion scenario is a better model for resolving the conflict than the race scenario. And it describes what the ultimate solution may be.

Will Gay Rights Trump Religious Freedom? (The Solution)

Julea Ward was a master's student in the counseling program at Eastern Michigan University, a few credits shy of graduating with a 3.9 GPA. One of her final tasks was to counsel real clients under faculty supervision.

She counseled her first two clients without incident. But as she reviewed the file before meeting her third client, she learned he was a gay man seeking counseling for a same-sex relationship. Ward was happy to counsel gay clients about a wide variety of life issues, but her religious beliefs wouldn't allow her to affirm a same-sex relationship. So she asked her faculty supervisor whether she could refer the client to another counselor.

Her supervisor wasn't happy. She assigned the client to another counselor but told Ward she was guilty of discrimination based on sexual orientation and would need to undergo a faculty review. During the review, Ward made it clear she was willing to counsel gay clients on a variety of issues. But her conscience wouldn't allow her to affirm a same-sex relationship. The faculty concluded that Ward was guilty of discrimination and expelled her from the university.[1]

Ward then filed a lawsuit, arguing that her expulsion violated her religious freedom. I helped her lawyers refine their legal arguments, and a federal court ultimately ruled in Ward's favor. The court recognized that counselors are allowed to refer clients to another counselor for a variety of reasons. For example, they can refer a client who is terminally ill and wants to explore assisted suicide if they can't in good conscience counsel a client in ending his life. They can refer a client who is grieving if they recently experienced a similar loss and are grieving themselves. They can refer a client who is seeking forms of therapy that may be harmful. In fact, the counseling code of ethics allows referral anytime a counselor is unable "to be of professional assistance to clients."[2]

Given all these permissible referrals, the fact that the university punished Ward for her religiously motivated referral suggested that the university was discriminating against her because of her religious beliefs. "Tolerance," the court said, "is a two-way street."[3]

After the court's ruling, the university erased the expulsion from Ward's record.

PROTECTING CONSCIENCE

Ward's case offers an example of how the "abortion" model can resolve conflicts between gay rights and religious freedom. In the abortion context, the law recognizes a right to abortion, but it also recognizes the right of conscientious objectors to live by a different moral view. It allows conscientious objectors to step aside. This doesn't mean doctors can stop women from getting abortions, but it means they can't be forced to participate.

In the same way, the law may recognize the right of individuals to enter various sexual relationships, but it can also recognize the right of conscientious objectors to live by a different moral view. It can allow conscientious objectors to step aside. This doesn't mean counselors can berate same-sex couples or try to force them to abandon same-sex relationships, but it means they can't be forced to further those relationships. Counselors like Ward should be allowed to step aside.

This sort of compromise makes sense for several reasons. First, it respects the basic human rights of conscientious objectors. For years, gay-rights advocates have sought to protect the dignity of LGBT individuals. They've argued that sexual orientation is a core aspect of human identity and that no one should be penalized because of her sexual orientation or choice of sexual partners. Now that the law recognizes same-sex marriage, conscientious objectors are asking for the same kind of protection. They argue that religion is a core aspect of human identity and that no one should be penalized because of his religious beliefs or practices. Protecting conscientious objectors ensures that religious people are not forced to violate a core aspect of their humanity.[4]

Second, this sort of compromise reduces social conflict. Our society is deeply divided over the morality of abortion and sex. Some people believe abortion is permissible and same-sex relationships are good. Others believe abortion is murder and same-sex relationships are immoral. That division isn't going away anytime soon. Given that division, we have to find a way for these groups to live together in peace. Protecting conscientious objection does just that.

Finally, at a purely practical level, everyone is better off when conscientious objectors are protected. As law professor Douglas Laycock, a leading scholar and supporter of gay rights, has said, "No same-sex couple in its right mind would want to be counseled by a counselor who believes that the couple's relationship is fundamentally wrong."[5] The couple would be better served by a counselor who is sympathetic to their views.[6] Similarly, many religious people want counselors who share their religious views. Protecting conscientious objectors ensures that everyone will have a diverse range of counselors to choose from.

In short, in a society that is deeply divided over human sexuality, the abortion model does the best job of respecting both sides. Same-sex couples are free to live according to their views; religious people are free to live according to theirs. The government doesn't force either side to violate their deeply held beliefs about human sexuality.

Why would anyone object to this kind of compromise?

THE ANALOGY TO RACE DISCRIMINATION

The most common objection is based on an analogy to race discrimination. According to this objection, sexual orientation is a fundamental, immutable aspect of human identity—just like race. Just as it's wrong to discriminate based on race, it's wrong to discriminate based on sexual orientation. So the law should prohibit both.

This objection also points out that many Christians opposed racial equality during the civil rights movement, often on religious grounds. Once laws prohibiting race discrimination were enacted, some Christians tried to use religious freedom as a defense against complying with those laws. For example, in *Bob Jones University v. United States*, a Christian university claimed the IRS violated its religious freedom by denying it tax-exempt status because of its rule against interracial marriage and dating.[7] But the Supreme Court rejected that defense, concluding that "the Government has a fundamental, overriding interest in eradicating racial discrimination in education" that "substantially outweighs" the university's claim of religious freedom.[8]

Thus, the objection concludes, just as religious freedom isn't a defense for race discrimination, it shouldn't be a defense for sexual-orientation discrimination. Julea Ward shouldn't be allowed to refuse to counsel a same-sex couple any more than she can refuse to counsel an interracial couple. And a Christian baker shouldn't be allowed to refuse to bake a cake for a same-sex wedding any more than a Christian lunch counter can refuse to serve African Americans.

This analogy is quite popular in debates over gay rights and religious freedom. But it is fundamentally flawed because it overlooks the important reasons our legal system treats race discrimination differently from any other kind of discrimination.

Our country has a uniquely tragic history of race discrimination. We had over three hundred years of dehumanizing slavery based on race. We fought a civil war based on race. We had government-imposed segregation based on race. And we've had three constitutional amendments addressing race.

Our history of racial injustice has imposed far more egregious harm on African Americans than on any other group, including the LGBT community. This is not to say LGBT individuals haven't suffered; they've suffered deeply. But African Americans were enslaved. Their families were torn apart. They were denied the right to vote. They were subjected to repeated mob violence that was ignored and sometimes supported by the state. They were denied education, housing, jobs, loans, and basic public accommodations. In short, they faced centuries of systematic, pervasive barriers to full participation in the economic, social, and political life of the nation.

To dismantle those barriers, the government adopted powerful legal tools to combat racism—tools it hasn't adopted for any other form of discrimination. Of course, our laws also prohibit discrimination on other grounds—such as sex, religion, age, marital status, disability, and personal appearance—but none of these traits are protected to the same degree race is. Rather, in each area, the law considers "the natural diversity of needs, situations, and histories of groups seeking protection."[9]

The same is true of sexual orientation. Take employment laws, for example. All fifty states ban employment discrimination based on race. Religious groups generally aren't exempt; they can be sued if they discriminate based on race. But when it comes to discrimination based on sexual orientation, only twenty-one states prohibit it, and all twenty-one have religious exemptions allowing religious groups to hire based on their religious beliefs about sexuality. This reflects a simple fact: different kinds of discrimination get different legal treatment. Sexual-orientation discrimination gets treated more like sex discrimination or marital-status discrimination (where religious exemptions are common) than like race discrimination.

The Supreme Court has also recognized this difference. When the court struck down a ban on interracial marriage in 1967, it condemned the beliefs underlying the ban as "invidious" relics of "White Supremacy."[10] But when it struck down bans on same-sex marriage in 2015, the court emphasized that the beliefs underlying traditional-marriage laws are "based on decent and honorable religious or philosophical premises" that "long ha[ve] been held—and continu[e] to be held—in good faith by reasonable and sincere people here and throughout the world."[11]

What the Supreme Court is getting at is yet another difference between race and sexual orientation. Bans on interracial marriage arose in the United States in connection with slavery. They were part of a belief system rooted in white supremacy that sought to dehumanize African Americans and suppress them as second-class citizens. Those who objected to interracial marriage didn't simply object to participating in an interracial wedding; they objected to any mixing of the races on equal footing as a threat to white supremacy. To address our sordid history of race discrimination, the law has labeled these beliefs "invidious" and sought to prohibit anyone from acting on them, with almost no exceptions. The goal is "to culturally marginalize the notion that African Americans are intrinsically inferior and unworthy."[12]

The belief in traditional marriage, by contrast, isn't rooted in a system of heterosexual supremacy designed to dehumanize gays and suppress them as second-class citizens. It is simply a reflection of the long-standing belief—almost universally held until quite recently—that marriage is limited to a relationship between a man and a woman. Those who hold this belief don't object to serving LGBT individuals generally or interacting with them on equal footing in society; they simply can't in good conscience support same-sex marriages. Accordingly, there is no need (or justification) for the law to label these beliefs "invidious" and prohibit everyone from acting on them. The law can fully protect LGBT individuals from discrimination while still recognizing that long-standing religious beliefs about sex are also reasonable and worthy of protection—not a form of "irrational hatred."[13]

Finally, if race and sexual orientation *aren't* different, we have to consider what the consequences would be. The government wields incredibly powerful tools to eradicate race discrimination. And if belief in traditional marriage is no different from racism, then the government can use all those tools against religious people. It can drive them from a variety of professions, like wedding-related industries, counseling, and medicine. It can punish religious groups for expecting their members and employees to agree with their views about sexual morality, making it difficult to form traditional religious groups. And it can strip the tax-exempt status of hundreds of Christian colleges and universities across the country. In short, if the law treats race and sexual orientation identically, it is a recipe for massive, long-term church-state conflict.

So the analogy between race and sexual orientation falls short. The law treats race differently because African Americans suffered a different and more severe kind of injustice than any other group in our nation's history.

What does this mean in practice?

It means sexual orientation shouldn't (and won't) be treated just like race is treated. Sometimes it will be treated like race, and conscientious objectors will lose. Other times it will be treated like abortion or sex or marital status, and conscientious objectors will be protected. Still other times it won't be uniquely protected at all. The outcome will depend on the context of the dispute, including the nature of the religious objection and the nature of the government's interest in prohibiting discrimination.

To understand what this means in practice, I'll examine three scenarios involving gay rights and religious freedom: (1) a religious school that fires a gay employee; (2) a local government that refuses to contract with a religious adoption agency unless it places children with same-sex couples;

and (3) a wedding photographer who declines to photograph a same-sex wedding. For each scenario I'll summarize the key arguments and how the conflict will likely play out. By the end, we'll have a much better understanding of how the lines between gay rights and religious freedom will likely be drawn.

Religious Hiring

First, consider a religious school that fires an employee for entering a same-sex marriage. This kind of scenario is already happening. In 2014, for example, a Catholic school in Georgia fired its band director for entering a same-sex marriage in violation of Catholic teaching. The band director sued the school for discrimination, and the case was settled out of court.[14]

If religious groups don't settle these cases, how will they be handled in court?

Although the law isn't perfectly clear, religious groups have a variety of good legal defenses, and in the long run I think they'll win most (but not all) of these cases.

The first line of defense is the fact that federal (and most state) employment laws don't prohibit discrimination based on sexual orientation. So gay-rights advocates have resorted to arguing that firing a gay employee is actually discrimination based on sex—because the employer lets female employees (but not male employees) marry men, and vice versa. Although a few courts have agreed with this argument, the Supreme Court probably won't because it stretches the word *sex* far beyond its ordinary meaning. If the Supreme Court rejects attempts to stretch the definition of *sex*, that will stop many of these lawsuits at the outset. But not all of them—because some states now prohibit employment discrimination based on sexual orientation, and federal law could always be amended to do the same.

The next line of defense will be the right of religious association, which I discussed at length in chapter 5. As you may recall, the Supreme Court's unanimous *Hosanna-Tabor* decision (involving a Lutheran schoolteacher) recognizes a broad right of religious groups to choose their religious leaders without interference from antidiscrimination laws. This is called the "ministerial exception." It means employees with important teaching or leadership responsibilities can't bring these sorts of lawsuits.

If the employee doesn't have teaching or leadership responsibilities, the next line of defense comes from the *Amos* decision (involving the Mormon gymnasium). Under *Amos,* religious groups have the right to require *all* their employees to be persons of a particular religion. So the key question is whether being a person of a particular religion means simply calling oneself a Christian or whether it also means *living* by the group's understanding of Christian conduct.

This is where the law is unclear and the results will be mixed (see chapter 5). In the short term, some courts will rule against religious groups in some of these cases—particularly where the religious group seems to have been unfair or inconsistent in how it has enforced its religious standards of conduct. But in the long run, if religious groups clearly articulate their standards of conduct in advance and consistently enforce them with gentleness and grace, I think they'll win most of these cases.

In fact, until recently, even the most ardent gay-rights organizations agreed religious groups *should* win these cases. Starting in 1994, gay-rights groups began pushing for a federal law called the Employment Non-Discrimination Act (ENDA). ENDA would make it illegal for employers to discriminate based on sexual orientation. But, like many similar state laws, ENDA also included a religious exemption—stating that the law wouldn't apply to religious organizations that have a right under federal law to hire persons of a particular religion.[15] Gay-rights groups uniformly supported this religious exemption until 2014, when many groups decided they wanted a more aggressive version of the law.[16]

Support for this kind of exemption also makes sense. Virtually all groups have some sort of mission, and virtually all groups hire employees based on their mission. The law doesn't force the Democratic Party to hire Republicans. It doesn't force pro-abortion groups to hire pro-lifers. And it doesn't force gay-rights groups to hire opponents of gay marriage. In the same way, the law shouldn't force religious groups to hire people who violate their core religious beliefs. Hiring people who agree with your core beliefs isn't invidious discrimination; it's simply hiring people who can best advance your mission.

CONTRACTS AND GRANTS

Next, consider a scenario where the government denies a contract or grant to a religious group that declines to affirm same-sex relationships. This, too, is already happening. The federal government has adopted a broad policy of denying contracts to any organization deemed to discriminate based on sexual orientation or gender identity.[17] The state of Maryland cut off vouchers from religious schools that required students or teachers to refrain from homosexual conduct.[18] And several jurisdictions have canceled contracts with religious adoption or foster-care organizations that declined to place children with same-sex couples.[19]

How will these conflicts be resolved?

One easy solution would be a compromise like the one gay-rights groups supported in ENDA: the law would generally prohibit recipients of government grants or contracts from discriminating based on sexual orientation, but religious organizations would be exempt. For example, adoption agencies would generally be required to place children with all couples (including same-sex couples), but religious groups would still be allowed to operate based on their religious principles (such as by placing children only with opposite-sex, married couples). This arrangement respects both sides of the debate: gay couples would still be able to adopt, and religious groups would still be able to serve children and families in accordance with their religious principles. This is how the law currently works in most places.

But what happens when a hostile government tries to upset this balance, threatening to shut down religious adoption agencies unless they violate their religious beliefs?

Here, although the law is unsettled, religious groups have several defenses. First, religious groups can make arguments based on the right of religious association, much like they do in the employment context. They can argue that the right of religious association protects their ability to form groups to carry out a religious mission—which is just what groups like religious schools and adoption agencies are doing. And just as the government can't punish these groups by enforcing employment discriminations laws, so also the government can't punish them by denying them licenses, grants, and contracts.[20] Beyond that, if there's evidence that the government is targeting religious groups rather than just evenhandedly enforcing nondiscrimination policies, religious groups will have a strong claim under the Free Exercise Clause.

On the other hand, some courts have concluded there's a difference between directly regulating religious groups—like requiring them to hire an employee on pain of being sued—and merely declining to partner with religious groups via grants or contracts.[21] The rationale of this argument is that the government should have extra control over how it spends its own funds.

Regardless of how this constitutional argument plays out, religious groups may also have a defense based on the Religious Freedom Restoration Act (RFRA) or similar state laws. As you may recall from chapter 4, RFRA provides extra protection for religious freedom. A religious group doesn't have to show that the government is targeting it because of its religion; it simply has to show that the government substantially burdened its religious exercise. If so, the government must prove it has a powerful reason for doing so.

A conflict involving World Vision (a Christian humanitarian aid organization) illustrates how RFRA can work in this context. In 2007, World Vision received a $1.5 million grant from the federal government to mentor at-risk youth. But the law authorizing the grant stated that no funds could go to an organization that "discriminat[ed] on the basis of religion."[22] That posed a problem for World Vision because it requires all its employees to be Christians. So World Vision asked for an accommodation: it wanted the government to let it keep the grant *and* keep its religious employment requirements.

The government not only granted World Vision's request but also concluded that denying the grant to World Vision would violate RFRA. Stripping World Vision of the funding would impose a substantial burden on World Vision's religious exercise by pressuring it to abandon its practice of hiring only fellow Christians, and the government had no powerful reason for pressuring World Vision to do so.[23]

In the same way, religious groups can argue that denying grants or contracts based on sexual-orientation nondiscrimination rules pressures them to abandon their religious practices without any powerful reason for doing so. This won't work in every case, because RFRA doesn't apply to every grant, and even when it does apply, some courts might still reject the argument. But RFRA provides an additional layer of defense.

So where does all this leave us? How will these cases play out?

I think most state and local governments, particularly in more conservative jurisdictions, will allow for compromise. If they prohibit discrimination based on sexual orientation, they'll include religious accommodations that allow religious groups to continue to serve. This is a commonsense political solution.

In more aggressive jurisdictions, the government will push the envelope, imposing nondiscrimination rules without religious accommodations. When that happens, some religious groups will shut down their ministries—as we've already seen Catholic Charities do with its adoption ministries in Boston, Illinois, and DC. But other religious groups will resist. In some courts they'll win, meaning they'll keep the freedom to serve in accordance with their religious beliefs. In some courts they'll lose, meaning they'll lose their license, grant, or contract and may have to curtail or shut down their ministry. It may be many years before the Supreme Court resolves the issue, so there will be no one-size-fits-all resolution. Religious groups will remain vulnerable to government-imposed penalties in hostile jurisdictions.

What should religious groups do about this?

First, they should try to make themselves and their ministries indispensable to their communities. Their schools should provide the best education to the neediest students. Their adoption agencies should find the most loving families for the most at-risk children. Their hospitals should provide the finest care for the sickest patients. As the apostle Peter said, "Who is there to harm you if you are zealous for what is good?" (1 Peter 3:13). If religious groups are indispensable to their communities, the government is less likely to shut them down. More importantly, providing loving care for the needy is what we're called to do.

Second, religious groups should make themselves and their ministries independent of government funds. Particularly in more hostile jurisdictions, it will be increasingly common for governments to attach burdensome nondiscrimination rules to a variety of government programs. As these nondiscrimination rules proliferate, more and more religious groups will face a difficult choice: Will they remain true to their religious principles and lose government funds, or will they surrender to the state to keep their ministries alive? In some cases, religious groups will have strong arguments for keeping *both* their religious beliefs and their government funds. But they won't win every case. In fact, religious groups are virtually guaranteed to lose some of these cases, so they must be ready to lose government funds.

Finally, religious groups should make a public case for why their work matters and why their religious freedom should be protected. Religious foster and adoption agencies, for example, are doing amazing work. States across the country desperately need more families willing to foster and adopt, and religious agencies often do the best job at recruiting those families and providing the support they need. Shutting down religious ministries due to politically motivated nondiscrimination rules doesn't help anyone. It doesn't help LGBT families, because many other agencies are already helping them adopt. And it doesn't help children, because it deprives them of families that might otherwise be willing to foster or adopt.

The same is true of other types of religious ministries. Cutting off scholarships to religious schools harms needy students who would benefit from the education. Cutting off funding for religious hospitals harms needy patients who can't afford other care. Cutting off grants to homeless shelters harms the homeless who have nowhere else to go.

Religious groups should make the case that respecting religious freedom isn't just about protecting their rights; it's about protecting the most vulnerable members of society. If they make that case effectively, they can dissuade the government from creating unnecessary religious freedom conflicts in the first place.

WEDDING VENDORS

Finally, what about religious business owners? They're already facing lawsuits for declining to support same-sex relationships or participate in same-sex weddings. For example, a religious photographer in New Mexico was penalized for declining to photograph a same-sex commitment ceremony.[24] A religious florist in Washington was sued for declining to design the flowers for a same-sex wedding.[25] And Betty and Dick Odgaard, whom I described in chapter 7, were sued when they declined to host and coordinate a same-sex wedding in their art gallery.

In 2018, the Supreme Court ruled in favor of a Christian baker who declined to design a cake for a same-sex wedding, emphasizing that the state commission that attempted to punish the baker showed overt hostility to his religious beliefs.[26] But as I indicated before, the Supreme Court left many questions unanswered, including the biggest one: How will these cases be resolved over the long term?

Given that the Supreme Court has legalized same-sex marriage, the most sensible solution, again, would be a compromise—much like the compromise that governs abortion. Gay couples would have the right to marry; conscientious objectors would have the right to refrain from participating in those marriages. Both sides would remain free to live according to their own values.

What are the main arguments for and against compromise?

As noted earlier, the main argument against compromise is based on the analogy to race discrimination. Just as we don't allow restaurants to refuse service to African Americans, we shouldn't allow bakeries to refuse cakes for same-sex weddings.

But conscientious objectors have several strong arguments in response. First, conscientious objectors aren't engaged in invidious discrimination. In the Jim Crow South, discrimination meant rejecting any intermingling of the races and refusing to serve all African Americans as a class simply because they were African American. Today's conscientious objectors, by contrast, gladly serve gay and lesbian customers in a wide variety of contexts, and they have no objection to serving gay and lesbian customers as a class simply because they're gay or lesbian. They're merely asking not to participate in a particular type of event. In that sense, they're no different from a pro-choice photographer who serves Christians generally but won't photograph a Christian pro-life rally. Or a lesbian florist who provides flowers to Catholics generally but won't provide flowers for an Easter Mass. None of these people are discriminating in the traditional, invidious sense.

More importantly, the scale of the legal problem is dramatically different. When the Civil Rights Act of 1964 was enacted, African Americans faced pervasive barriers to participating in the economic, social, and political life of the nation. Entire areas of economic life were completely shut off to them, and racist attitudes were so pervasive that market forces didn't correct them.

Here, by contrast, we're talking about a small number of conscientious

says you can't run a business unless you abandon your religious beliefs. In short, as one supporter of gay rights has acknowledged, when the cost of finding another baker or florist is "trivial" and the cost of shutting down a business is "serious," refusing to accommodate conscientious objectors is "irrational."[33]

So there are strong arguments for finding a compromise that respects both sides.

But how will these conflicts play out in court? What will happen when a same-sex couple sues a religious business owner for declining to participate in a same-sex wedding?

Conscientious objectors have three main legal arguments. The first is that they don't discriminate based on sexual orientation; they simply object to promoting a particular message or participating in a particular event.

In many of these cases, business owners have willingly employed gay workers and served gay customers for many years, showing that they have no objection to anyone's sexual orientation.[34] So their refusal to promote a particular message or participate in a particular event shouldn't be treated as discrimination. In 2018, the United Kingdom Supreme Court agreed with this argument, concluding that refusing to bake a cake with the message "support gay marriage" was not discrimination based on sexual orientation. Rather, "the objection was to the message, not the messenger."[35]

The difficulty with this argument is that some courts have refused to recognize a distinction between the message and the messenger, or between the event and the customer's status. They've concluded that if only same-sex couples enter same-sex marriages, then refusing to participate in a same-sex marriage is effectively discriminating based on the couple's "status."

Second, conscientious objectors can make an argument based on the right of free speech—particularly when their business is expressive. Under modern free-speech jurisprudence, the government can't compel people to engage in expression they disagree with. So the argument would be that compelling people to photograph a wedding, design floral arrangements, or create a wedding cake is effectively forcing them to communicate a message they disagree with. Just as the government can't force an artist to paint a mural celebrating a cause she disagrees with, the government can't force a baker to design a cake celebrating a cause he disagrees with. The right of free speech trumps the right to be free from discrimination.

The difficulty with this argument is that it's limited to businesses that are expressive, and it can be difficult to define what counts as expressive. Painting a portrait or writing a speech obviously counts; selling a bottle of wine or renting a tuxedo doesn't. But many businesses fall somewhere in between. So when the case of the baker reached the Supreme Court, the justices spent much of the argument debating what kinds of businesses are expressive and what aren't. Are florists expressive? Are makeup artists? Are architects? Is a wedding cake expressive? Does it matter whether the cake is plain or instead has a rainbow on top? Ultimately, arguments based on free speech will protect only expressive businesses but not others.

Third, conscientious objectors can make an argument based on religious freedom. The argument would be that a wedding is a ceremony with tremendous religious significance and that the government can't force people to participate in ceremonies that violate their religious beliefs—regardless of whether their participation is expressive.

The difficulty with this argument is the Supreme Court's decision in *Smith* (see chapter 4), which usually requires conscientious objectors to show that the government was targeting them because of their religious beliefs. Although some conscientious objectors will be able to demonstrate this kind of targeting—as the baker in *Masterpiece* did by showing that the government made hostile comments about his religious beliefs—other times the targeting will be hidden or nonexistent.

So how will these cases turn out? Who will win?

The easiest cases to predict are the ones that involve the most expressive businesses with the most direct participation in a wedding—such as musicians, wedding coordinators, and wedding celebrants. These types of individuals will have strong free-speech arguments and will typically win.

Harder to predict are cases involving businesses that are less obviously expressive, like wedding venues, florists, or caterers. Some of these businesses may win on free-speech grounds. But they'll also need to rely on arguments that they aren't discriminating and that they can't be forced to participate in a religiously significant ceremony like a wedding. Although these arguments may eventually prevail, that is not guaranteed. And given how slowly constitutional issues are resolved by the Supreme Court—a process that can take many years—we shouldn't expect a uniform, national answer anytime soon. Instead, most conflicts in the near term will be resolved by lower courts, some of which are friendly to religious freedom and some of which aren't. So we can expect a messy mix of results, with some wins and some losses.

What does this mean for religious business owners? What should they do?

First, they should assess their risk. Some businesses are more likely to be sued than others; some have stronger legal defenses than others; and some will face lawsuits in better jurisdictions than others. An experienced attorney can help a business assess its risks.

Second, business owners should consider ways to reduce their risks. There are several possibilities.

Some businesses aren't dependent on weddings for their profitability, so they might simply exit the wedding industry altogether.

Other business owners might reconsider the scope of their conscientious objection. Although some owners may believe that baking a cake for a same-sex wedding makes them complicit in sin, other owners, upon reflection, may decide that while they firmly believe same-sex marriage is sinful, merely selling a wedding cake to a same-sex couple doesn't implicate them in sin. Or they may decide they want to "love their enemies" by giving the same-sex couple a cake for free.

Still other business owners may find ways to avoid conflict altogether. Perhaps they can arrange with another business owner to handle same-sex weddings for them. Or maybe they find ways to decline same-sex weddings without revealing their religious reasons for doing so. This is not to suggest that business owners should abandon their religious beliefs, but there may be ways to reduce the likelihood of conflict.

Finally, business owners should be ready for potential losses in court. Sometimes conflict can't be avoided. Sometimes we'll suffer for our faith. I address this at greater length in chapters 11–13.

SUMMING UP

Where does all this leave us? How should we think about the conflict between gay rights and religious freedom?

Let me suggest five key takeaways.

First, there are strong arguments for protecting religious freedom in the context of gay rights. Just as we don't force conscientious objectors to participate in war or abortion, we don't force conscientious objectors to support same-sex relationships. Instead, when our society is deeply divided on an important moral issue, we look for ways to protect both sides. Protecting conscientious objectors respects the fundamental right of religious freedom and allows our divided society to live together in peace.

Second, the analogy to race discrimination is weak. Our country had over three hundred years of slavery based on race, fought a civil war based on race, and had government-imposed segregation based on race. Because of that horrific injustice, African Americans faced widespread racism and pervasive barriers to even basic participation in the economic, social, and political life of the nation. Thus, our legal system rightly puts race discrimination in a category of its own.

While LGBT individuals have also suffered severe injustice, it doesn't compare to what African Americans have endured. Nor do LGBT individuals face anything like the pervasive barriers to full participation in society faced by African Americans in the Jim Crow South. Instead, they face a small number of small businesses with a narrow religious objection—not to serving LGBT individuals generally but to participating in a specific, religiously significant event. Given these important differences, the law rightly treats sexual-orientation discrimination less like race discrimination and more like sex or marital-status discrimination, where religious accommodations are common.

Third, religious groups will likely retain the right to require their employees to live by their religious principles. This right is strongest with respect to religious leaders. But even for lower-level employees, religious groups will be able to require employees to live by religious standards of conduct, particularly if religious groups are gracious and consistent in the way they apply those standards.

Fourth, religious groups will face significantly more risk when they partner with the government in their ministries, such as by receiving government grants or contracts for adoption services, homeless shelters, hospitals, and schools. In this context, religious groups should first make the case for why respecting religious freedom benefits all of society— particularly the needy—and why pressuring religious groups to abandon their beliefs is harmful and unnecessary.

If they don't prevail in the political context, religious groups should make sure they're not overly dependent on government funds. Lawsuits in this context will produce mixed results and will likely be a source of significant conflict for years to come.

Fifth, religious business owners should assess their risks and start thinking about mitigation now. Highly expressive businesses will have strong free-speech claims. Less expressive businesses will face mixed results. Some will win; some will lose. Some will reconsider the scope of their conscientious objection; some will find creative ways to avoid conflict. Given the small number of conscientiously objecting businesses nationwide, along with the various ways of reducing or avoiding conflict, I expect these conflicts will become fairly rare fairly soon.

Ultimately, Christians should realize that conflicts between gay rights and religious freedom are a significant risk. Some of those conflicts are already occurring, and more are sure to come. Some will result in painful

losses for religious freedom. But there are also strong arguments for protecting religious freedom in the context of gay rights. Some of those arguments have already prevailed, and there are good reasons to believe they
will increasingly do so. The rise of gay rights shouldn't be the cause of fear
or alarm; it should be the cause of increased devotion to God.

We should also remember that conflicts between gay rights and religious freedom aren't the only pressing religious freedom issue of our time.
Many other conflicts exist, both for Christians and for people of other
faiths.

As the next chapter explains, these conflicts can be linked in surprising
and important ways.

Will Muslims Take Over?

Some religious freedom issues rarely grab headlines yet still affect churches almost daily. One is the fascinating issue of zoning.

Yes, zoning is fascinating. Stick with me.

Unless a church meets on an airplane or in a boat, it has to meet on land. It might meet in a home. It might meet in a park. It might meet in a movie theater. But wherever it meets, it meets on land. And that means the church has to deal with zoning laws.

Zoning laws restrict how land can be used. The goal is to keep incompatible uses apart—so we don't end up with a smelly pig farm next to suburban homes, or a day care next to a strip club.

The problem is that churches are the unwanted stepchild of zoning. They're unwanted in residential zones because they bring traffic and noise. They're unwanted in commercial zones because they don't generate enough business during the week. And they're unwanted by local governments because they don't pay local property taxes.[1]

So churches often face resistance in the zoning process. Sometimes this resistance is legitimate, like when a megachurch would bring major traffic to a residential area. But often zoning officials use "traffic" or "noise" or "the character of the neighborhood" as a pretext for opposing churches—either because they want more tax revenue or because they just don't like the church.

I once represented a small church in Texas that wanted to buy a vacant church building and use it as a sanctuary. But the city refused. It had designated the street as a retail corridor and said it was "very undesirable" for a "church to displace sales tax generating business[es]" and "have a giant 'hole' in a retail area."[2] It would let the church have its administrative offices and day care in the building—because it could tax those—but not Sunday worship.

I also represented an evangelical church in liberal Boulder County, Colorado. The church wanted to expand its sanctuary and add classrooms for its Christian school. Even though a local school had done the same thing just a mile away, the county refused, saying the church was getting too big. County officials were overtly hostile to the church, vowing that "there will never be another mega church in . . . Boulder County."[3]

We won both cases because the courts ruled that zoning officials had treated the churches unfairly.

But one zoning case in particular stands out.

A growing church in Dearborn, Michigan, urgently needed a larger building. Because of the cramped sanctuary, services often spilled outside, with members standing in the parking lot. Other members watched services on closed-circuit TV in an overflow room. There was no room for a children's ministry, so some families stopped attending altogether.

To accommodate its growth, the church bought property on the outskirts of town and sought permission to build a new sanctuary. At first, the government was receptive and approved their plans. But then local opposition began to grow. Dearborn is home to the largest Muslim population in the United States, and some residents were hostile to a growing Christian church.

First a sign marking the property as the church's future home was vandalized—with the words *Not Welcome* spray-painted on it. Then construction equipment at the site was set on fire. On September 5, the church received an expletive-ridden phone call saying a bomb would be planted in their building on September 11. The church canceled services, and many families were afraid to return.

Finally, a group of neighbors filed a lawsuit opposing the church. Shortly before construction on the new sanctuary was complete, a local judge revoked the church's permission to use its property, reasoning that because the church was "a matter of tremendous public interest," zoning officials should have provided more detailed public notice before approving the project. The church now had a nice, new building—but they were forbidden to use it.

I filed a lawsuit in federal court defending the church. I explained that the local government had approved several mosques using the same type of public notice and that it was illegal to apply a double standard to the church just because some neighbors opposed it. The federal court agreed, and the congregation was able to move into its new building.

Legally, this was an open-and-shut case. The law is clear that the government can't apply stricter rules to one house of worship than to another just because neighbors are hostile to its beliefs. But the case stands out to me for two reasons.

The first is the level of hostility experienced by the church. I'd never represented a church that faced vandalism, arson, and a bomb threat.

The second is the identity of the church. The case didn't actually involve a Christian church. It involved a Muslim mosque. And the hostility came not from Muslims in Dearborn, Michigan, but from professing Christians in Murfreesboro, Tennessee.[4]

TESTING OUR INTUITIONS

That's right—I tweaked the facts of the case as I was just describing it. Law professors do this all the time. We take a real case and change a couple of key facts to test our intuitions about what the law should be. I do this with my wife, too, but I can never get one past her anymore. Every time I introduce a new case, she asks, "Are those the *real* facts? Or did you change something?"

That's what I did here. All the facts I just described are true—the cramped services, the purchase of new property, the vandalism, the bomb threat, the lawsuits. The only difference is that the conflict erupted over a mosque, not a church, and it took place in Murfreesboro, Tennessee, where the government had approved twenty Christian churches in a row before it rejected the mosque.

Should that change the way we think about the case? Should we view religious freedom for Muslims differently than we view religious freedom for Christians?

That is the subject of this chapter.

Given that I represented the mosque, you might think you already know my answer. But as the apostle Paul once said, "I beg you to listen to me patiently" (Acts 26:3).

I'm not going to argue that Islam is a religion of peace and we should all just find a way to get along. I believe Jesus is the only way to God (John 14:6), and Islam denies that fundamental truth.

I also believe Islamic terrorism is one of our most significant national security threats. I remember exactly where I was on the morning of 9/11, and the images of those terrorist attacks are seared into my memory. I watch with horror what Islamic State terrorists are doing to Christians in the Middle East. I attend church with a Pakistani man whose parents survived Muslim terrorist attacks on their own house of worship. I believe Islamic terrorism poses a serious threat to Christians and others throughout the world.

Yet I also believe that Christians should care about the religious freedom of Muslims—and other non-Christians too.

In this chapter, I'll offer three arguments for this:

1. **An argument from self-interest:** Protecting religious freedom for Muslims helps protect religious freedom for Christians.
2. **An argument from evangelism:** Protecting religious freedom for Muslims helps more Muslims come to Christ.
3. **An argument from justice:** Protecting religious freedom for Muslims is the right thing to do.

These arguments apply equally to other non-Christian faiths, not just Islam. But I focus on Islam because it is currently treated as the most controversial minority religion in American public life—much like Quakers, Baptists, Catholics, Mormons, and Jehovah's Witnesses have been treated in other eras.

After offering these arguments, I'll also address the three most common objections to protecting religious freedom for Muslims: (1) that protecting Muslims is a form of relativism that speeds people on their way to hell, (2) that protecting Muslims threatens national security, and (3) that Islam isn't really a religion but a political movement bent on imposing Islamic law throughout the world.

SELF-INTEREST

Recall how you felt while reading about the "church" in Michigan that faced hostile opposition from Muslims. Angry? Alarmed? Worried that something similar might happen to you or your church?

These feelings are not necessarily bad. They're natural.

Houses of worship of various faiths face similar problems all the time. Of course, bomb threats and arson attacks are rare. But unjust obstacles to building houses of worship are not.

I offered two examples from churches in Texas and Colorado. But in the late 1990s, Congress systematically examined this problem and found "massive evidence" of widespread discrimination against churches.[5] So Congress enacted a new law to address it, called the Religious Land Use and Institutionalized Persons Act (RLUIPA). (It's pronounced ar-LOO-puh or RUH-loo-puh, depending on whom you ask.)

RLUIPA gives religious groups special protection from zoning laws. It prohibits the government from treating a "religious assembly" (like a church) worse than a "nonreligious assembly" (like a movie theater or private club). It prohibits the government from treating some religious groups (like Muslims) worse than others (like Christians). And it prohibits the government from imposing a substantial burden on any religious group unless the government has a powerful justification for doing so.

My law firm, Becket, won the nation's first case under RLUIPA,[6] and since then, the law has protected thousands of religious groups across the country—from Jews in Florida[7] to Sikhs in California[8] to Muslims in New Jersey[9] to Christians in almost every state.

Critically, RLUIPA applies to all these religions equally. So if the government blocks a mosque based on the hostility of neighbors in Tennessee, it creates a precedent for blocking a church based on the hostility of neighbors in Michigan. Conversely, if a court protects the mosque, it sets a precedent that protects churches.

This happens in my cases all the time. When I won the zoning case for the small Christian church in Texas, my argument rested primarily on a case involving a Jewish synagogue in Florida.[10] The Florida court ruled that it violated RLUIPA to allow "private clubs" in the business district but not a synagogue.[11] The Texas court then adopted the same logic, saying that, like the synagogue, "the Church and a private club must be treated the same."[12] Simply put, a victory for Jews led to a victory for Christians.

This principle is easy to understand in zoning cases because all houses of worship face the same basic problem: they're unpopular in the zoning context.

But the principle also holds true in other cases, even when they seem to have nothing to do with each other. Take my law firm's victory in *Hobby Lobby* (see chapter 6), where the Supreme Court ruled that the owners of a family business couldn't be forced to pay for abortion-causing drugs in violation of their conscience. The court of appeals ruled in our favor based primarily on a case called *Abdulhaseeb v. Calbone,* which involved a Muslim prisoner who was denied a halal diet in prison. According to the court, just as the government had forced the Muslim prisoner to choose between violating his faith and not eating, so also the government was forcing the owners of Hobby Lobby to choose between violating their faith and paying multimillion-dollar fines. Hobby Lobby, the court said, faced "precisely the sort of Hobson's choice described in *Abdulhaseeb*."[13] In other words, a victory for a Muslim prisoner led straight to victory for the Christian family business Hobby Lobby.[14]

The same principle also works in reverse: a loss for non-Christians often leads directly to losses for Christians. The prime example is the landmark *Smith* decision (see chapter 4), where the Supreme Court ruled that the government could punish Native Americans for using peyote in their religious ceremonies. The precedent set in *Smith* led directly to our loss in *Stormans* (see chapter 6), where the court held that the government could punish Christian pharmacists for refusing to sell abortion-inducing drugs. (Notably, the three best precedents we relied on in *Stormans* all involved religious minorities: Jews who faced a land-use problem,[15] Santeros who wanted to engage in animal sacrifice,[16] and a Muslim police officer who wanted to grow a beard.[17]) The *Smith* decision has also led to losses in many other religious freedom cases—demonstrating that religious freedom for Native Americans is vitally important for Christians.

In short, Martin Niemöller's famous lines about the Holocaust apply equally to religious freedom:

> First they came for the [Muslims], and I did not speak out—
>   Because I was not a [Muslim].
> Then they came for the [Native Americans], and I did not speak out—
>   Because I was not a [Native American].
> Then they came for the Jews, and I did not speak out—
>   Because I was not a Jew.
> Then they came for me—and there was no one left to speak for
>   me.[18]

In a very real sense, if we ignore religious freedom for Muslims, Native Americans, Jews, and others, we're undermining it for ourselves. And if we defend religious freedom for non-Christians, we're defending it for ourselves.

Evangelism

While protecting our own freedom is a logical motive, it's not necessarily the most Christian one. Jesus said, "Whoever wishes to save his life will lose it, but whoever loses his life for My sake, he is the one who will save it" (Luke 9:24, NASB). We are called not to self-preservation but to self-denying love, which compels us to make disciples of all nations.

That brings us to the second (and better) reason for protecting religious freedom for Muslims: it helps more Muslims come to Christ.

This is a simple theological argument. Scripture doesn't instruct us to use government power to make disciples. Neither Jesus nor the early church did so. Instead, we're called to "preach Christ" in word and deed (1 Corinthians 1:23), trusting the Holy Spirit—not the government—to "convict the world concerning sin and righteousness and judgment" (John 16:8). As Paul said, "The weapons of our warfare are not of the flesh"—such as government power—but of "divine power" (2 Corinthians 10:4).

Some people point to ancient Israel as an exception to this rule. They note that the Torah (Old Testament law) commanded the rulers of Israel to punish blasphemy and idolatry and enforce true worship of God (e.g., Deuteronomy 17:3–5; Leviticus 24:16). So isn't God commanding us to use government power to make disciples?

The problem with this argument is that it equates ancient Israel with modern America, as if the Torah were simply a blueprint for modern American government. But it's not. The Torah was part of God's covenant with His chosen people Israel—"a kingdom of priests and a holy nation" through whom God promised to bless the whole world (Exodus 19:6). That covenant is fulfilled in Christ. And despite long-standing theological debates about the precise relationship between Israel and the church, nobody believes that the Torah's command to stone idolaters is a model for modern civil governments. It is instead pointing ahead to God's final judgment—not telling us to use government power to make disciples.

This understanding is also consistent with how God created us and interacts with us (see chapter 2). God never forces anyone to love Him, because forced love is not love at all. And if God doesn't force anyone to love Him, how much less should the government try to do so?

Using government power to suppress false religion is also counter-productive. Preventing a mosque from being built or preventing a Muslim from wearing a headscarf doesn't bring any Muslims closer to Christ. At best, it may pressure them to feign Christianity—which is not a saving faith. At worst, it can harden them against Christ and entrench them even more deeply in non-Christian religion.

By contrast, defending religious freedom for Muslims can lead directly to opportunities for sharing the gospel. For example, I'm now good friends with the imam from the Murfreesboro mosque. We've had multiple conversations about the differences between Christianity and Islam. He tries to convince me the doctrine of the Trinity makes no sense; I try to convince him we can't earn God's favor and must turn to Jesus as our savior instead. I never would have had that opportunity if I hadn't defended his religious freedom.

Similarly, which churches do you think have more opportunities to share the gospel with their Muslim neighbors—churches that vehemently oppose the construction of nearby mosques, or churches that recognize their neighbors' legal rights, welcome them to the neighborhood, and offer to show them a better way?

Ultimately, the argument rooted in evangelism invites us to examine our own hearts. Why would we try to use the power of government to stop a mosque from being built? Is it because we love our Muslim neighbors and think restricting their religion will help lead them to Christ? Or is it possible we're motivated, at least in part, by something else? Fear of terrorism, fear of losing our way of life, or fear of people who are different from us.

Of course, fear may be a natural response when encountering people who are different from us and when memories of 9/11 remain raw. But we're expressly commanded *not* to fear (Matthew 10:28–31). Instead, we're commanded to view Muslims as people who bear God's image and need God's love.

So the argument from evangelism urges us to confess our fears and love our Muslim neighbors as ourselves. That means caring about their religious freedom, even as we show them there is a better way.

JUSTICE

Finally, we should care about religious freedom for Muslims not just as a matter of self-interest or evangelism but also as a matter of justice.

As I explained in chapter 2, a violation of religious freedom is an act of injustice. God created each one of us for a loving relationship with Him—a relationship that can be entered only voluntarily. It can't be coerced by the government. So when the government needlessly interferes in our relationship with God, it is committing an injustice in two respects. First, it's exceeding its God-given realm of authority and attempting to exercise authority that belongs to God alone. Second, it's taking away something every human being deserves—an opportunity to respond freely (even if erroneously) to God.

To use an analogy, imagine the government adopted a policy of taking custody of children whose parents taught them a pernicious worldview—say, white supremacy. We'd all immediately condemn this policy as unjust. We'd agree that raising children to be white supremacists is dangerous and immoral, but we'd also recognize that the government was invading the God-ordained authority of the family and depriving the parents and children of the familial relationship they deserve.

It is likewise unjust to prohibit Muslims from building a house of worship simply because we oppose their religion. That doesn't mean parents (or houses of worship) can do anything they want. If parents abuse or ne-

founder of the first Baptist church in North America, wrote in 1644, "It is the will and command of God that, since the coming of his Son the Lord Jesus, a permission of the most Paganish, Jewish, Turkish, or anti-Christian consciences and worships be granted to all men in all nations and countries: and they are only to be fought against with that sword which is only, in soul matters, able to conquer: to wit, the sword of God's Spirit, the word of God."[22]

But some Christians still have concerns about supporting religious freedom for other faiths, especially Islam. So I will address three of the most common concerns.

The first is this: Isn't supporting religious freedom for Muslims a form of relativism? Or as one Tennessee pastor put it, "If we defend the rights of people to construct places of false worship are we not helping them speed down the highway to hell?"[23]

No. Precisely the opposite is true.

We support religious freedom for Muslims not because we're relativists but because we believe a particular absolute truth: God created us for loving relationship with Him, and no one can enter that relationship via coercion. We also believe Christianity will flourish on a level playing field because Christianity is true. Far from speeding anyone down the highway to hell, we believe that allowing people to choose freely will enable more people to choose rightly.

By contrast, relying on state power to restrict Islam suggests we lack confidence in the absolute truth of Christianity. It also tends to harden Muslims against the faith. James Madison may have put it best, saying that using the state to prop up Christianity tends to "weaken in those who profess this Religion a pious confidence in its innate excellence . . . and to foster in those who still reject it, a suspicion that its friends are too conscious of its fallacies, to trust it to its own merits."[24]

In short, we support religious freedom for Muslims precisely because we know Christianity is true and precisely because we want Muslims to have the opportunity to freely embrace it.

What About Terrorism?

The second objection is this: Doesn't protecting religious freedom for Muslims endanger national security? Multiple terrorist attacks have been carried out by Muslims on American soil. If we allow Islam to take root and proliferate, won't we suffer more terrorist attacks?

This objection to protecting religious freedom has an important kernel of truth: religious freedom should never be used to protect terrorism. Religious freedom doesn't mean religious people are immune from government regulation. It means the government needs a powerful reason before it interferes in religious practices. National security is just such a reason. So if members of a mosque ever plot a terrorist attack, they can and must be stopped and punished. The government can punish religiously motivated acts of violence just as much as it can punish any other act of violence. In that sense, I fully agree with this objection.

The problem comes when the government wants to punish not just acts or attempted acts of violence but also the *beliefs* that might lead to violence. This is when the government says, "Islam is a dangerous ideology that leads to terrorist attacks; therefore, we can suppress Islam"—such as by searching Muslim homes, monitoring Muslim sermons, or shutting down Muslim mosques even with no evidence they're plotting or committing any criminal acts.

That is a dangerous power, and history shows that it invariably results in tragic abuse. It's how China justifies tight restrictions on Christian house churches. It's how Iran justifies the imprisonment of Christian missionaries. And it's how North Korea justifies the torture of anyone who professes Christianity. All claim Christianity is a dangerous ideology that threatens national security. It's no coincidence that China uses the same coercive tactics on both Christians and Muslims.[25]

Nor are we immune from this temptation in our own country. In 1838, the governor of Missouri deemed Mormons a threat to the state, resulting in the infamous "extermination order." Also in the 1800s,

Protestants deemed Catholics a threat to the state because of their loyalty to the pope, resulting in numerous anti-Catholic laws.

It's difficult to find *any* historical examples of governments that claimed the power to stamp out dangerous belief systems and then wielded that power well.

So we must pick our poison. Which is more dangerous: Allowing Muslims to practice their faith, subject to the government's power to prohibit any acts or attempted acts of violence? Or giving the government power to deem Islam a dangerous ideology and restrict its spread?

That's not a difficult choice. The government that has the power to deem Islam a dangerous ideology has the power to do the same to Christianity. And given the way Christianity is viewed as a threat to modern culture (see chapter 4), I wouldn't be surprised if Christianity were deemed a dangerous ideology in this country long before Islam is.

We're right to be concerned that religious freedom not be used as a cover for terrorism. But the way to address that concern is to ensure that the government has authority to punish acts or attempted acts of violence, whether religiously motivated or otherwise. We shouldn't go beyond that by giving the government authority to deem particular religious beliefs a threat and suppress them. That cure is worse than the disease. It is unjust, and it sows the seeds of our own destruction.

Is Islam Really a Religion?

The third objection to protecting religious freedom for Muslims is that Islam isn't really a religion; it's a totalitarian sociopolitical movement bent on imposing Islamic law (sharia) throughout the world. According to this view, a dangerous sociopolitical ideology shouldn't receive First Amendment protection as a religion.

This objection is hard to take seriously. But enough people have made it—including several politicians[26]—that it should be addressed.

One common response is to try to defend Islam, arguing that it's not violent but peaceful and that it's merely been distorted by a small number of radical terrorists using it for political ends. Although it's fairly obvious that most Muslims are law-abiding citizens, this response doesn't seem to convince anyone who believes Islam is inherently violent. So I won't try to defend Islam here.

Instead, even assuming Islam is a dangerous ideology, this objection still fails for several reasons. First, Islam easily qualifies as a religion under any plausible interpretation of the First Amendment. The most famous definition of religion comes from James Madison, who defined it as "the duty which we owe to our Creator, and the manner of discharging it."[27] Islam obviously involves duty to a Creator (Allah) and a manner of discharging it (such as reciting the declaration of faith, praying, giving, fasting, and making the pilgrimage to Mecca). Since Madison's day, the legal definition of *religion* has only broadened. It now includes any belief in transcendent truth—truth that is outside oneself and higher than oneself—that imposes obligations on one's conscience. So the idea that the government could interpret the First Amendment in a way that excludes Islam is absurd.

More importantly, empowering the government to suppress any religion it labels a dangerous ideology is itself dangerous. Many people in this country would gladly label Christianity a dangerous ideology bent on imposing its values throughout the world. They would point out that Christianity has produced deadly terrorist attacks on abortion clinics and would insist the Bible supports violent punishment of idolaters, adulterers, and gay people. If the government can use these kinds of arguments to suppress Islam, it can do the same to Christianity. Indeed, some local governments have already declared various forms of Christianity *fides non grata*—like when San Francisco issued a formal resolution calling the Catholic Church's teaching on adoption and homosexuality "hateful," "insulting," "callous," and "discriminatory" and urging Catholics to "defy" it.[28]

Finally, acknowledging that Islam is a religion doesn't reduce our power to stop terrorism one whit. As noted above, the government retains broad authority to investigate, prevent, and punish acts of violence or attempted violence against the state. Religious freedom isn't a defense. So the way we resist a dangerous ideology is not by repressing the people who hold it but by persuading them they're wrong or punishing their illegal deeds.

Summing Up

In sum, Christians should care about religious freedom for people of all faiths, including Muslims. Protecting religious freedom for Muslims is common sense because their religious freedom is inextricably linked with ours. It is consistent with the Great Commission because it gives Muslims an opportunity to freely embrace the gospel of Jesus Christ. And it is consistent with the biblical view of justice because all human beings have a right to seek and embrace transcendent truth without undue coercion by the state.

This doesn't mean we're relativists. Just the opposite: we defend religious freedom for Muslims because we're confident in the absolute truth of the gospel. This doesn't mean religious freedom is a license to commit terrorism. Rather, religious freedom is limited by the government's power to prevent and punish acts of violence against the state.

When we defend religious freedom as a matter of justice—rather than as a matter of preserving our own rights or saving our own skin—it also affects how we think about religion in the public square. How should we think about religious symbols on government property, prayer in public schools, or government funding of religious groups? Should we seek a robust place for religion in the public square as a way of patting ourselves on the back and reminding everyone else that Christianity is true? Should we seek it because we're a Christian nation?

Or should we have a different approach to the public square altogether?

That is what the next chapter is about.

Will *God* Become
a Dirty Word?

N othing illustrates our fights over the public square like a cross in a public park. In 1941, as the nation faced World War II, the citizens of Pensacola, Florida, gathered in a waterfront park at sunrise on Easter morning, erected a simple pine cross, and prayed for peace.

During the war, the local Easter gathering became an annual tradition. Citizens gathered at the cross to pray for the nation's leaders and brought flowers for soldiers in nearby hospitals. The tradition continued after the war, and in 1969, a local service group replaced the aging wooden cross with a larger concrete version.

The government never paid for the cross or promoted any religious services. It simply allowed local citizens to gather in the park as they saw fit. The cross has now been a popular gathering place for over seventy-five years and is one of many monuments displayed in the city's parks. It's a small piece of Pensacola's history and a tangible reminder of how citizens came together on the eve of World War II.

But you know what happened next.

An atheist organization sued to have the cross torn down. The main plaintiff was a Satanist who regularly biked past the cross and had lived in Pensacola for twenty-three years. He said he found the cross offensive. In 2016, he asked the city for permission to reserve the area around the cross on Easter Sunday. A church had already reserved the site, but when he complained, the church agreed to move to another area of the park. He then used the cross for satanic purposes on Easter morning and filed his lawsuit two months later.

How do you think the case turned out?

The district judge ruled that the cross must come down. He acknowledged that "the Founding Fathers . . . would have most likely found this lawsuit absurd."[1] But he said he was bound to follow Supreme Court precedent, and because the cross has a "religious purpose," it "runs afoul of the First Amendment as currently interpreted by the Supreme Court."[2]

I helped Pensacola appeal this case to the Supreme Court, and as I write this, the Supreme Court is considering a similar lawsuit challenging a nearly century-old cross erected in Maryland to honor fallen World War I heroes.[3] The court's decision will be released shortly before this book.

THE QUESTION

These cases illustrate one small part of a much larger question: How should the government treat religion in the public square?

There are two common answers. The first comes from secularists: the government should scrub religion from the public square. According to the secularists, we're a diverse nation and people are offended when the government endorses religion. So there should be no religious symbols in the public square, no prayer in public schools, and no government funding of religious groups. Religion should be private, and the public square should be secular.

The second answer comes from many Christians: the government should promote religion in the public square. According to many Christians, we're a Judeo-Christian nation and religion is good for society. So the government should display religious symbols, encourage prayer in schools, and fund religious groups. The public square should promote Christianity because Christianity is true.

The secularists accuse Christians of trying to cram religion down their throats. The Christians accuse secularists of waging war on religion. Everyone else gets exasperated with both sides, wishing the conflict would go away.

We need a better way.

That's what this chapter is about. My thesis is simple. The government shouldn't *promote* religion in the public square. Neither should it *scrub* religion from the public square. Instead, it should treat religion as a *natural* part of the public square. It should acknowledge that religion is a fundamental aspect of human history and culture, and it should try to leave religion as uninfluenced by government power as possible.

Why is this a better approach? And what would it look like in practice?

To answer these questions, we need to remember how these conflicts began.

What Is an Establishment of Religion?

It all begins with the first ten words of the First Amendment: "Congress shall make no law respecting an establishment of religion." This is called the Establishment Clause, and it's the primary source of our modern conflicts over religion in the public square.

The problem is that it's been so long since we've had a real establishment of religion in this country—almost two hundred years—that we've forgotten what it is.[4] At the time of the founding, however, an establishment of religion was a well-known concept. Nine of the thirteen colonies had established churches, as did Great Britain. Many of the colonists were familiar with established churches in other parts of Europe. As leading scholar Michael McConnell has observed, an "establishment of religion was a familiar institution, and its pros and cons were hotly debated from Georgia to Maine."[5]

What is an establishment of religion? Simply put, it is the use of

for serving the poor (at taxpayer expense); staffing local schools; maintaining public records of births, deaths, and marriages; and prosecuting moral offenses like swearing, Sabbath breaking, drunkenness, and adultery.

These practices now strike most of us as highly unusual, but they were widespread at the founding. Even today, many of these practices are present in milder form in countries that still have established churches, like England and Germany.

What made an establishment of religion so attractive? There were two main rationales—one theological, one political.

The theological rationale is exemplified by the New England Puritans, who saw themselves as a city on a hill—a model of a community based on biblical truth. They believed that Scripture was clear and that the government should use its power to promote and enforce scriptural truth. When the government punished someone for violating Scripture, it was not, as Puritan minister John Cotton explained, "persecut[ing] [him] for cause of conscience, but for sinning against his own conscience."[10] The government, in their view, had both the right and the duty to use its power to support the church.

The political rationale was less concerned with religious truth than with the fact that religion could be harmful (or useful) to the state. The philosopher Thomas Hobbes, for example, worried that religion could harm the state by encouraging citizens to "disobey the laws, and thereby overthrow the commonwealth, and introduce confusion and civil war."[11] Others, including the British statesman Edmund Burke, emphasized that religion could be useful to the state by encouraging citizens to be honest, charitable, and loyal to the king.[12] That is partly why the 1604 Canons of the Church of England "required ministers at least four times each year to deliver sermons teaching that the king 'is the highest power under God.'"[13] The idea was that by supporting and controlling the established church, the government could harness the power of religion to maintain order and peace.

Although some of the early colonies justified their establishments on theological grounds, by the time of the Revolutionary War, the dominant rationale was political.[14] The main argument was that democratic self-government required citizens of virtue, and virtue was produced by public support of religion. As the Massachusetts Constitution of 1780 put it, "The happiness of a people and the good order and preservation of civil government essentially depend upon piety, religion, and morality . . . [and] these cannot be generally diffused through a community but by the institution of the public worship of God and of public instructions in piety, religion, and morality."[15]

WAS IT A GOOD THING?

That explains what an establishment was and why it was viewed as useful. But how did it work out in practice?

Not well. The theologically based establishment in Massachusetts produced brutal persecution of religious minorities, especially Quakers, who were banned from preaching, exiled from the colony, imprisoned, flogged, tortured, and even killed for their faith.[16] Even under the more tolerant establishment in Virginia, dozens of Baptists were imprisoned for preaching without a license.[17]

Nor was persecution of dissenters the only problem. The most vocal critics of the established church were devout evangelicals who were inspired by the Great Awakening of the mid-1700s. They believed that established churches were ultimately beholden to the state and were therefore prone to corruption, indifference, or worse. They witnessed "the generally low quality and sometimes questionable morality of the settled ministers of the established church,"[18] and they criticized established churches as fostering "a watered-down, rationalistic, nonsectarian style of religion."[19] Instead, they argued that each church should be left to stand or fall on its own merits. In short, they "sought disestablishment in order to strengthen and revitalize Christianity."[20]

Nonevangelicals recognized the same phenomenon. David Hume, the

British philosopher who saw religion as a threat, favored an establishment precisely because it would *weaken* the church. He argued that the government should "bribe [the clergy's] indolence, by assigning stated salaries to their profession, and rendering it superfluous for them to be farther active, than merely to prevent their flock from straying in quest of new pastures."[21] That way, "ecclesiastical establishments . . . prove in the end advantageous to the political interests of society."[22] James Madison saw the opposite effect after the colonies disestablished their churches, writing that "the number, the industry, and the morality of the priesthood & the devotion of the people have been manifestly increased."[23]

The same issues can be seen in established churches today. Theologically based establishments in Muslim countries often brutally repress dissenters. Politically based establishments in Europe are associated with dwindling religious fervor. But the United States, with its tradition of disestablishment, remains far more religiously observant than other wealthy nations.[24]

Why does this matter? First, it reveals a great irony in modern fights over separation of church and state. At the founding, the most fervent advocates of separation of church and state were religious evangelicals who thought establishment weakened the church by making it dependent on the state. Those who wanted government support for religion offered secular arguments based on the social utility of religion. Today, the polarities are often flipped, with secularists arguing for less government involvement in religion and religious evangelicals wanting more.

Second, it suggests Christians should be careful what we wish for. No doubt, the Supreme Court has taken the idea of "separation of church and state" far beyond what the founders intended, and it is overdue for a correction (as we will soon discuss). But in our eagerness to right the ship, we sometimes forget the dangers of government support for religion—including not only the trampling of religious dissent but also the fostering of a tepid civil religion that obscures the distinctive truth of the gospel.

What Did the Founders Do About It?

So what did the founders decide to do about establishments of religion? There were two main camps. In the first camp were evangelicals, who wanted to eliminate religious establishments to free the church from interference by the state. They were joined by Enlightenment rationalists like James Madison and Thomas Jefferson, who wanted to free the state from interference by the church.

In the second camp were the civic republicans, who viewed government support for religion as the best way to promote the virtue necessary for self-government. Patrick Henry, for example, proposed a bill in Virginia that would levy a tax for the support of Christian ministers.[25] Although his proposal was opposed by Madison and ultimately voted down, almost every colony "witnessed a movement to institute or strengthen a religious establishment" after the Revolutionary War.[26] Commenting on Massachusetts, John Adams reportedly observed, "We might as soon expect a change in the solar system, as to expect they would give up their establishment."[27]

So when the framers debated the Bill of Rights in 1789, establishment of religion was a contested issue. Some favored disestablishment; others believed establishment was essential for democratic self-government.

An early draft of the Establishment Clause provided that "no religion shall be established by law." This reflected Madison's view that no religion should be established at the *national* level. But when the language was debated in the House, several members worried it might be interpreted to prohibit existing establishments in the *states*.[28] After significant debate, Congress reached a compromise, which is now reflected in the final language of the Establishment Clause: "Congress shall make no law respecting an establishment of religion." This ensured that the Establishment Clause restricted only *Congress,* not the states. It also ensured Congress could make no law *respecting* an establishment of religion—meaning no law establishing a national religion and no law interfering with establishments in the states. This was a compromise rooted in the idea of federalism—the principle that power should be divided between the national government and the states. Establishment of religion would be off-limits to the national government, but states would remain free to choose their own way.[29]

Over the next forty years, all the states voluntarily ended their establishments. The last to do so was Massachusetts in 1830. However, the move toward disestablishment was not the result of "increasing secularism or rationalism."[30] Rather, "the strongest support for disestablishment c[ame] from the most evangelical denominations."[31]

How Did the Supreme Court Mess It Up?

That brings us to the story of how the Supreme Court messed up its modern Establishment Clause jurisprudence. For the first 150 years after the Constitution was ratified, the Supreme Court left the Establishment Clause alone. It operated, if at all, only as a restriction on Congress.[32]

But in 1947, in a case called *Everson v. Board of Education,* the Supreme Court ruled that the Establishment Clause also applied to the states. This was the culmination of a series of rulings, beginning in the 1920s, which concluded that various provisions of the Bill of Rights applied to the states. These rulings were based on the language of the Fourteenth Amendment, which was ratified in 1868 and which says no "state" shall deprive any person of "liberty" without "due process of law." Without getting into the details, the basic idea is that the Bill of Rights, including the Establishment Clause, protects fundamental liberties that no state can deny.

Everson meant that the Supreme Court was free to apply the Establishment Clause to the states. This kicked off seventy years of conflict over the many interactions between church and state—from prayer in public schools, to religious displays on public land, to public funding of religious groups, and many more.

Throughout those seventy years, the Supreme Court has adopted various approaches to interpreting the Establishment Clause. Sometimes the court has focused on the historical meaning of the Establishment Clause and early practices under it. Relying on this historical lens, the court has upheld Sunday closing laws, tax exemptions for churches, and prayers at the beginning of legislative meetings.[33]

But the court's dominant approach has been to apply something called the *Lemon* test—named after a case called *Lemon v. Kurtzman*. The *Lemon* test asks three questions: (1) Does the government's action lack a secular purpose? (2) Does it have the primary effect of advancing or endorsing religion? and (3) Does it excessively entangle the government in religion? If the answer to any of these questions is yes, the government's action is unconstitutional.

Using the *Lemon* test, the court has struck down a variety of government practices—from prayer in public schools,[34] to government funding of religious groups,[35] to religious symbols on government property.[36] In each of these cases, it's fairly easy to claim that there is some kind of religious purpose or effect and that the government's action is therefore unconstitutional. Thus, the *Lemon* test has had a decidedly secularist bent.

But the results under the *Lemon* test have also been inconsistent. For example, the court has upheld programs allowing public-school children to receive religious instruction during the school day.[37] It has upheld tax credits and grants for religious education.[38] And it has upheld religious symbols on government property.[39]

The reason for these inconsistent results is that the *Lemon* test is highly subjective. The concept of a religious purpose or effect is somewhat vague. Compounding the vagueness, the court says the existence of a religious purpose or effect should be assessed through the eyes of a hypothetical reasonable observer who is aware of all the facts of the case. In practice, however, the reasonable observer ends up looking like whichever justice holds the deciding vote. So the court strikes down one nativity display and upholds another[40] or strikes down one program supporting religious schools but not another[41]—often without giving any consistent rationale for its decisions.

Because of this, the *Lemon* test has been the subject of withering criticism from lower-court judges, scholars, and even many of the Supreme Court justices themselves. Perhaps the most famous criticism came from the late Justice Scalia, who compared the inconsistent application of the *Lemon* test to "some ghoul in a late-night horror movie that repeatedly sits up in its grave and shuffles abroad, after being repeatedly killed and buried. . . . It is there to scare us (and our audience) when we wish it to do so, but we can command it to return to the tomb at will."[42]

Horror movies aside, the problem with the *Lemon* test is real. Not only has it produced a host of inconsistent decisions, but it has also introduced into the Supreme Court's jurisprudence a strain of hostility toward religion that never belonged there in the first place.

How Can It Be Fixed?

The good news is that the court appears poised to get rid of the *Lemon* test for good—or, as Justice Scalia put it, "personally driv[e] pencils through the creature's heart."[43] Recent decisions suggest the court has been quietly laying the groundwork for a major change in its Establishment Clause jurisprudence.

What will that change look like?

The most dramatic alternative to *Lemon* would be to reject the court's 1947 ruling in *Everson,* which first applied the Establishment Clause to the states. This would leave the states free to support religion as much as they would like (subject to their own state constitutions). Although Justice Thomas has advocated for this approach, no other justice has.[44] So it is largely an academic theory. Also, given the way religious establishments tend to harm religion, prohibiting state establishments is probably a good thing.

The more likely alternative to *Lemon* is a return to the historical meaning of "an establishment of religion." We can see the beginnings of this approach in the court's 2014 ruling in *Town of Greece v. Galloway.* There, a town council opened its meetings with a prayer led by local clergy. A federal court struck down this practice as an endorsement of religion under the *Lemon* test. But the Supreme Court reversed that ruling. Instead of applying the *Lemon* test, the court said "the Establishment Clause must be interpreted 'by reference to historical practices and understandings.'"[45] It noted that the First Congress appointed legislative chaplains just days after approving the language of the Establishment Clause—so the framers obviously didn't view legislative prayer as an establishment of religion. And because the town council's prayer policy fit "within the tradition long followed in Congress and the state legislatures," it was constitutional.[46]

Although *Town of Greece* leaves many questions unanswered, it points toward a way out of the Establishment Clause mess. Instead of asking whether a reasonable observer would think the government's action endorses religion (the key question under the *Lemon* test), the court can ask whether the government's action bears any of the hallmarks of "an establishment of religion" as understood at the time of the founding—namely, government control over the doctrine or personnel of the church, government coercion of religious practices, government funding of the church, or government use of the church to carry out civil functions. If not, the government's action would be constitutional.

The Establishment Clause would no longer be used as a weapon to eliminate religion from the public square. Nor would the Establishment Clause allow the government to promote a bland, majoritarian, least-common-denominator civil religion. Instead, the government would be free to acknowledge religion as a vital part of our history and culture while leaving religion as untouched by government influence as possible.

What Will It Look Like?

What would this approach look like in practice? Consider three examples: (1) a cross in a public park, (2) prayer in public schools, and (3) government funding of religious schools.

A Cross in a Park

Let's start with the example from the beginning of this chapter—a seventy-five-year-old cross in a city park. Under the *Lemon* test, the court treated the cross as an inherently suspect endorsement of religion. In fact, courts have often struck down similar displays unless they are surrounded by enough secular symbols to neutralize any religious meaning. Sometimes they strike them down even when secular symbols abound.[47] This approach generates a huge amount of litigation, and it tends to communicate a message of hostility toward religion in the public square.

Under a historical approach, by contrast, the cross in a city park wouldn't be inherently suspect because it doesn't share the characteristics of an establishment at the time of the founding. It doesn't control the doctrine or personnel of any church; it doesn't coerce anyone to engage in religious practices; it doesn't provide funding to religious institutions; and it doesn't use religious institutions for civil functions. Religious acknowledgments like this were common at the founding—even after disestablishment—and a court could uphold the cross as a simple acknowledgment of the role of religion in the city's history and culture.

Although it may seem counterintuitive, this approach also has the effect of leaving religion as untouched by government power as possible. If we lived in a world where the government owned little property and had little voice in the culture, the government could be entirely secular and have little influence on religion. But we live in a world where the government owns vast amounts of property and has a massive voice in the culture. As Professor McConnell has observed, "Silence about a subject can convey a powerful message."[48] If the government uses its property and cultural influence to celebrate a variety of nonreligious ideas and symbols but excludes religious ideas and symbols, it "marginalizes religion" and "profoundly distort[s] public culture"—just as if the government excluded the "viewpoints and contributions of women" or "African American and other minority citizens."[49]

By contrast, "if the aspects of culture controlled by the government (public spaces, public institutions) exactly mirrored the culture as a whole, then the influence and effect of government involvement would be nil: the religious life of the people would be precisely the way it would be if the government were absent from the cultural sphere."[50] That, ultimately, is how the government can be neutral toward religion on government property. This kind of neutrality isn't achieved by having courts police every religious symbol in a flood of litigation. It is achieved primarily through the political process, where citizens can argue about what symbols should be displayed in the public square and where decisions are made by politically accountable officials. Moving most of these disputes to the political realm—rather than having them decided in high-profile court battles—would also go a long way toward cooling the temperature on these cultural disputes.[51]

Prayer in Public Schools

Next, consider the issue of prayer in public schools. Few church-state conflicts generate so much emotion.

The Supreme Court has struck down several laws requiring or permitting prayer in public schools. In *Engel v. Vitale,* its first school-prayer case in 1962, the court struck down a law requiring every class to start the school day by reciting a prayer written by a government agency: "Almighty God, we acknowledge our dependence upon Thee, and we beg Thy blessings upon us, our parents, our teachers and our Country."[52] In *Wallace v. Jaffree,* in 1985, the court struck down a state law allowing teachers to begin the school day with a "moment of silence for meditation or voluntary prayer."[53] And in *Santa Fe Independent School District v. Doe,* in 2000, the court struck down a high school's policy permitting student-initiated, student-led prayer over the loudspeakers before home football games.[54]

How should these cases turn out under a historical approach?

Engel would come out the same way. A key feature of the established Church of England was that Parliament approved and adopted the Book of Common Prayer, which "set out in minute detail the accepted form and content of prayer."[55] That is essentially what the government was doing in *Engel:* it was, as the court said, "prescrib[ing] by law [a] particular form of prayer which [wa]s to be used as an official prayer in carrying on [a] program of governmentally sponsored religious activity."[56] As Christians, we should shudder at the thought of government officials composing prayers and requiring our children to say them each morning. That is a recipe for bland, gutless civil religion at best and tyranny and heresy at worst.

Wallace and *Santa Fe,* however, would come out differently. The government was not initiating, requiring, or composing the prayers. It was not controlling the content of the prayers. It was simply creating space for students to pray if they desired. This is a good result. While no one should want the government composing prayers and making students say them, we should want the government to create room for private prayer. This doesn't pressure anyone to pray. It simply reflects the fact that religion is an important part of our culture, and it leaves religion as untouched by government power as possible.

The same principle applies across a variety of public-school conflicts. For example, this would mean public schools themselves wouldn't offer religious instruction, because we don't want government bureaucrats deciding whether our children will be taught Calvinism or Arminianism, Catholicism or Protestantism. But public schools could allow students to receive *private* religious instruction during the school day, and they could even award school credit for students who do so. This kind of religious instruction is currently offered through released-time programs throughout the country.[57] The idea is that students are free to receive religious instruction and that the public school creates neither an incentive nor a disincentive for doing so.[58]

Funding for Religious Schools

Finally, consider the question of government funding of religious schools—such as vouchers, tax credits, or direct grants that can be used by religious schools. Under the *Lemon* test, any kind of funding for religious

glect their children, the government can take custody and prosecute the parents. And if a mosque disrupts traffic or plots a terrorist attack, the government can intervene. But the rights of the mosque and the rights of the parents remain important matters of justice.

Even apart from our theological understanding of justice, a violation of religious freedom is a violation of basic human rights. As I explained in chapter 3, all human beings are born with a religious impulse—a desire to seek and embrace transcendent truth. But by our very nature, we can seek and embrace the truth authentically only if we do so freely. So when the government coerces us to go against our understanding of transcendent truth, it is forcing us to go against our very nature as human beings and is violating a human right.

This analysis doesn't depend on the understanding of transcendent truth we embrace. It applies to everyone—even those who are mistaken about transcendent truth. This is not because we're relativists but because the government simply can't coerce anyone to embrace transcendent truth.

Thus, we should care about religious freedom for Muslims not simply because their freedom is inextricably linked with ours or because we hope to lead them to Jesus, but also because it is the right thing to do.

ARE WE PROMOTING RELATIVISM?

Many Christians already support religious freedom for people of all faiths. When I represented the Murfreesboro mosque, Christians of all stripes signed a letter supporting the mosque's right to use their property—Catholics and Protestants; evangelicals and mainliners; conservatives and liberals; Baptists, Lutherans, Methodists, Presbyterians, and more.[19] This support echoes the official teaching of many branches of Christianity, from the Roman Catholic Church's statement on religious freedom (*Dignitatis Humanae*)[20] to Article XVII of the Baptist Faith and Message.[21] Nor is this support new. As Roger Williams, the

ernment preference for some religious denominations—namely, those that toe the government's line on sexuality—over others. Thus, these kinds of strings are constitutionally problematic under a historical approach.

Summing Up

So what are the main takeaways? How should we think about religion in the public square?

First, we should beware of government support for religion. The government that supports religion becomes the government that controls religion. And the government that controls religion invariably goes wrong in one of two ways: either it coercively represses dissent, as in colonial Massachusetts and in some Muslim countries today; or it fosters a tepid civil religion that is subservient to the state, as in colonial Virginia and in some European countries today. So James Madison and the Great Awakening evangelicals were right: Christianity doesn't need "the support of human laws," and giving it that support produces only "pride and indolence in the Clergy" and "ignorance and servility in the laity."[63]

In practice, this means we shouldn't want government bureaucrats composing prayers that schoolchildren must say. We shouldn't want the government funding religious schools and then using that funding to dictate what the religious curriculum should contain. We shouldn't want the government pressuring people to embrace Christianity. Separation of church and state—rightly understood—is a good thing.

Of course, this doesn't mean religion should be scrubbed from the public square either. The government routinely recognizes various aspects of human culture, such as race, ethnicity, sex, and art. Because religion, too, is an essential part of our history and culture, it's only natural for religion to be part of the public square. Anything less would send a message of government hostility toward religion.

So what kind of public square should we be aiming for?

We should aim for a public square that neither promotes religion nor suppresses it, but instead welcomes religion as an essential part of human culture. We don't need the government to pat us on the back for our Christianity or pressure other citizens to join us. Nor do we want the government to treat *God* like a dirty word and pretend religion doesn't exist. Instead, the government can leave religion free to flourish or not and to influence the public square or not, "according to the zeal of its adherents."[64]

After many years of misguided jurisprudence, the Supreme Court appears poised to head in this direction by interpreting the Establishment Clause according to its historical meaning. Among other things, this would mean the government couldn't pressure anyone to attend religious services, but it could let citizens display religious symbols in the public square. It couldn't require students to say a prayer, but it could create space for students to pray on their own. It couldn't give preferential funding to religious schools, hospitals, and soup kitchens, but it could fund religious organizations on the same terms as nonreligious ones.

This would be a good result—avoiding the twin problems of government support and government hostility toward religion. In short, the government would leave religion as untouched by government power as possible. That is a result all Christians can celebrate—not because we're relativists, but because we're confident in the truth and persuasiveness of the gospel.

Now that we've considered the most significant religious freedom conflicts—in the areas of nondiscrimination, abortion, gay rights, Islam, and the public square—the next question is, What can we *do* about it? How do we respond to the religious freedom challenges ahead? That is the subject of part 3.

Part 3

WHAT CAN BE DONE?

Let Go of Winning

I've been in court many times as a lawyer but only once as a defendant. It started as a conflict with my landlord in Washington, DC. My wife and I rented a house in DC for four years. Before we left DC for Utah, we gave the landlord thirty days' notice as provided in the lease. He stopped by the house to receive our last rent check, looked around the property, and told us we were the best tenants he'd ever had.

After we moved across the country, he sent us a letter saying the property manager found "issues" with the house—like uncut grass and trash in the yard—so he was withholding the entire $2,100 security deposit. He also said we weren't allowed to end the lease with thirty days' notice, and he sued us in small-claims court for an additional $1,661 in rent. It was an obvious attempt to soak us for extra cash.

I was shocked. I was angry. I wanted to give the landlord a piece of my mind. I wanted to win.

WE WANT TO WIN

Religious freedom conflicts can be a little like that, only the stakes are much higher and the emotions more intense. We're not fighting about a security deposit but about a fundamental human right. We're not accused of failing to cut the grass but of bigotry. We're not facing a loss of cash but of conscience.

objectors—a handful of small-business owners unwilling to personally support or participate in a same-sex marriage. There's no evidence that same-sex couples can't find other photographers, florists, or bakers for their weddings or that they've been shut out of entire areas of the economy. If anything, other vendors are clamoring for their business, and there are "powerful economic incentive[s]" *not* to conscientiously object.[27] Thus, the reasons for adopting sweeping antidiscrimination laws aren't present here.

In response, gay-rights advocates sometimes claim that antidiscrimination laws aren't just about preventing economic harms; they're about preventing dignitary harms. These are the feelings of distress, embarrassment, or pain that someone feels when he's denied service based on a personal trait like race or sexual orientation.[28]

But preventing dignitary harm isn't by itself a sufficient basis for restricting First Amendment rights. In the free-speech context, for example, the law allows people to impose dignitary harms all the time. The Supreme Court has recognized the right of Nazi protestors to march through a neighborhood of Holocaust survivors[29] and the right of anti-gay protestors to picket a funeral, shouting slogans that are deeply hurtful and offensive to gay people.[30] This conduct is far more reprehensible, and it imposes far greater dignitary harms, than when a business owner who otherwise gladly serves gay and lesbian customers politely declines to participate in a same-sex wedding. Yet the court has long recognized that "the government may not prohibit the expression of an idea simply because society finds the idea itself offensive or disagreeable."[31]

Dignitary harms also occur on both sides of these conflicts. No one denies it's painful for a same-sex couple to encounter someone who won't photograph their wedding. But they can find another photographer with little or no hardship. Conscientious objectors, however, can face financial ruin—like the baker in Oregon who lost her business and was ordered to pay $135,000 in fines.[32] And while it may harm your dignity to hear that a fellow citizen disapproves of your marriage, it harms your dignity even more when your own government brands you a bigot and

Given these stakes, religious freedom conflicts naturally generate strong emotions. We feel surprised that we're facing hostility for our faith. We feel angry that people are attacking us. We feel afraid that our rights will be taken away. We want justice.

We want to win.

So when we ask, "What can we *do* about religious freedom conflicts?" often what we're really asking is "How can we *win*?" We want practical steps we can take to avoid being blindsided by lawsuits and losing our rights. We want a strategy for winning.

That's a natural desire, and I'll certainly offer some practical steps for winning.

But I also think starting with a strategy for "winning" is the wrong way to approach the question. It assumes the primary goal in religious freedom conflicts is to "win," and it's often driven by fear—fear that our rights will be taken away or other bad things will happen if we lose. That fear, in turn, produces anger, hostility, frustration, and despair.

Scripture, however, calls us to a radically different approach. We're called not to win but to be like Jesus; not to fear suffering but to fear God; not to be surprised at hostility but to expect it; not to complain when we lose but to rejoice; not to lash out at our opponents but to love them. We're called not to avoid losing at all costs but to glorify God at all costs.

So before we address what we're going to *do* about religious freedom, we need to reconsider what type of people we're called to *be* in the midst of religious freedom conflicts. Only if we become those people can we "win" religious freedom fights in any meaningful sense. That's what this chapter is about.

Scripture is packed with teaching on how to be faithful to God in suffering and persecution. But American Christians, secure in the comfort of our Judeo-Christian nation, have often lost sight of this teaching. The following are seven principles that are especially challenging for us today.

Expect Suffering

First, Scripture teaches that we should expect to suffer for our faith. As American Christians, we're used to having our religious freedom protected; we feel entitled to it, and we're surprised when it's taken away. But Scripture teaches the opposite.

When Jesus sent out the twelve apostles, He told them to expect suffering: "Behold, I am sending you out as sheep in the midst of wolves. . . . Beware of men, for they will deliver you over to courts and flog you in their synagogues. . . . You will be hated by all for my name's sake. . . . If they have called the master of the house Beelzebul, how much more will they malign those of his household?" (Matthew 10:16–25).

He said the same during the last supper: "If the world hates you, know that it has hated me before it hated you. . . . 'A servant is not greater than his master.' If they persecuted me, they will also persecute you" (John 15:18–20).

The same expectation of suffering is repeated in the epistles. Peter tells us, "Do not be surprised at the fiery trial [of persecution] when it comes upon you to test you, as though something strange were happening to you" (1 Peter 4:12). Paul put it even more bluntly: "*All* who desire to live a godly life in Christ Jesus will be persecuted" (2 Timothy 3:12).

So we need to reject the idea that just because we live in America, we won't suffer for our faith. We've enjoyed many years of extraordinary religious freedom in this country. By the grace of God, we may enjoy many more. But we aren't supposed to expect it, much less assume we're entitled to it.

Rejoice When It Comes

Second, Scripture teaches us that our primary response to persecution should be to rejoice. In the Sermon on the Mount, Jesus said, "Blessed are you when others revile you and persecute you and utter all kinds of evil against you falsely on my account. *Rejoice and be glad,* for your reward is

government power to promote and inculcate a common set of religious beliefs.[6] An establishment might be narrow—focusing exclusively on a particular church, like the Church of England. Or it might be broad—promoting multiple Christian denominations. It might be coercive—imposing harsh penalties on anyone who dissents. Or it might be more tolerant—allowing for worship in dissenting churches. The colonial establishments took different forms at different times, but they all had several key features in common.

First, the government controlled the doctrine and personnel of the established church. In Virginia, for example, the General Assembly required that worship be conducted only in accordance with the Canons of the Church of England, which were prescribed by the British Parliament. Ministers had to be approved by the governor.[7] In Massachusetts, the law regulated who could preach and how local ministers would be selected.[8]

Second, the government mandated attendance in the established church. For example, Virginia, Massachusetts, and Connecticut all imposed fines for failing to attend church services.[9]

Third, the government allocated land and money to support the established church. Most of the colonies dedicated public land for the construction of church buildings. They gave ministers income-producing land for their financial support, and they levied taxes (called "tithes") to support churches and ministers.

Fourth, the government restricted worship in dissenting churches. Massachusetts, for example, banned preaching outside the established church, resulting in severe persecution of Quakers, Catholics, and Baptists. Virginia repeatedly imprisoned Baptists for preaching without a license. And multiple colonies adopted laws prohibiting Catholic churches.

Fifth, the government limited political participation to members of the established church. This meant dissenters were barred from voting or holding political office.

Finally, the colonies used the established churches to carry out various civil functions. For example, the established church was often responsible

great in heaven, for so they persecuted the prophets who were before you" (Matthew 5:11–12). In Luke, Jesus added that when people hate, revile, and exclude us, we should "leap for joy" (6:23). Similarly, Peter, right after telling us not to be surprised, said, "*Rejoice* insofar as you share Christ's sufferings, that you may also rejoice and be glad when his glory is revealed. If you are insulted for the name of Christ, you are blessed, because the Spirit of glory and of God rests upon you" (1 Peter 4:13–14).

Why should we rejoice in persecution? Not because it is pleasant or good, but because we "share Christ's sufferings" and our "reward is great in heaven." Persecution also creates opportunities to spread the gospel. As Jesus said, it "will be your opportunity to bear witness" (Luke 21:13). Paul confirmed this, writing that his imprisonment "has really served to advance the gospel, so that it has become known throughout the whole imperial guard and to all the rest that my imprisonment is for Christ. And most of the brothers, having become confident in the Lord by my imprisonment, are much more bold to speak the word without fear" (Philippians 1:12–14).

So our first response to persecution shouldn't be surprise or anger, but rejoicing.

Fear God, Not Men

Third, not only should we expect persecution and rejoice in it, but we should also have no fear of it. Scripture repeatedly calls us to reject the fear of men and to fear God alone. Jesus said it best: "*Do not fear* those who kill the body but cannot kill the soul. Rather fear him who can destroy both soul and body in hell" (Matthew 10:28).

Peter echoed this teaching, saying, "Even if you should suffer for righteousness' sake . . . *have no fear of them,* nor be troubled, but in your hearts honor Christ the Lord as holy" (1 Peter 3:14–15). And speaking to the church at Smyrna, Jesus said, "*Do not fear* what you are about to suffer. Behold, the devil is about to throw some of you into prison, that you may be tested, and for ten days you will have tribulation. Be faithful unto death, and I will give you the crown of life" (Revelation 2:10).

How can we resist fear? The answer is not to grit our teeth and pretend suffering doesn't hurt. Instead, it's to cultivate a holy fear of God. As Jesus said, "Fear him who can destroy both soul and body in hell" (Matthew 10:28). And as Peter said, "Honor Christ the Lord as holy" (1 Peter 3:15). This means recognizing that we serve a holy God and that our actions have eternal consequences far more significant than anything that might happen on earth. It also means remembering that God is sovereign and cares about us. As Jesus said right after commanding us to fear God, "Are not two sparrows sold for a penny? And not one of them will fall to the ground apart from your Father. . . . Fear not, therefore; you are of more value than many sparrows" (Matthew 10:29–31).

So our fearlessness comes both from fearing God and from knowing His sovereign love for us.

Strive for Peace

Fourth, just because we expect suffering, rejoice in it, and have no fear of it doesn't mean we should go looking for it. Some Christians seem to *want* religious freedom conflicts. They look for ways their faith might conflict with the law and use inflamed rhetoric to stoke the conflict even when it might be avoided. But Scripture commands the opposite.

Paul, no stranger to conflict, urged us, "If possible, so far as it depends on you, live peaceably with all," including "those who persecute you" (Romans 12:18, 14). Immediately afterward, he commanded that "every person be subject to the governing authorities" (13:1). Similarly, the author of Hebrews urged us to "strive for peace with everyone" (12:14).

This doesn't mean we compromise our faith to keep the peace. Scripture has plenty of examples of faithful people who engaged in civil disobedience—from Daniel, who braved the lions' den, to the apostles, who said, "We must obey God rather than men" (Acts 5:29). Jesus and the apostles often spoke truth that provoked conflict (Luke 11:37–54; Acts 23:6–7). But it means we don't go looking for conflict for conflict's sake, and we don't stoke conflict for self-serving reasons. Instead, we look for ways to obey both God and government, to protect both our conscience and the peace. This is part of what it means when Jesus said, "Be wise as serpents and innocent as doves," and "When they persecute you in one town, flee to the next" (Matthew 10:16, 23). The goal is not to win religious freedom conflicts but to "lead a peaceful and quiet life, godly and dignified in every way" (1 Timothy 2:2).

Continue Doing Good

Fifth, sometimes it's impossible to keep the peace and still obey God. In that case, Scripture is clear: we must obey God.

When we face suffering for doing good, it's tempting to compromise our behavior or the truth of the gospel. Peter experienced this firsthand. On the night Jesus was betrayed, Peter denied Him three times (Mark 14:66–72).

But Peter also got it right. He boldly told the Sanhedrin that he must keep preaching about Jesus, even though it led to a beating (Acts 5:29, 40). So Peter was speaking from personal experience when he told persecuted Christians that "those who suffer according to God's will should commit themselves to their faithful Creator and *continue to do good*" (1 Peter 4:19, NIV). We can't let the prospect of conflict or suffering stop us from doing good.

This is not only the right thing to do but also a path to greater religious freedom. Recall "The Quakers' Lesson" from chapter 6. The Quakers were brutally persecuted by the early colonies for refusing to serve in the militia. They were fined. They were beaten. They "joyfully accepted the plundering of [their] property" (Hebrews 10:34), and they refused to budge. Eventually, the colonies realized that punishing them was futile. So the colonies gave in and exempted the Quakers from military service.

Sometimes religious freedom is gained not through political power but through patiently suffering and continuing to do good.

Love Our Enemies

Sixth, sometimes being faithful to God and doing good means we'll have hostile enemies. Then Scripture is clear: we must love our enemies.

Jesus's words are the most challenging: "Love your enemies, do good to those who hate you, bless those who curse you, pray for those who abuse you" (Luke 6:27–28). This is not merely a prohibition on retaliating against our enemies; it's an affirmative command to do good to them in word and deed. Jesus expanded on what this means in practice: "Do not resist the one who is evil. But if anyone slaps you on the right cheek, turn to him the other also. And if anyone would sue you and take your tunic, let him have your cloak as well. And if anyone forces you to go one mile, go with him two miles" (Matthew 5:39–41).

Peter and Paul further applied this teaching in passages about persecution. Peter said, "Do not repay evil for evil or reviling for reviling, but on the contrary, bless, for to this you were called, that you may obtain a blessing" (1 Peter 3:9). Paul said the same thing (Romans 12:14, 17), and then he offered practical ways we can love our enemies: "If your enemy is hungry, feed him; if he is thirsty, give him something to drink" (verse 20). In short, "Do not be overcome by evil, but overcome evil with good" (verse 21).

This doesn't mean we approve of what our enemies do or join them in doing evil. For example, we don't love our enemies by helping them perform abortions. In fact, loving our enemies may include exposing their deeds as evil. As Paul said, "Take no part in the unfruitful works of darkness, but instead expose them" (Ephesians 5:11). Similarly, we must be "prepared to make a defense to anyone who asks," but we must "do it with gentleness and respect" (1 Peter 3:15) and "always be gracious" (Colossians 4:6).

So loving our enemies means changing our speech—to bless them and speak with graciousness, gentleness, and respect. It means changing our prayers—to pray for them. And it means changing our actions—to find ways to do good to them without participating in their evil deeds.

Our primary concern is not defeating our enemies but loving them.

Care for One Another

Finally, Scripture commands us to care for fellow Christians who are suffering. We must "remember those who are in prison, as though in prison with them, and those who are mistreated, since you also are in the body" (Hebrews 13:3). We must remember that "if one member suffers, all suffer together" (1 Corinthians 12:26). And we must "weep with those who weep" (Romans 12:15).

Accordingly, the early church made "earnest prayer" for Peter when he was imprisoned (Acts 12:5). It sent help to Paul in prison multiple times (Philippians 4:10, 14, 16). And it "made great lamentation" over Stephen when he was killed (Acts 8:2). So even if we aren't personally suffering, we're called to actively remember, pray for, and encourage those who are.

This includes caring for Christians we might disagree with. Take, for example, a scenario where a Christian baker is asked to provide a cake for a same-sex wedding. Some Christians might agree that same-sex marriage is wrong but still disagree over how the baker should respond. Some might believe the baker should never provide a cake for a same-sex wedding because it makes him complicit in immorality. Others might believe the baker can provide a cake because he isn't personally participating in the wedding ceremony. Still others might believe the baker should provide the cake for free as a way of blessing people who need to experience the love of Christ.[1]

The point is that sometimes Christians will disagree on questions of conscience. And sometimes we'll be tempted to condemn Christians we disagree with. The ones who would provide the cake may accuse the ones who wouldn't of being unloving toward gay couples, stoking an unnecessary culture war, or giving Christianity a bad name. The ones who wouldn't provide the cake may accuse the ones who would of failing to be good witnesses, being "soft" on marriage, and caving to the culture.

This is not a new phenomenon. Early Christians disagreed over another matter of conscience: whether they could eat food sacrificed to idols. Some believed eating such food (like providing a wedding cake for a same-sex couple) made them complicit in evil; others believed they could eat it in good conscience. Amid that disagreement, Paul urged Christians to "pursue what makes for peace and for mutual upbuilding" (Romans 14:19). That means not despising or passing judgment on those who disagree (verses 3, 10, 13). It also means "walking in love" and not putting a "stumbling block" in the way of fellow Christians (verses 13, 15, 20–21; 1 Corinthians 8:9, 12–13).

There's room to debate how these passages apply to modern disagreements over questions of conscience. But the command to walk in love and pursue peace and mutual upbuilding is a good starting point. Rather than quickly condemning fellow Christians who reach different conclusions on questions of moral complicity, we should try to build one another up, reason together frankly, and work together in community to discern how to love our neighbors as ourselves.

SUMMING UP

In sum, Scripture calls us to radically reorient our thinking about suffering and persecution. We're called not to "win" but to be like Christ. That means we expect suffering, respond with joy, fear God, strive for peace, keep doing good, love our enemies, and care for one another in suffering. In short, we don't try to win a culture war; we try to glorify God by being like Christ.

We obviously can't do this on our own. We can't flip a switch and suddenly make ourselves rejoice in suffering and love our enemies. We must "be transformed by the renewal of [our] mind[s]" (Romans 12:2). That starts with repenting of ways we've sought comfort over Christlikeness and feared men rather than God. It continues with cultivating humility toward those we disagree with and presenting ourselves daily as living sacrifices to God (Romans 12:1). Ultimately, how we respond to violations of religious freedom will be dictated by the nature of our relationship with God. We'll respond faithfully only if we've "been with Jesus" (Acts 4:13).

What does this faithful response to violations of religious freedom look like in practice?

Scripture offers numerous examples of just that—stories of how God's people responded to violations of religious freedom. The problem is that, aside from an occasional Sunday school lesson on Daniel and the lions' den, we've largely overlooked them.

So the next chapter briefly highlights eight of the most significant religious freedom conflicts in Scripture—underscoring how God's people responded and what we can learn from it. The lessons are not always what you would expect.

❧

The lawsuit with my landlord, which I described at the start of this chapter, also didn't end as I expected. After I recovered from my initial shock and anger at getting sued, I considered simply letting go of our $2,100 security deposit, sending him a check for the $1,661 in extra rent he demanded, and including a gift card and conciliatory note. As Jesus said, "If anyone would sue you and take your tunic, let him have your cloak as well" (Matthew 5:40). I could pat myself on the back for being so radically righteous.

But after discussion and prayer with my wife and pastor, we decided the more loving approach, given our long-standing relationship with the landlord, would be to meet with him in person, explain why we thought he was doing something wrong, and give him an opportunity to make it right. So I flew across the country to meet him in small-claims court, where I requested the return of our security deposit.

The small-claims court sent us to a mediator, who explained that my interpretation of the lease wasn't as obvious as I thought and that the landlord's demands weren't as reasonable as he thought. The mediator recommended we resolve the lawsuit by having the landlord return one-quarter of the security deposit ($500) and drop his claims. But the landlord was unwilling to do that.

The landlord said he was angry at the tone of some of my prior communications and upset that we left some items in the front yard when we moved out. I apologized for that. I said we were upset that he seemed to be taking advantage of us and exaggerating about alleged damage to the property. He apologized for that.

The landlord then suggested we both drop our claims and he'd buy me lunch. I agreed. So we dropped our claims, walked across the street, ate lunch together, shook hands, and said, "No hard feelings."

That was not what I expected. I thought I was completely in the right and either the landlord would repent or I would win the case. Instead, I realized my legal claims weren't as strong as I thought and my own sin had contributed to the conflict. I also thought the most important thing was winning the case and making sure justice was done. Instead, I learned that God wanted to do something in my heart and my relationship with my landlord—and that I needed a lesson in humility.

Religious freedom conflicts can be the same way. We often think we're completely in the right and the most important thing is for justice to be done. But sometimes God is doing something we don't expect, and we need to approach the conflict in a different way. Nothing illustrates this better than the wide variety of religious freedom conflicts described in Scripture.

Learn from Scripture

Remember the case of the courageous pharmacists in chapter 6? For four generations, the Stormans family owned a small grocery store and pharmacy in Olympia, Washington. When they decided not to sell drugs that could cause an abortion, abortion-rights activists targeted them—protesting the store, disrupting traffic, and filing multiple complaints with the state. The governor then issued a new regulation requiring the family to either sell abortion pills or lose their pharmacy license and their livelihood. It's one of the clearest cases of antireligious targeting I've ever litigated.

The trial court ruled in favor of the family. The Ninth Circuit reversed that ruling on appeal. Then we appealed to the Supreme Court. But shortly after we appealed, Justice Scalia died, leaving us one vote shy of what we needed to move forward with the case.

It was a gut-wrenching loss.

How should we think about a loss like this? Does Scripture have anything to say about it?

Of course! In fact, the Bible tells a story of two women who faced almost the same dilemma as the Stormans family over three thousand years ago. Do you remember it?

If not, you're in good company. Most Christians don't. But this means we may be missing some important lessons Scripture teaches about religious freedom.

There are *dozens* of religious freedom stories in Scripture—places where God's people faced a conflict between the demands of God and the demands of government. So if you're looking for concrete examples of what faithfulness in a religious freedom conflict looks like, this is the place to start.

We'll begin with the very first religious freedom conflict in Scripture—a story remarkably similar to that of the Stormans family: the story of the courageous Hebrew midwives.

THE MIDWIVES REFUSE TO KILL

The story is told in Exodus 1:8–22. The Israelites were slaves in Egypt, but their population was growing rapidly, and the Egyptians were afraid of them. The Egyptians thought war might break out and the Israelites would join their enemies (verse 10). So they viewed the Israelites as a national security threat.

To combat this threat, Pharaoh summoned the leading Hebrew midwives, Shiphrah and Puah, and commanded them, "When you serve as midwife to the Hebrew women and see them on the birthstool, if it is a son, you shall kill him, but if it is a daughter, she shall live" (verse 16).

Here we have the first religious freedom conflict in Scripture: the Egyptian government commanded the midwives to do something contrary to God's commands—to destroy human life.[1] This is eerily similar to the dilemma faced by the Stormans family: either sell a drug that can destroy human life or face punishment.

We aren't told what the punishment for disobeying Pharaoh would have been, but we know he ruthlessly enslaved and slaughtered entire nations. So the punishment would have been severe—probably death (Genesis 40:22). The midwives faced immense pressure to bow to Pharaoh's demands.

So what did they do?

"The midwives feared God and did not do as the king of Egypt commanded them, but let the male children live" (Exodus 1:17). They disobeyed Pharaoh—and they did it because they "feared God" more than they feared Pharaoh.

Next, Pharaoh investigated them: "The king of Egypt called the midwives and said to them, 'Why have you done this, and let the male children live?'" (verse 18).

This created another dilemma. Should the midwives tell the truth, or should they deceive Pharaoh?

They deceived him: "The midwives said to Pharaoh, 'Because the Hebrew women are not like the Egyptian women, for they are vigorous and give birth before the midwife comes to them'" (verse 19).

I wish I could find a way to interpret this passage so that the midwives are telling the truth. But it can't be done without stretching the text. It clearly says the midwives "did not do as the king of Egypt commanded them"—not because the Hebrew women gave birth too quickly, but because the midwives "feared God" (verse 17).

What was God's response?

"So God dealt well with the midwives. . . . And because the midwives feared God, he gave them families" (verses 20–21). God rewarded the midwives for fearing Him. He not only protected them from punishment but also gave them families of their own.

This story teaches several important lessons. First, it gives us a classic example of a religious freedom conflict: the government commands something that God forbids. But think about how this conflict came about. Pharaoh was *not* sitting around thinking, *I hate Judaism. How can I force the midwives to violate their faith?* Rather, he was pursuing a *different* goal—national security—through the killing of Hebrew boys.

This is how religious freedom conflicts usually arise. Government officials don't usually sit around saying, "I hate Christianity. How can I stop Christians from practicing their faith?" Rather, the conflicts arise because government officials are pursuing another goal—like national security, nondiscrimination, or access to abortion—and religious practices conflict with that goal.

Second, this story shows that we may face immense pressure to obey the government rather than God. But the key to standing strong is not our smarts, our courage, or our political power. It is the *fear of God.* Do we know God and honor His commands? Do we fear God more than we fear men? That will determine whether we stand strong.

Third, fearing God is not the same as recklessness. The midwives could have told Pharaoh that they disobeyed his command because it was contrary to God's law. But they didn't. They deceived him. There's no easy formula for deciding when deception might be permissible. But there's ample precedent for it—like Rahab deceiving the king of Jericho (Joshua 2), Jonathan deceiving Saul (1 Samuel 20), and Hushai deceiving Absalom (2 Samuel 15–17).[2] The broader point is that fearing God doesn't mean picking every possible fight.

Would this ever apply to modern religious freedom conflicts? For example, could a Christian photographer say she's too busy to photograph a same-sex wedding if the real reason is that she believes same-sex marriage is wrong? Or could she offer an evasive response that isn't entirely false? (I discuss this further in chapter 13.)

Finally, this story teaches us that God deals well with us when we're faithful (Exodus 1:20). He protected the midwives and gave them families, and He's fully able to protect and reward us too.

But that doesn't mean He always will. Sometimes our faithfulness leads to suffering—as our next story shows.

Jeremiah Commits Treason

In the sixth century BC, two world powers were competing for control of Jerusalem—Babylon and Egypt. Babylon captured Jerusalem in 597 BC and installed Zedekiah as its puppet king. As a puppet king, Zedekiah had a choice: he could keep serving the king of Babylon, or he could revolt and declare his independence.

The prophet Jeremiah urged Zedekiah to "serve the king of Babylon and live" (Jeremiah 27:17). But Zedekiah and his officials refused to listen. They revolted against Babylon and allied with Egypt instead. The king and other leaders viewed Jeremiah with suspicion and imprisoned him as a traitor (Jeremiah 37).

Then the stakes got even higher. The king of Babylon besieged Jerusalem and tried to starve it into submission. Zedekiah and his army resisted, hoping the Egyptians would save them (verses 6–10).

At this crucial moment—with an army surrounding the city—Jeremiah prophesied, "Thus says the LORD: He who stays in this city shall die by the sword, by famine, and by pestilence, but he who goes out to the [Babylonians] shall live. . . . This city shall surely be given into the hand of the army of the king of Babylon and be taken" (38:2–3).

Jeremiah was essentially prophesying treason. He told the people to desert Zedekiah and surrender to the Babylonians.

Not surprisingly, the officials of Jerusalem were furious. They said to Zedekiah, "Let this man be put to death, for he is weakening the hands of the soldiers who are left in this city, and the hands of all the people, by speaking such words to them. For this man is not seeking the welfare of this people, but their harm" (verse 4). In other words, Jeremiah was a national security threat.

King Zedekiah granted their request: "Behold, he is in your hands, for the king can do nothing against you" (verse 5). "So they took Jeremiah and cast him into the cistern of Malchiah, the king's son, which was in the court of the guard, letting Jeremiah down by ropes. And there was no water in the cistern, but only mud, and Jeremiah sank in the mud" (verse 6). They planned to starve Jeremiah to death.

This is another vivid example of a religious freedom conflict. Like the midwives, Jeremiah's faithfulness to God conflicts with the government's national security demands. Only this time the government isn't a cruel

Egyptian pharaoh but the supposedly righteous leaders of Jerusalem. And Jeremiah is not spared punishment; he is imprisoned and left for dead.

This was not the first time Jeremiah suffered a violation of his religious freedom. Earlier in his life, the leaders of his hometown threatened him with death if he kept prophesying (11:21). Others plotted to kill him (18:18, 23). The chief temple officer beat him and put him in stocks because of his harsh message (20:2). A crowd of priests and prophets nearly convinced the leaders of Judah to put him to death (chapter 26). And government officials beat him and imprisoned him on false charges of deserting to the Babylonians (chapter 37).

If Jeremiah's story teaches us anything, it's that faithfulness to God doesn't guarantee freedom or safety. It often leads to suffering. Many other prophets experienced the same thing. Micaiah and Hanani were imprisoned (1 Kings 22:26–27; 2 Chronicles 16:7–10). Elijah and Elisha were threatened with death (1 Kings 19:1–4; 2 Kings 6:31–32). Uriah was killed with the sword (Jeremiah 26:20–23). Zechariah was stoned in the temple (2 Chronicles 24:21). John the Baptist was beheaded (Matthew 14). All were punished by the government because of their faith.

Jeremiah's story also shows that this suffering really hurts. Consider how he prayed after suffering for his faith (11:18–20; 12:1–4; 18:19–23; 20:7–18). He questioned God: "Why does the way of the wicked prosper? Why do all who are treacherous thrive?" (12:1). He accused God: "O LORD, you have deceived me, and I was deceived" (20:7). He complained to God: "I have become a laughingstock all the day; everyone mocks me" (verse 7). He cursed his life: "Cursed be the day on which I was born!" (verse 14); "Why did I come out from the womb to see toil and sorrow, and spend my days in shame?" (verse 18). He called for vengeance: "Pull them out like sheep for the slaughter" (12:3); "Forgive not their iniquity, nor blot out their sin from your sight" (18:23).[3]

These are not the prayers of someone who is happy to suffer. They are the prayers of someone experiencing real pain and discouragement. We shouldn't forget that lesson: violations of religious freedom cause real people to suffer real pain and discouragement.

Thankfully, Jeremiah's story doesn't end with starvation in a muddy cistern. A servant of King Zedekiah—an Ethiopian eunuch named Ebed-melech—heard that Jeremiah had been put into the cistern. Ebed-melech thought this was unjust. So he went to King Zedekiah and said, "My lord the king, these men have done evil in all that they did to Jeremiah the prophet by casting him into the cistern, and he will die there of hunger, for there is no bread left in the city" (38:9).

This was a remarkably bold move. Powerful officials had *just* convinced King Zedekiah to put Jeremiah to death for treason. There was no reason to think Zedekiah would change his mind, and every reason to think the same officials would go after Ebed-melech next—for calling them "evil" and for supporting Jeremiah's treason. Ebed-melech was not even a Jew; he was a Gentile eunuch. Yet he cried out for justice anyway.

Remarkably, it worked: "Then the king commanded Ebed-melech the Ethiopian, 'Take thirty men with you from here, and lift Jeremiah the prophet out of the cistern before he dies'" (verse 10). So Ebed-melech did so, rescuing Jeremiah from death.

You might call him the first religious freedom advocate.

Then God gave Jeremiah a message for Ebed-melech:

Go, and say to Ebed-melech the Ethiopian, "Thus says the LORD of hosts, the God of Israel: Behold, I will fulfill my words against this city for harm and not for good, and they shall be accomplished before you on that day. But I will deliver you on that day, declares the LORD, and you shall not be given into the hand of the men of whom you are afraid. For I will surely save you, and you shall not fall by the sword, but you shall have your life as a prize of war, because you have put your trust in me, declares the LORD." (39:16–18)

God promised to save Ebed-melech from two things—"the men of whom you are afraid" (i.e., the same officials who wanted to kill Jeremiah) and "the sword" of the Babylonians. And He did it because Ebed-melech "put [his] trust" in Him.

Ebed-melech teaches us several lessons. First, we should reject fatalism. Ebed-melech had every reason to abandon hope. But he didn't give up; he still sought justice. We should do the same. We should reject the fatalism that says our religious freedom is already lost, and we should continue to seek justice.

Second, we should seek justice even when it's risky. Ebed-melech took a huge risk: the same officials who went after Jeremiah would probably come after him. He was afraid of them (verse 17), but he sought justice anyway.

Third, we should consider where we put our trust. Ebed-melech's boldness wasn't based on his trust in King Zedekiah. It wasn't based on having a conservative majority on the Israelite Supreme Court. It was based on his "trust in [God]" (verse 18). Our pursuit of justice has to be rooted in the same trust.

Finally, God rewards the pursuit of justice. God saved Ebed-melech from hostile government officials and an invading army. God will reward us for pursuing justice too. That doesn't mean we'll always escape hardship. But we'll always be rewarded.

Our next two stories—both from the book of Daniel—expand on these themes of hope, risk taking, trust, and reward. But they also show that religious freedom conflicts can take unexpected forms.

DANIEL REFUSES THE KING'S FOOD

Daniel and his three friends (Shadrach, Meshach, and Abednego) were contemporaries of Jeremiah. They all lived through the Babylonian conquest of Jerusalem in 597 BC. But while Jeremiah was left in Jerusalem with the puppet king, Daniel and his friends were taken to Babylon. There they were educated in the literature and language of the Babylonians and given a daily portion of the king's food and wine (Daniel 1:3–5).

This was a great benefit. Instead of being imprisoned or enslaved, Daniel and his friends would be the king's advisers and eat from the king's table. But this also created a conflict: the food wasn't kosher, and if they ate it, they would be violating God's law.

The Bible doesn't suggest the Babylonian officials were trying to attack the Jewish faith. They thought eating the king's food would make Daniel and his friends healthier (verse 10). So, unlike Jeremiah, this is an example of an *unintentional* religious freedom conflict—where the government adopts a policy it thinks will help people but ends up causing problems instead.

There are many such conflicts today. School districts require students to wear uniforms, not realizing this can pressure students to abandon religious articles of clothing. Police departments forbid officers from growing beards, not realizing this can exclude Jews, Sikhs, and Muslims. Towns require new construction projects to use new technology, not realizing this can create conflicts for the Amish. So even when the government isn't "out to get" religious people, it can still create religious freedom conflicts.

Intentional or not, this conflict created a dilemma for Daniel and his friends. If they ate the king's food, they would be disobeying God. But if they refused, they could be punished or lose their privileged status. Nevertheless, "Daniel resolved that he would not defile himself with the king's food" (verse 8). He chose devotion to God over noble status.

But notice what Daniel *didn't* do. He didn't exacerbate the conflict. He didn't stage a hunger strike, condemn the leaders, or draw attention to himself. Instead, he quietly "asked the chief of the eunuchs [the king's official] to allow him not to defile himself" (verse 8). That is, he asked for a *religious accommodation*—an exception to the rules to let him practice his faith.

The official could have rejected this request outright. But instead "God gave Daniel favor and compassion in the sight of the chief of the eunuchs" (verse 9). God Himself was working through a government official in favor of religious freedom.

But there was still a problem: "The chief of the eunuchs said to Daniel, 'I fear my lord the king, who assigned your food and your drink; for why should he see that you were in worse condition than the youths who are of your own age? So you would endanger my head with the king'" (verse 10). In other words, the eunuch wanted to give Daniel a religious accommodation, but he was afraid he'd get in trouble for doing so. This is not uncommon: government officials often want to respect religious liberty, but they succumb to other pressures not to do so—whether hostile opposition from neighbors or mere administrative convenience.

So Daniel asked for a test: "Test your servants for ten days; let us be given vegetables to eat and water to drink. Then let our appearance and the appearance of the youths who eat the king's food be observed by you, and deal with your servants according to what you see" (verses 12–13). This shows great faith. It also shows that Daniel was a shrewd negotiator. He didn't criticize the official or demand his way; he merely asked for a chance to prove himself.

This can also be a model for our own religious freedom advocacy. While there is a place for civil disobedience, there is also a place for negotiation. And there is a place for *proving* that religious freedom is a good thing. If we show by our good works that religious freedom leads to human flourishing—through our religious schools, hospitals, soup kitchens, and other ministries—the government will be more willing to respect us.

Daniel's negotiation was a success. The steward let Daniel and his friends take the test, and after ten days they were healthier than any of the other youths. "So the steward took away their food . . . and gave them vegetables"—granting their request for religious freedom (verse 16). Daniel and his friends had gained religious freedom by trusting God and negotiating for it.

It was the first successful religious freedom negotiation. But, of course, religious life in Babylon didn't always go so smoothly.

SHADRACH, MESHACH, AND ABEDNEGO
REFUSE IDOLATRY

Two chapters later, Daniel's friends were embroiled in another religious freedom conflict. King Nebuchadnezzar set up a huge golden image—a symbol of his powerful empire—and commanded every government official to "fall down and worship" it (3:5). It was a test of loyalty to the empire. If any official refused, he would be cast into a fiery furnace.

This conflict was unlike any that came before. The government wasn't just pursuing a goal like national security in a way that happened to create a religious freedom conflict. It wasn't offering a benefit that created a conflict accidentally. It was putting itself directly in the place of God and commanding worship on pain of death.

Shadrach, Meshach, and Abednego would have faced strong temptation to comply. Disobedience would lead to a grisly death. And they weren't being asked to formally renounce the God of Israel; they simply had to bow down one time to a golden image. Perhaps they could comply while asking for God's forgiveness—as Naaman the Syrian did (2 Kings 5:17–18). Perhaps by keeping their noble position, they could save other Israelites from an even worse fate.

But they refused to succumb to the temptation. They refused to bow to the golden image.

When their refusal came to light, their fellow officials "maliciously accused" them to King Nebuchadnezzar, who flew into a "furious rage" (Daniel 3:8, 13). He summoned them and demanded an answer: "Is it true, O Shadrach, Meshach, and Abednego, that you do not serve my gods or worship the golden image that I have set up?" (verse 14). He also gave them one last chance to obey: "Now if you are ready . . . to fall down and worship the image that I have made, well and good. But if you do not worship, you shall immediately be cast into a burning fiery furnace. And who is the god who will deliver you out of my hands?" (verse 15).

In contrast with Nebuchadnezzar's rage, Shadrach, Meshach, and

Abednego's response was calm and resolute: "O Nebuchadnezzar, we have no need to answer you in this matter. If this be so, our God whom we serve is able to deliver us from the burning fiery furnace, and he will deliver us out of your hand, O king. But if not, be it known to you, O king, that we will not serve your gods or worship the golden image that you have set up" (verses 16–18).

This is the most defiant response to a religious freedom conflict yet. The midwives deceived Pharaoh. Jeremiah simply kept prophesying. Daniel negotiated a compromise. But Shadrach, Meshach, and Abednego defiantly declared they would never obey. This shows tremendous faith. It also shows that different religious freedom conflicts can call for different responses.

We all know what happened next. Filled with fury, Nebuchadnezzar ordered the furnace heated seven times hotter than usual and had Shadrach, Meshach, and Abednego thrown into the fire. But God miraculously rescued them. Nebuchadnezzar saw *four* men walking in the furnace, unhurt—and "the appearance of the fourth [was] like a son of the gods" (verse 25). He called Shadrach, Meshach, and Abednego out of the furnace, and they emerged unharmed. Then Nebuchadnezzar praised the God of Israel: "Blessed be the God of Shadrach, Meshach, and Abednego, who has sent his angel and delivered his servants, who trusted in him, and set aside the king's command, and yielded up their bodies rather than serve and worship any god except their own God" (verse 28).

This is one of the most dramatic religious freedom conflicts in Scripture. Most didn't end so miraculously. Just ask Jeremiah, after he was beaten and imprisoned, or John the Baptist, who was beheaded. But this dramatic story teaches several important lessons.

First, it shows that God is far more powerful than any human authority and that He can rescue us from any situation, no matter how desperate. This should give us confidence to live faithfully no matter what kind of religious freedom conflict we might face.

Second, it teaches us to put our trust in God even when a miraculous rescue isn't guaranteed. That's what Shadrach, Meshach, and Abednego did. They were willing to honor God even if He *didn't* rescue them (verse 18). We're called to the same faithfulness.

Finally, it shows how faithfulness in response to a religious freedom conflict can glorify God. It can even cause a prideful pagan king to acknowledge the God of Israel.

Still, there is one part of the story we haven't considered. After acknowledging God, Nebuchadnezzar issued a dramatic new decree: "Any people, nation, or language that speaks anything against the God of Shadrach, Meshach, and Abednego shall be torn limb from limb, and their houses laid in ruins, for there is no other god who is able to rescue in this way" (verse 29). What should we make of this decree?

In modern legal terms, this is an antiblasphemy law. Antiblasphemy laws are historically common, and they've long been used to punish people for speaking against the majority faith. They were used for over a century in the United States to punish those who spoke against Christianity. And they remain common in Muslim-majority countries, where there are severe punishments for speaking against Islam. Is this passage commending antiblasphemy laws?

Although it has sometimes been interpreted that way, that's a dubious interpretation because it's contrary to the overall message of the book of Daniel. First, the antiblasphemy law came from Nebuchadnezzar, who is portrayed not as a godly, humble king but as a rash, prideful king who swings wildly from one misguided decree to another.

Second, one of the main messages of the book of Daniel is that God is supreme over all earthly kingdoms. In light of that message—and the miracle of the fiery furnace—Nebuchadnezzar's antiblasphemy decree is almost comical. God doesn't need Nebuchadnezzar to defend His reputation. Indeed, when the next king, Belshazzar, committed blasphemy against God's temple, God dealt with it Himself: He sent a miraculously written message, and Belshazzar was killed that very night (chapter 5).

So Nebuchadnezzar's antiblasphemy law isn't a model for modern governments to follow. Rather, it's one more example—repeatedly condemned in Daniel—of the government claiming power that belongs to God alone.

But government power can also be used in more positive ways. That's what the next story is about.

ESTHER AND MORDECAI RESCUE THE JEWS

Esther and Mordecai were Jewish exiles in the Persian Empire. Esther was taken into the king's harem and made queen (Esther 2:17). Mordecai was made one of the king's servants (verse 19).

One day, the king promoted Haman the Agagite as his chief official and commanded all the king's servants to bow down to him. But Mordecai refused. When his fellow servants asked him, "Why do you transgress the king's command?" Mordecai told them he was a Jew (3:3–4).

Scripture doesn't explain why Mordecai perceived a conflict between being a Jew and bowing down to Haman. Some have suggested he had an ethnic motivation because Haman was an Amalekite, a longtime enemy of the Jews. But the more traditional explanation is that Mordecai had a religious motivation because he believed bowing to Haman was a form of idolatry. Either way, Mordecai was not simply acting on a personal preference; he was acting in accordance with his conscience. The king's command had created a religious freedom conflict.[4]

When Haman saw that Mordecai refused to bow, he was "filled with fury" (verse 5). But he didn't want to punish only Mordecai. When he found out Mordecai was a Jew, he wanted to destroy all Jews. So he told the king that there was "a certain people" in the kingdom whose "laws are different from those of every other people" and who "do not keep the king's laws" (verse 8). He thus convinced the king to authorize the destruction and plunder of the Jews.

This is a new kind of religious freedom conflict. It's not a conflict that occurred unintentionally, like when Daniel was offered the king's food. It's not a restriction on religious practices deemed a threat to the state, like

Jeremiah's treason. And it's not a case of government mandated idolatry, like with Shadrach, Meshach, and Abednego. Instead, it's an attempt by a government official to destroy an entire religious group.

In response to this dire threat, Mordecai urged Esther to go to the king and beg for mercy for the Jews. But Esther was hesitant. It was illegal for her to approach the king without being called, and she would risk death by doing so. Mordecai then offered his famous reply: "Do not think to yourself that in the king's palace you will escape any more than all the other Jews. For if you keep silent at this time, relief and deliverance will rise for the Jews from another place, but you and your father's house will perish. And who knows whether you have not come to the kingdom for such a time as this?" (4:13–14).

Three aspects of this reply are noteworthy. First, Mordecai was a realist. He didn't pretend everything was fine. He recognized the threat was real, and he warned Esther that she and her family would die if she did nothing. Like Mordecai, we should be realistic about the threats we face— even though they are not as dire as Mordecai and Esther's.

Second, Mordecai had deep faith. He believed that even if Esther did nothing, God would still bring "relief and deliverance . . . from another place." In the same way, our realism must be coupled with faith. No matter how bad our circumstances seem, we have to remember that God is in control. No violation of religious freedom can thwart His plans.

Third, Mordecai believed that God wanted to work through Esther. He believed that God put her in a place of power "for such a time as this" and that she was called to use her influence for justice. In the same way, God often places us in situations where we are called to use our influence for justice.

Esther's response is equally instructive. She called on the Jews to fast for three days (verse 16). She risked her life by going to the king (5:1). After the king welcomed her, she didn't immediately plead her case. Instead, she invited the king to two feasts and waited until the perfect moment to reveal Haman's plot (chapters 5–7).

So we see that Esther's actions were rooted in fasting and prayer. She was brave—to the point of facing death. She was wise—waiting until the ideal moment to make her request. And her prayerful, brave, and wise use of power saved the Jews.

These stories demonstrate that God can protect religious freedom in a variety of ways. In the midwives' case, He let them deceive Pharaoh. In Jeremiah's case, He raised up an Ethiopian eunuch to advocate for freedom. In the case of the king's food, He gave Daniel favor so he could negotiate a compromise. In the case of the fiery furnace, He miraculously intervened. And in Esther's case, He put her in a position of power, which she used to rescue her people.

These stories also show that God is on the side of religious freedom and able to rescue His people. But what about when God *doesn't* rescue His people? We see this in several stories in the New Testament.

THE APOSTLES KEEP PREACHING

The book of Acts records the first religious freedom conflict in the early church—a conflict between the apostles and the Jewish leaders.

Shortly after Pentecost, Peter and John healed a blind beggar—an event that drew a large crowd—and began preaching about Jesus. This "greatly annoyed" the Jewish leaders (Acts 4:2). So they threw Peter and John in jail overnight and commanded them "not to speak or teach at all in the name of Jesus" (verse 18).

This was a command Peter and John couldn't obey. As they explained, "Whether it is right in the sight of God to listen to you rather than to God, you must judge, for we cannot but speak of what we have seen and heard" (verses 19–20). After their release, they "continued to speak the word of God with boldness" (verse 31).

This led to further conflict. As the apostles continued performing miracles and gathering crowds, the Jewish leaders were "filled with jealousy" and "arrested the apostles and put them in the public prison" (5:17–18).

"But during the night an angel of the Lord opened the prison doors and brought them out, and said, 'Go and stand in the temple and speak to the people all the words of this Life'" (verses 19–20). So that's what they did.

The next morning, the Jewish leaders sent for the prisoners, but they were gone. They eventually found them preaching in the temple again, brought them to trial, and accused them of violating their prior orders: "We strictly charged you not to teach in this name, yet here you have filled Jerusalem with your teaching, and you intend to bring this man's blood upon us" (verse 28).

Peter and the apostles didn't deny the charge. Instead, they asserted their duty to follow their conscience: "We must obey God rather than men" (verse 29). They also accused the Jewish leaders of disobeying God.

This sent the Jewish leaders into a rage, and they wanted to kill the apostles. But one of the leaders, Gamaliel, advised them to leave the apostles alone—arguing that if the apostles were wrong, their plans would fail anyway. So instead of killing the apostles, the council "beat them and charged them not to speak in the name of Jesus, and let them go" (verse 40). The apostles left the council, "rejoicing that they were counted worthy to suffer dishonor for the name. And every day, in the temple and from house to house, they did not cease teaching and preaching that the Christ is Jesus" (verses 41–42).

There is much to learn from this conflict. First, consider how it started: with the Jewish leaders' jealousy (verse 17). As the apostles gained more followers, they were viewed as a threat (verse 13). This dynamic has repeated itself throughout church history. As the church grows, it is viewed as a threat to the authorities—whether a first-century Jewish council or a totalitarian Communist regime. Church growth often leads to religious freedom conflicts.

Second, God gave the apostles great boldness. Even though the same leaders had crucified Jesus just months earlier, the apostles confronted them and declared that they "must obey God rather than men" (verse 29). The Jewish leaders were "astonished" at the boldness of these "uneducated, common men," and "recognized that they had been with Jesus" (4:13). This boldness was a fulfillment of Jesus's earlier promise: "When they bring you before the synagogues and the rulers and the authorities, do not be anxious about how you should defend yourself or what you should say, for the Holy Spirit will teach you in that very hour what you ought to say" (Luke 12:11–12). In the same way, when we face religious freedom conflicts, we can trust that the Holy Spirit will teach us what to say.

Third, God rescued the apostles, but He also let them suffer. The rescue came in the middle of the night when an angel opened the prison, brought the apostles out, and told them to preach in the temple (Acts 5:19–20). But the rescue also led them to suffering: they went back to the temple, back to trial, and back to a beating (verse 40). This is a crucial lesson: we serve a sovereign God who can rescue us from any situation; but sometimes God *doesn't* rescue us.

Why not? That's a natural question, and it's tempting to offer pat answers like "Their suffering glorified God" or "It made them more Christlike." But the story doesn't answer that question. Instead, it highlights the apostles' obedience. When they were miraculously rescued, they obeyed the angel and immediately began preaching at great risk to their lives (verse 21). When they were beaten, they rejoiced, just as Jesus commanded (Matthew 5:11–12). So the story *doesn't* teach us why God sometimes rescues us and sometimes doesn't. It teaches us what a faithful response to persecution looks like: joyful obedience to God.

We see another joyful response—with a much sadder ending—in another story from the early church.

Stephen Is Killed for Speaking the Truth

Stephen was an early Christian who got into a dispute over Jesus in his local synagogue. The members of the synagogue "could not withstand the wisdom and the Spirit with which he was speaking" (Acts 6:10). So they falsely charged Stephen with blasphemy and brought him to trial before the Jewish council.

During the trial, Stephen recounted Israel's history, highlighting how they had rejected Moses and the prophets, and then accused the council of rejecting Jesus in the same way. As the council filled with rage, Stephen saw the heavens opened and Jesus standing at the right hand of God. The council then "cried out with a loud voice," "rushed together at him," and "cast him out of the city and stoned him" to death (7:57–58). As he died, he cried out, "Lord, do not hold this sin against them" (verse 60).

Stephen's death prompted a wave of persecution against the church, and "they were all scattered throughout the regions of Judea and Samaria, except the apostles" (8:1). "Those who were scattered went about preaching the word" (verse 4). And "devout men buried Stephen and made great lamentation over him" (verse 2).

Stephen's story reinforces several important lessons. First, being full of wisdom and the Holy Spirit didn't bring Stephen peace and prosperity. It brought him conflict with the Jewish leaders. In the same way, when we faithfully live the gospel, we can expect conflict.

Second, during that conflict, Stephen was bold, prophetic, and steeped in Scripture. He quoted Amos and Isaiah and didn't shy away from calling out the leaders' stubbornness. He was "full of the Holy Spirit" (7:55), just as Jesus had promised (Luke 12:11–12). In the same way, we don't need to manufacture boldness or wisdom. We can trust that it will be given by the Spirit in our time of need.

Third, Stephen's last words were a prayer of forgiveness for his enemies: "Lord, do not hold this sin against them" (Acts 7:60). Even as they killed him, he obeyed Jesus's command to "love your enemies and pray for those who persecute you" (Matthew 5:44). In the same way, we're called to love and pray for those who persecute us.

Fourth, Stephen died. God could have miraculously rescued him, but He didn't. Again, this shows there is no guarantee of rescue.

Fifth, the church "made great lamentation" over Stephen (Acts 8:2). His murder was not intrinsically good. It was unjust and worthy of lament. So are violations of religious freedom today.

Finally, even though Stephen's murder was worthy of lament, God still brought good out of it. "Those who were scattered went about preaching the word" (verse 4), which resulted in the immediate spread of the gospel to Samaria and Ethiopia (verses 5–39). Similarly, God can bring good out of violations of religious freedom today.

We see similar themes—with a different twist—demonstrated in the life of Paul.

PAUL FLEES, FLOURISHES, AND FIGHTS

Paul's missionary journeys not only took the church into new territory but also generated new religious freedom conflicts. In Acts alone, there are at least a dozen incidents where Paul's ministry comes into conflict with the governing authorities.

These conflicts had two main sources. The first were Jewish leaders, who grew jealous as Paul gained new converts (Acts 17:5). They used a variety of tactics to oppose his work. Sometimes they convinced local leaders to persecute Paul and drive him from their region, as in Pisidian Antioch (13:50) and Iconium (14:5–6). Other times they caused disturbances or used mob violence, as in Lystra (14:19), Thessalonica (17:5), and Berea (17:13). Still other times they brought formal charges against Paul in Roman tribunals, as in Thessalonica (17:6–9), Corinth (18:12–17), and Caesarea (chapters 24–26).

The other source of conflict was the Gentiles, who viewed Paul's ministry as a financial threat. In Philippi, for example, Paul cast an evil spirit out of a slave girl who made money for her owners through fortune telling (16:16–18). When the owners realized their profit was gone, they charged Paul in front of the local magistrates, who beat and imprisoned him (verses

19–23). Similarly, in Ephesus, Paul turned so many people from idolatry that local silversmiths began losing business (19:23–27), so they started a riot to cause trouble for Paul (verses 28–41).

Paul's responses to these conflicts varied, but they teach us several important lessons. First, violations of religious freedom often caused Paul to flee. In Pisidian Antioch, for example, the city leaders "stirred up persecution against Paul and Barnabas, and drove them out of their district" (13:50). Paul and Barnabas didn't try to stay; "they shook off the dust from their feet against them and went to Iconium" (verse 51). In Iconium, the local leaders plotted to stone them, so they "fled to Lystra" (14:6). In Lystra, Paul was stoned, so "the next day he went on with Barnabas to Derbe" (verse 20). He similarly fled Damascus, Philippi, Thessalonica, and Berea after facing arrest, imprisonment, legal charges, and hostile crowds (Acts 16:40; 17:10, 14; 2 Corinthians 11:32–33). This echoes Jesus's instructions when He first sent out the twelve apostles: "When they persecute you in one town, flee to the next" (Matthew 10:23). Sometimes the appropriate response to a religious freedom conflict is not fight but flight.

But that doesn't mean Paul was afraid. He faced danger countless times, including multiple beatings, shipwrecks, imprisonments, and attempts on his life (2 Corinthians 11:23–27). Sometimes his friends had to restrain his boldness—like when he wanted to address a violent crowd in Ephesus (Acts 19:30–31). Other times they tried but couldn't—like when he went to Jerusalem despite their dire warnings (21:13). Paul didn't flee conflicts because he was afraid. He fled when he thought it was best for the spread of the gospel—either because he could be more effective elsewhere or because his continued presence would endanger the fledgling church. In the same way, sometimes we may be called to flee conflict—not from fear but for the sake of the gospel.

Second, although violations of religious freedom often prompted Paul to flee, protection of religious freedom often had the opposite effect: it allowed Paul's ministry to flourish. One example was in Corinth, where "the

Lord said to Paul one night in a vision, 'Do not be afraid, but go on speaking and do not be silent, for I am with you, and no one will attack you to harm you, for I have many in this city who are my people'" (18:9–10). Because of this freedom, Paul "stayed a year and six months, teaching the word of God among them," and many people were saved (verse 11).

When a new governor was appointed, the Jews in Corinth "made a united attack on Paul and brought him before the tribunal," alleging that he was "persuading people to worship God contrary to the law" (verses 12–13). But the governor refused to rule against Paul, saying, "If it were a matter of wrongdoing or vicious crime, O Jews, I would have reason to accept your complaint. But since it is a matter of questions about words and names and your own law, see to it yourselves. I refuse to be a judge of these things" (verses 14–15). Because of this protection of his religious freedom, "Paul stayed many days longer" (verse 18).

Similarly, Paul was able to stay in Ephesus for over two years without any religious freedom conflicts—"so that all the residents of Asia heard the word of the Lord, both Jews and Greeks" (19:10). Although some spoke against Paul's teaching in the synagogue, there were no legal threats or violence (verse 9). And while Paul awaited trial in Rome, he was given significant freedom, including being "allowed to stay by himself," and he "welcomed all who came to him." He stayed "two whole years . . . proclaiming the kingdom of God and teaching about the Lord Jesus Christ with all boldness and without hindrance" (28:16, 30–31). It's no accident that three of the places where Paul was given the most freedom—Corinth, Ephesus, and Rome—were three of the places with the most vibrant churches.

Finally, when Paul experienced religious freedom conflicts, he often invoked his legal rights. We see this first in Philippi, where Paul and Silas were falsely charged with "disturbing [the] city" and the local magistrates beat and imprisoned them without a trial (16:20–23). This violated Roman law, which required trials and prohibited the beating of Roman citizens. So when the magistrates ordered their release the next morning, Paul and

Silas refused to leave and invoked their rights: "They have beaten us publicly, uncondemned, men who are Roman citizens, and have thrown us into prison; and do they now throw us out secretly? No! Let them come themselves and take us out" (verse 37). When the magistrates heard they were Roman citizens, "they were afraid," and "they came and apologized to them" and brought them out of prison (verses 38–39).

Why did Paul and Silas invoke their legal rights in this way? It was *not* to avoid suffering. If they wanted to avoid suffering, they could have left at night when God sent an earthquake (verses 25–28) or in the morning when the magistrates released them. Yet they chose to stay in prison and invoke their rights. Nor was it to get even with the magistrates, which they could have done by pressing charges with a higher authority. That was why the magistrates "were afraid" (verse 38).

Instead, Paul and Silas were concerned about the reputation of the gospel and the common good. If they left "secretly" (verse 37), everyone would assume they were criminals who had been punished justly—which would undermine the reputation of the gospel and invite similar injustice. But by insisting on a public apology and release, they showed that they had done nothing wrong, and they deterred similar conduct by the magistrates in the future.

In the same way, there will be times when we should invoke our legal rights. But it shouldn't be for our personal comfort or revenge. It should be for the sake of the gospel and the common good.

We see a similar theme when Paul invoked his legal rights in Jerusalem and Caesarea. In Jerusalem, Roman soldiers arrested Paul as he was being beaten by an angry mob of Jews. As the soldiers stretched him out for flogging, Paul invoked his legal rights: "Is it lawful for you to flog a man who is a Roman citizen and uncondemned?" (22:25). Upon confirming Paul's citizenship, the soldiers "withdrew from him immediately, and the tribune also was afraid" (verse 29).

The Roman authorities then placed him on trial in Caesarea—first before Felix, then Festus, then Agrippa. At each trial, he proclaimed his innocence. He also argued that the Jews couldn't prove their charges, refused to be tried in Jerusalem, and invoked his right to appeal to Caesar (24:13; 25:10–11). But again, his motive for making these legal arguments wasn't personal comfort or revenge. In fact, Agrippa said he "could have been set free if he had not appealed to Caesar" (26:32), and Paul acknowledged that he "had no charge to bring against [his accusers]" (28:19). Instead, Paul was acting on the calling given to him by Jesus Himself: "As you have testified to the facts about me in Jerusalem, so you must testify also in Rome" (23:11). By invoking his legal rights, Paul was "brought before kings and governors for [Jesus's] name's sake" and was able to preach the gospel "to small and great" alike—not just in Jerusalem but "to the end of the earth" (Luke 21:12; Acts 1:8; 26:22).

SUMMING UP

Taken together, these stories offer several broader lessons.

First, they illustrate the radically different way Christians are called to approach suffering and persecution. The goal is not to win but to be like Christ. That means expecting suffering, rejoicing when it comes, fearing God rather than men, striving for peace, doing good, loving our enemies, and caring for one another. Each story illustrates these principles in different ways.

Second, these stories teach us that there's no formula for responding to religious freedom conflicts. As Christians, we often want simple answers. We want to say, "Boldly confront persecution!" But the midwives deceived Pharaoh, Daniel negotiated, and Paul fled. We want to say, "God will rescue you!" But Jeremiah suffered, and Stephen was put to death. We want to say, "Rejoice!" But Jeremiah was angry, and the early church lamented. Rather than offering simple answers, Scripture calls us to know God. We can't understand how to respond to religious freedom conflicts unless we know God.

Finally, these stories invite us to keep God's broader purposes in mind.

We tend to want to focus on our own behavior—our boldness, our rescue, our justice. Are we doing the right thing? But Scripture teaches us that there is much more going on, because there is a much bigger story of God bringing His kingdom into this world. So Paul's imprisonment was not just about his behavior or his circumstances. It was an opportunity for the church to participate in his suffering and for the gospel to spread. He invoked his rights and defended himself in court not because he wanted to win his case or punish his enemies, but because he wanted to proclaim the gospel and glorify God. In the same way, as we face our own religious freedom conflicts, God's kingdom purposes should inform everything we do.

With that in mind, we can address one of the most important lingering questions: What practical steps can we take to prepare for the religious freedom challenges ahead?

institutions was often treated as suspect because it had the effect of "advancing" religion.[59] How would government funding be treated under a historical approach?

At the founding, a key element of established religion was government financial support for the established church—typically taking the form of government land grants for the established church or mandatory taxes ("tithes") for the support of the established minister. But as Professor McConnell pointed out, this financial support "singled out religion" for a special benefit, and "secular institutions, activities, and ideologies received no comparable form of assistance."[60]

Translated into a modern context, this would mean that singling out religious schools for a special benefit—such as providing grants or vouchers that could be used only at religious schools—would be constitutionally suspect. But providing grants or vouchers to religious *and* nonreligious schools on equal terms would be permissible. And providing grants or vouchers only to nonreligious schools, while excluding the religious, would be "to penalize [religious schools] for being religious."[61] Again, the goal is to leave religion as untouched by government power as possible—meaning that government funding programs should create neither an incentive nor a disincentive for attending religious schools.

The same analysis applies to government funds that come with strings attached, such as nondiscrimination rules. For example, Maryland provides vouchers that can be used at both religious and nonreligious schools. But to participate in the voucher program, religious schools must agree not to discriminate based on sexual orientation—meaning Christian schools can't require their students or teachers to refrain from sex outside traditional marriage.[62] The government in these cases argues that it should have discretion over how it spends its own funds and that it shouldn't have to use its funds to support what it views as discrimination. But in practice, these kinds of strings pressure religious organizations to change their doctrines and practices, exerting the same type of government control over religion that was a hallmark of establishment. They also represent a gov-

Prepare for the Future

Emily Herx was an English teacher at a Catholic junior high. After giving birth to her first child, she and her husband began struggling with infertility. Their doctor said their best hope for another child was in vitro fertilization—a process in which sperm and egg are united in a lab, and the resulting embryo is implanted in the mother's womb. So Emily informed her principal that she would be taking time off for treatment, and the principal offered her support and prayers.

After the first round of treatment was unsuccessful, Herx informed the principal that she was starting a second round. At that point, something clicked for the principal, and she realized in vitro fertilization was against Catholic teaching. (This is in part because in vitro fertilization typically results in the creation and destruction of multiple human embryos.) So the principal informed the priest who oversaw the school.

The priest then met with Herx. He informed her that in vitro fertilization is gravely immoral and against Catholic teaching. This came as a surprise to Herx, who wasn't aware of Catholic teaching. She also didn't think the priest fully understood her medical procedure and told him that no embryos would be destroyed. When she asked whether her job was at risk, the priest told her he would need to research the matter further. Because Herx thought it was medically impossible to stop the second round of treatment, she completed it. The priest then consulted with other clergy and ended Herx's employment.

Herx sued the church, alleging it had discriminated against her because of her sex. She argued that the church punished moral violations by women more severely than moral violations by men. In support, she offered evidence that the church had a "don't ask, don't tell" policy for enforcing its standards of conduct. So if immoral conduct was obvious—like becoming pregnant outside of marriage or missing work for in vitro fertilization treatments—the church would punish it; but if a violation was hidden, the church would ignore it. This, Herx argued, disproportionately affected women, who are the ones who have to miss work for pregnancy or fertility treatments. She also pointed out that a male teacher had gone to a strip club to celebrate his birthday and was never disciplined.

The church, in response, argued that it enforced its standards of conduct equally between men and women, that destroying multiple human embryos is a far graver offense than going to a strip club, and that the male teacher had shown remorse, while Herx hadn't. It argued that it shouldn't be forced to employ a teacher who unrepentantly violated core church teachings.

The jury sided with Herx and ordered the church to pay her $2 million in damages.[1]

How Do We Prepare Ourselves?

What does this case teach us?

In the abstract, the church had a strong religious freedom claim. In vitro fertilization is clearly contrary to Catholic teaching—as serious as getting multiple abortions. Herx had signed an employment contract agreeing to live by Catholic teaching. And federal law protects the right of churches to employ only people who follow their religious teachings.

Yet the church lost.

The reason the church lost is that it made several mistakes that increased its risk of conflict and liability. It didn't clearly communicate its religious values throughout the organization—which is why Herx was surprised at the church's teaching, and why even the principal missed the issue at first. It wasn't careful enough in hiring and training its employees. And it lacked a consistent process for enforcing its standards of conduct. Many Christian organizations make similar mistakes, leaving them vulnerable to the religious freedom challenges ahead.

In this chapter, then, I identify several mistakes Christians commonly make, along with practical steps they can take to prepare for the challenges ahead. Some of these steps are primarily for Christian organizations like churches and schools. Others are for Christian business owners. Still others are for pastors and individuals in the pews.

Of course, this book is not a substitute for legal advice addressing a specific situation. The law in every jurisdiction is different, and different kinds of organizations face different risks. So if you have a specific legal question, you need to consult an attorney in your jurisdiction.

But many of these steps can help Christian organizations and individuals strengthen their witness and reduce their likelihood of conflict and loss.

As we consider these steps, it's crucial to remember *why* we're taking them. We're not taking these steps because we're trying to win the culture war, afraid of losing our rights, or itching for a fight. We're not taking them because we fear suffering, want to avoid litigation, or need to prove a point. We're not taking them to "win."

We're taking these steps because we want to be faithful to God. Faithfulness includes being "wise as serpents and innocent as doves" (Matthew 10:16). Part of being wise is prudently assessing our risks and preparing for the challenges ahead. Part of being innocent is checking our motives—making sure we're motivated not by fear or self-preservation, but by the desire to glorify God.

With that in mind, I start with the most common problems I see in Christian ministries and businesses and the steps they can take to fix them. I then offer practical suggestions for pastors and other individuals.

CLEARLY DEFINE AND PURSUE YOUR MISSION

First, many religious organizations haven't clearly articulated their religious mission or adequately communicated it throughout the organization. That was one of the problems in the *Herx* case. Although Catholic teaching on in vitro fertilization is clear, neither the school's principal nor Herx were familiar with it. So Herx never thought twice about pursuing treatment, and the principal initially encouraged her to do so. Understandably, then, when the priest confronted and fired her, Herx felt betrayed. This made her more likely to sue and made the church more likely to lose.

The lesson here is that religious organizations need to clearly articulate their religious mission, vision, values, and expectations. And they need to cultivate support for those values throughout the organization.

This can be done in a variety of ways. A key starting point is the organization's official documents, such as its articles of incorporation, bylaws, and written policies. These should clearly articulate a religious mission grounded in religious principles. They should also include the doctrinal foundation of the organization's values and the religious basis for any standards of conduct.

But having clear official documents is only a starting point. Religious organizations also need to communicate their religious values throughout their organization. For example, churches might require all employees and volunteers to attend basic classes on the church's doctrine and mission. Religious schools might require their teachers to attend training on their religious principles. Religious ministries might require their employees to attend retreats emphasizing the organization's religious character. The idea is not simply to put employees "on notice" of religious values they should "watch out for," but to actively cultivate top-to-bottom *support* for the organization's religious principles and mission. That not only makes for a more effective organization but also reduces the likelihood of mission-based conflicts and lawsuits.

A good example of clearly defining and pursuing a religious mission is

Hobby Lobby. Hobby Lobby is a for-profit business, but its official state-ment of purpose commits its leaders to "[honor] the Lord in all we do by operating the company in a manner consistent with Biblical principles."[2] Each trustee signs a statement of faith and promises to "honor God with all that has been entrusted" to them and to "create, support, and leverage the efforts of Christian ministries."[3] These commitments are reflected throughout the business.

For example, the company closes on Sundays, provides employees with cost-free chaplains and spiritual counselors, refrains from selling or otherwise promoting alcohol, and donates millions of dollars to ministries every year. It's no accident, then, that when Hobby Lobby had to defend its religious freedom in the Supreme Court, the court issued a ruling that recognized Hobby Lobby's religious identity.[4]

ALIGN YOUR EMPLOYMENT WITH YOUR MISSION

In addition to clearly defining and pursuing their religious mission, reli-gious organizations need to make sure their employment practices are fully aligned with their mission. Many Christians seem to think religious free-dom conflicts come primarily from hostile opposition on the outside. But conflicts often come from within—and flawed employment practices are a major culprit. The problems can take several forms.

First, many religious organizations are not sufficiently attentive on the front end of their employment practices—when they're first deciding whom to hire. Whether from necessity, expediency, or inattention, they hire employees who aren't fully aligned with their mission. Herx and her principal, for example, weren't aware of basic Catholic teachings. Some Christian schools hire non-Christian teachers. Other Christian organiza-tions hire people who call themselves Christians but aren't deeply commit-ted to their faith or aren't fully committed to the mission. When employees aren't fully committed to the organization's mission, conflicts and lawsuits are more likely.

This is not to say every Christian organization should adopt a detailed statement of faith and require every employee to agree with it. Some religious schools will value excellence in teaching over uniformity in faith. Some organizations need an excellent social worker more than they need a faithful Christian. Every organization needs to decide for itself how important it is for its employees to share its faith and mission.

But religious organizations must be aware of the full scope of the trade-off. When a Christian school hires an excellent English teacher who isn't a Christian, the school isn't just gaining good classroom instruction at the expense of teacher-led prayer or evangelism. It's also bringing in a potential source of conflict with its mission. If it tries to require multiple non-Christian employees to live by Christian standards of conduct, it's far more likely to experience conflict and litigation. And if it ends up in court, the fact that it hires non-Christians will be used to try to undermine its religious freedom defenses.[5] So loose hiring practices ultimately expose religious organizations to more religious freedom conflicts.

Religious organizations can control the front end of their hiring process in various ways. Some organizations require all employees to be members in good standing of a particular church or denomination.[6] This provides the most protection because if an employee loses his church membership, the organization is free to dismiss the employee, and courts will not second-guess decisions about church membership. Other organizations require all employees to sign a statement of faith. Still others merely require employees to support the organization's religious mission. The most appropriate method will depend on the ultimate goals of the organization and how it views the trade-offs. But each organization should keep in mind that it is less risky to pass over a candidate at the hiring stage than to fire him later.

Second, in addition to controlling hiring on the front end, religious organizations can strengthen their religious freedom defenses on the back end by clearly articulating the religious significance and requirements of each employment position. If an employee plays an important religious role in the organization, that role should be reflected in her job title, position description, job duties, training requirements, supervision, and evaluation. If an employee has a religiously significant title (such as "minister"), leads others in prayer or worship, is required to have religious training, and is evaluated on religious criteria, that employee is much more likely to qualify as a "minister" under the First Amendment—which means the government can't interfere in the organization's hiring decisions.

Even if an employee is not a "minister," the organization should make clear what the religious expectations are. That means more than just putting religious expectations in an employee handbook. It means going over those expectations with employees in person, evaluating employees in light of those expectations, and including those expectations in a signed employment contract.

Religious organizations should also avoid including boilerplate language in their contracts and employee handbooks that undermines their religious freedom defenses—such as saying they are an "equal opportunity employer" that doesn't "discriminate" based on "religion." Disgruntled employees often try to use such language against religious organizations in litigation.[7] So if the organization has religious requirements for employment, it should consistently say so throughout its employment documents.

Third, religious organizations should be consistent and gracious in enforcing their religious requirements. That was a problem in the *Herx* case. The jury heard testimony that a male employee went to a strip club, showed no remorse, and was never disciplined; instead, when the priest met with him, the subject quickly changed to "a discussion of the upcoming Cubs' [baseball] season."[8] Herx, by contrast, didn't know she was violating church teaching, was initially encouraged to continue by the principal, and was fired before she was ever clearly told to stop. The process looked inconsistent and harsh, and the jury responded accordingly.

There is no easy solution to this problem. It requires sustained effort. Religious organizations need to think through matters of employee discipline before they happen. They need to decide which standards of conduct they're truly going to enforce. They need to put clear procedures in place for enforcing them. And they need to apply those procedures consistently, being aware of inevitable tendencies toward hypocrisy and self-righteousness.

Perhaps most importantly, religious organizations need to consider *why* they're enforcing religious standards of conduct. What is the point? Some religious organizations seem primarily concerned about organizational purity—as if having a "sinner" on staff will pollute the organization. These organizations tend to focus on investigating the nature of the sin and dismissing the employee as quickly as possible. Others seem primarily concerned about the organization's public reputation. If the conduct remains private, they take no action; but if it becomes public, they address it. There may be circumstances where either of these approaches makes sense.

But many Christian organizations would benefit from viewing violations of religious standards more pastorally—as opportunities for discipleship. Under this view, the primary goal is not to purify the organization or protect its image but to bring employees closer to Christ. The first response is not firing but an invitation to repentance and restoration. Of course, some employees will still reject the invitation. But it can be a more gracious, pastoral, and biblical approach. It can also reduce the risk of litigation.

Finally, all Christian organizations should be models of kindness, grace, and generosity toward their employees. Pay employees well. Treat them fairly. Care for their interests. Speak kindly to them. Even in conflict, love them, bless them, pray for them. These are biblical mandates, and they reduce litigation.

Strive for Peace with Outsiders

So far we've focused primarily on threats from the inside, such as the failure to pursue a clear religious mission or align employment practices with that mission. But religious organizations also face threats from the outside. These tend to be more varied, depending on the type of organization and its location, and therefore harder to predict.

So an important first step for any religious organization is to assess its risks. What are the most likely sources of religious freedom conflicts? Does the organization provide services to the general public? Does it rent space to outsiders? Does it provide housing? Does it participate in weddings? Does it provide medical services? Does it work with families and children? Does it need a government license or accreditation? Does it receive government funds? All these factors present different kinds of risks. Consulting with an experienced attorney can help identify those risks.

Take, for example, an organization that allows part of its space to be used by the general public. Perhaps it hosts a homeschooling convention or a job fair. Then it's asked to host a same-sex wedding or an LGBT health fair. If it declines, it could be sued under a public accommodations law. To reduce this risk, religious organizations can develop a facilities-use policy describing the conditions under which they make their space available and how they use their space to further their religious mission.

But there is no one-size-fits-all solution. And it's important not to overstate the risk. For example, some states clearly exempt churches from public accommodations laws. So churches in those states shouldn't fear public accommodations lawsuits. In fact, adopting restrictive facilities-use policies might even cause some churches to miss out on valuable ministry opportunities. So it's important to seek individualized legal advice.

Second, after assessing their risks, religious organizations should look for ways to minimize conflict without compromising their religious convictions. Consider, for example, various ways a Christian baker might minimize conflicts over requests to serve a same-sex wedding. The baker might proactively partner with another bakery that has no objection to same-sex weddings. Formally or informally, they could agree to refer customers to each other, cover for each other in emergencies, and swap business. If a same-sex couple asked the first baker to serve their wedding, he could in good conscience say yes, knowing the other baker would cover it for him.

Alternatively, if weddings were only a small portion of his business, the baker could simply decide to no longer serve weddings and focus on other areas with less risk.

Or the baker could carefully pray through the difficult moral questions of complicity. The Hebrew midwives, for example, evaded Pharaoh when asked why they weren't killing the Hebrew baby boys. Would it ever be permissible for a baker to give an evasive answer when asked to serve a same-sex wedding? Could she truthfully decline to bake the cake because she was extremely busy, without mentioning that even if she weren't extremely busy, she would have a conscientious objection? Is that failing to "[speak] the truth in love" (Ephesians 4:15)? Or is it being wise and striving for peace? The answer is not always easy.

Or the baker could consider a counterintuitive act of love. Jesus told His followers that if someone sues you and tries to take your shirt, "let him have your cloak as well," and if someone makes you go one mile, "go with him two miles" (Matthew 5:40–41). Maybe the baker could tell the same-sex couple she believes in traditional marriage but also wants to give them her best cake for free. Does this make the baker complicit in celebrating the marriage? Or is it an effective way to embody the love of Christ?

I obviously can't answer these moral questions for most Christians in their unique situations. The conflicts faced by a baker will differ from those faced by an adoption agency, hospital, or homeless shelter. Nor am I suggesting religious people should alter their convictions or violate their consciences. I'm suggesting we should examine our motives. Are we trying to win the culture war? Are we trying to prove a point? Or are we seeking to glorify God and live in peace? It is not cowardice to prayerfully consider ways to minimize conflict.

Finally, religious organizations should carefully think through the risks of relying on government funds. Over time, government funds will increasingly have hostile strings attached, such as broad "nondiscrimination" rules that require religious organizations to violate their convictions. Organizations dependent on government funds will face immense pressure to either cut back their service or violate their faith. Sometimes it's possible to find compromises that allow religious organizations to do both—keep government funds and keep their convictions. And those compromises are worth seeking. But in practice, many religious organizations should consider what it would look like to operate without government funds.

It can be done. Grove City College and Wyoming Catholic College are examples of colleges that operate without government funds. Other colleges, and other types of organizations, should consider whether they might need to do the same.

Religious organizations face similar risks from relying on other outside organizations, such as accreditors or professional licensing organizations. Religious schools, for example, may face pressure to change their convictions or lose their accreditation. Religious counselors may face pressure to counsel same-sex couples or lose their license. Sometimes these conflicts can be reduced by changing the way an organization operates—such as by providing only spiritual counseling instead of licensed professional counseling and thus avoiding licensing restrictions. Other times it may be possible to set up parallel institutions, like a religiously informed accreditation agency. Either way, religious organizations should begin assessing and mitigating these risks.

GET GOOD LEGAL ADVICE

In all these matters, it is essential to have good legal advice. Far too often, religious organizations wait until a conflict is already upon them before seeking legal advice. By then it's often too late.

Legal advice can help in all the areas I've mentioned. A good lawyer can help a religious organization think about the scope of its religious mission and ensure that its mission is reflected in all its organizational documents.

She can give advice on how to screen employees on the front end, how to communicate religious requirements to employees, and how to enforce those requirements when conflicts arise. And she can identify risks from outsiders and devise strategies to minimize those risks.

But religious organizations need to budget for good legal advice. Relying on a fellow church member who offers to help you for free but who has never advised a religious organization may help a little. But lawyers who don't specialize in religious organizations will miss things, just as a lawyer who does specialize in religious organizations would miss things in other kinds of cases. Most organizations will need to pay for legal advice, and the advice needs to come from an experienced attorney who has handled similar matters before. (My law firm, Becket, typically doesn't provide this kind of prelitigation advice because we focus instead on precedent-setting litigation in courts of appeals. But we often refer inquiring churches to lawyers who do handle this sort of work.)

Religious organizations should also beware of overlawyering and overestimating risk. Some lawyers seem to view their job as pushing organizations to eliminate every possible risk no matter how small. But every organization faces trade-offs. In some cases, it may be wise to incur legal risks to advance the organization's mission. In other cases, the risks are so small that they should be ignored. As I've noted, in some jurisdictions, churches are exempt from public accommodations lawsuits. So they're more likely to face a lawsuit with local zoning authorities over the size of their parking lot than with a same-sex couple over a wedding. Religious organizations should feel free to ask their lawyers challenging questions about the magnitude of various risks and the trade-offs involved in mitigating them.

CONSIDER POLITICAL INVOLVEMENT

In addition to assessing their risks under current laws, religious organizations can try to change those laws through the political process. Every day, the federal, state, and local governments in this country consider laws and regulations that could affect religious freedom. This includes everything from major federal legislation like the Religious Freedom Restoration Act (RFRA), to municipal nondiscrimination ordinances, to rules on state university campuses. An important part of protecting religious freedom is remaining involved in the processes that shape these laws.

That means, first, staying informed of proposed laws that might affect religious freedom.

Second, religious organizations should cultivate relationships with those who may share common interests. That obviously includes other Christians, but it might also include people of other faiths or no faith at all. On university campuses, for example, Christian student groups have effectively worked across faith lines to ensure that universities protect the right of all student groups to choose their leaders without university interference. Christians can often be more effective when they're working together with people of other faiths.

Third, religious organizations should speak up when laws or regulations might affect them. That includes opposing bad laws, asking for religious accommodations when necessary, and voting for candidates who respect religious freedom.

In all this, it's important not to make political influence an idol. Our ultimate hope is not in passing the right laws or winning in the Supreme Court; our hope is in God. We participate in the political process not to win a culture war or protect our rights, but to seek justice and glorify God. Political involvement is just one area among many where we seek to be faithful to God.

TEACH THE TRUTH

So far I've focused on ministries and businesses. But what about pastors and other religious leaders? They also have important roles to play. Most importantly, they can help ground the church in the truth of Scripture so we're ready to face the challenges ahead.

That means, first, teaching the truth of Scripture even (and especially) when it conflicts with modern culture. This includes not only explaining the basic message of the gospel but also drilling down on how the gospel applies to controversial topics—such as human sexuality, respect for life, minority religions, and religion in the public square. It also means offering a robust theology of religious freedom, suffering, and persecution. This isn't the same as rallying Christians to a culture war. It may mean just the opposite: calling Christians to abandon our fixation with comfort, safety, and status, and to rejoice in suffering, strive for peace, and love our enemies. This can be done in sermons or classes. It can be part of the curriculum of a religious school. Or it can take place in one-on-one discipleship. But the goal is the same: calling on Christians not to preserve our status but to be like Christ.

Pastors will also need to be ready to advise Christians who are involved in religious freedom conflicts. Some church members may own businesses and be asked to participate in same-sex weddings. Others may work for a company where they risk losing their job if they don't toe the company's cultural line. Still others may lead ministries that have to make hard decisions about their religious mission, employment, or government funding. It's important to recognize how difficult and complicated these situations can be.

I've worked with one couple who lost their pastor's support when they took a stand on a religious freedom issue their pastor disagreed with. I've worked with another couple whose pastor seemed to be urging them to stoke a religious freedom conflict when they probably didn't need to. And there are other times when church members are told, in effect, "You're on your own," because a pastor wants to avoid a difficult topic.

All of us have gut-level intuitions we bring to conflicts like these. We need to check those intuitions against Scripture so we're calling people not to our own version of truth but to Jesus. Sometimes that means encouraging people to take a stand and endure suffering. Other times it means encouraging people to seek peace and to love their enemies. Always it means encouraging people toward a deeper relationship with Jesus.

Finally, pastors can urge their churches to support religious freedom in practical ways. Pray for congregants who are involved in religious freedom conflicts. Participate in the International Day of Prayer for the Persecuted Church. Call local officials when they're considering religious freedom legislation. Talk to neighboring pastors, rabbis, or imams when they're facing a religious freedom conflict and ask how you can help.

It may seem like no single action will change the course of religious freedom in this country. But that's not the only goal. The goal is faithfulness to Jesus.

PURSUE CHRISTLIKENESS

There are also practical steps *all* Christians can take to respond to the challenges ahead. The first step is to cultivate a different mind-set and let go of "winning," as described in chapter 11. We need to abandon the idea that just because we're Christians in America, we deserve a privileged place in society and will never suffer for our faith. We should expect suffering, rejoice when it comes, fear God, strive for peace, continue doing good, love our enemies, and care for one another. We can't do this on our own; we have to be transformed by God. So before anything else, we must pursue a transformative relationship with God.

As our mind-set changes, we'll respond to religious freedom conflicts in different ways. First, we'll reject fear and gloom. Too many Christians talk about religious freedom with an attitude of fear and hopelessness. They predict worst-case scenarios, such as business owners being thrown into jail, ministries being shut down, and pastors being forced to perform same-sex marriages. And they treat these scenarios as if they're losses from which the church could never recover. It's as if we get an odd sense of pleasure from complaining about how bad things are and predicting how bad they're going to get.

But these dire predictions are often inaccurate. Religious freedom remains well protected in this country. In the last ten years, my firm has won nearly 90 percent of our cases, and we're undefeated in the Supreme Court. I believe some things will get worse, but we can also expect a lot of victories. Many of the worst-case predictions are simply poorly informed fiction.

More importantly, even the worst-case scenarios are not grounds for despair. To be sure, they're potential injustices to be resisted. But we're called to resist them with joyful trust in the goodness of God, not in fear of losing our rights. So we should stop speaking and writing as if we're without hope. We should stop exaggerating and complaining about our circumstances. We should be marked by joy no matter what we face. And our joy should be rooted not in the composition of the Supreme Court, nor in the caliber of our latest victory, but in the character of our suffering and victorious Savior.

Second, in addition to rejecting fear and gloom, we should reject anger and hostility toward our opponents. Instead, we're commanded to speak to them "with gentleness and respect" (1 Peter 3:15). We're commanded to bless them, pray for them, do good to them, and love them (Luke 6:27–28).

When was the last time we prayed for the gay couple in a religious freedom dispute? When was the last time we tried to do something good for someone who was hostile to us? When was the last time we went out of our way on social media to say something kind to someone we sharply disagreed with? The primary characteristic of our tone toward our opponents, both in person and online, should be kindness, gentleness, humility, and love. Of course, we also speak the truth, but we do it with gentleness and respect.

Third, when we engage in conflict—whether a religious freedom lawsuit or an online debate—we should check our motives. Are we driven by a desire to "win"—to prove our point and preserve our rights? Or are we driven by a desire to be like Christ, spread the gospel, and glorify God? When we're driven by the former, we should confess, apologize, and change our approach.

Fourth, we should stand up for the religious freedom of non-Christians. If we really believe religious freedom is a matter of justice, rooted in how God created us and interacts with us, then we should care about religious freedom for everyone.

What do we do when the government destroys a Native American sacred site or denies approval for the construction of a new mosque? Do we sit in silent approval? Or do we call our elected officials and urge them to protect religious freedom for all? It doesn't take much effort to speak up. Doing so strengthens religious freedom for everyone. It demonstrates confidence in our own faith. And it's the right thing to do.

Fifth, we should remember Christians who are suffering as if we were suffering with them (Hebrews 13:3). This applies to Christians both here and abroad. When we read about the latest religious freedom lawsuit, we should pray for all involved. When we hear about persecution overseas, we should pray for the believers there too. We can also write notes of encouragement to those who are involved in religious freedom conflicts. It can be very difficult to endure a multiyear religious freedom lawsuit, and many of my clients have sometimes felt alone. Look them up online and write them a note telling them you're praying for them and you appreciate them. It's a simple way to care for fellow brothers and sisters in Christ.

Sixth, we should be kind to Christians with whom we disagree. As we face increasing pressure on our religious freedom, we'll naturally have disagreements over the best response. Some Christians will bake a cake for a same-sex wedding; others will refuse. Some Christians will seek legal compromises that respect both gay rights and religious freedom; others will view any compromise as selling out. When we find ourselves disagreeing with fellow Christians, we should remember that the legal and cultural dynamics are complex and that Scripture often doesn't provide a simple answer. So we should approach our disagreements with humility and a desire to build one another up, not with condemnation and a desire to tear one another down.

Finally, we should rest in the completed victory of Christ. Far too often we treat each new religious freedom conflict as a life-or-death battle with the future of the country and the gospel hanging in the balance. But God is on the throne. Our eternal victory is secure. No religious freedom conflict is beyond God's control. So we can face each conflict not with fear of losing but with joyful confidence in the goodness of God. We can receive each loss not with anger toward our opponents but with hope in the justice of God. And we can celebrate each victory not with confidence in the Supreme Court but with thankfulness for the mercy of God.

Summing Up

There is no simple formula for responding to the religious freedom challenges ahead. But there are some concrete steps we can take. We can define our religious mission more clearly, pursue our mission more comprehensively, and design our employment practices more carefully. We can strive for peace with outsiders, seek good legal advice, and stay politically involved. And we can teach the truth of Scripture, pursue Christlikeness, and live more faithfully.

Ultimately, though, our calling is not to respond to the religious freedom challenges ahead. Our calling is to respond to Jesus. Sometimes that means we'll win religious freedom cases, transform the culture, and make society more just. Other times it means we'll lose religious freedom cases, oppose the culture, and suffer injustice. We have to be prepared for both. The only way to be prepared is to be transformed by Jesus Christ.

So I end this book close to where it began. We worship a Savior who suffered. He told us, "In this world you will have trouble" (John 16:33, NIV). And we should expect trouble.

But we also worship a Savior who is victorious. He is with us. And He tells us, "Take heart! I have overcome the world" (verse 33, NIV).

Acknowledgments

Many generous people have helped me in writing this book. Stuart McAlpine and Bo Parker at Christ Our Shepherd Church first invited me to teach on religious freedom and pushed me to unite my work and my faith. Kyle Costello, Nate Tunnell, and others at Missio Dei Community walked with me throughout the process, providing counsel, friendship, and prayer. Nish Weiseth gave me hope as an author and generously shared her experience, connections, and book proposal. Josh Butler gave me a jolt of enthusiasm, insightful comments, and a vital introduction to his (now my) agent.

Don Jacobson has been much more than an agent—a fantastic partner and friend. He's offered invaluable wisdom, advice, and insight every step of the way.

The team at Multnomah has been outstanding. Andrew Stoddard immediately caught the vision for the book and was willing to think outside the box. Bruce Nygren provided a wise and gentle editorial hand. (I'm still trying to be warmer and more human, Bruce!) The entire team brought tremendous energy and expertise.

Several people read all or part of the manuscript and improved it: Ryan Colby, Ben Goodman, Angela Wu Howard, John Inazu, Adele Keim, Hyewon Kraemer, Brandon Prichard, Eric Rassbach, Levi Rogers, Rabbi Dr. Meir Soloveichik, and Asma Uddin. Meg Schilling kindly tracked down sources and meticulously rechecked every note.

Three people have uniquely shaped my thinking on law and religious freedom. Michael McConnell risked hiring me out of law school and, ever since, has been a generous mentor, hiking companion, co-counsel, and friend. His scholarship has shaped a generation, including me. Douglas Laycock let me litigate beside him in cases like *Hosanna-Tabor* and *Holt*, incorporating some of my ideas and bluntly (and correctly) rejecting others. His intellectual honesty and fierce independence are inspiring. Seamus Hasson brought me to Becket and repeatedly unsettled me with his combination of philosophical depth, creativity, wit, wisdom, faith, and street smarts. More importantly, he modeled what it means to put first things first.

Working in the trenches with my Becket colleagues has been a gift and a blast. Eric Rassbach has taught me as much about religious freedom and the practice of law as anyone, all while embodying selfless humility, strategic thinking, and good humor. (He rightly requires me to add this disclaimer: the views expressed in this book do not necessarily reflect the views of the Becket Fund or its clients.) Eric Baxter and Mark Rienzi have shared their wisdom countless times. Bill Mumma and Montse Alvarado have offered unflagging support and taught me vital lessons on leadership. Every member of the staff has made Becket the most amazing place to work.

There would be no religious freedom if there weren't people who sought transcendent truth and tried to live their lives accordingly. My clients at Becket have taught me more than I ever knew about suffering, sacrifice, faithfulness, endurance, patience, and love—constantly reminding me that there are more important things in life than winning lawsuits.

My parents, on both sides, have encouraged and prayed for me, modeling what it means to seek God.

My children: Thank you for cheering me on as I wrote my "Bible." I love you!

Sarah: You prayed and talked with me about this book when it was only a germ of an idea. You listened as I fleshed out each chapter on our walks around the park. You critiqued each chapter after the kids went to bed. You gave birth to Lily in the middle of chapter 7! You're my best encourager, best critic, and best friend. Thank you for letting this book be one small part of our work together. We're one. I love you. Eighty more years!

Notes

Introduction

1. "Hosannas for the Court," *Wall Street Journal*, January 13, 2012, www
.wsj.com/articles/SB10001424052970204124204577154932994154936
[https://perma.cc/JU9Y-QG4N].
2. C. S. Lewis, *Mere Christianity* (New York: Macmillan, 1952), 65.
3. Lewis, *Mere Christianity*, 65.
4. Hosanna-Tabor Evangelical Lutheran Church & School v. EEOC, 565
U.S. 171, 196 (2012).

Chapter 1: How Christians Get It Wrong

1. Kevin Seamus Hasson, *The Right to Be Wrong: Ending the Culture War
over Religion in America* (San Francisco: Encounter, 2005), 29–44.
2. Michael W. McConnell, "Establishment and Disestablishment at the
Founding, Part I: Establishment of Religion," *William & Mary Law
Review* 44, no. 5 (2003): 2128–29, 2166–67; Kurt T. Lash, "The
Second Adoption of the Establishment Clause: The Rise of the
Nonestablishment Principle," *Arizona State Law Journal* 27 (1995):
1118–24.
3. Stansbury v. Marks, 2 Dall. 213 (Pa. 1793).
4. David Hume, *The History of England from the Invasion of Julius Caesar
to the Revolution in 1688,* vol. 3 (Indianapolis: Liberty Fund, 1983), 91,
http://lf-oll.s3.amazonaws.com/titles/790/Hume_0011-03_EBk
_v6.0.pdf [https://perma.cc/3Z2R-24W3].
5. Michael W. McConnell, John H. Garvey, and Thomas C. Berg,
Religion and the Constitution, 3rd ed. (New York: Aspen, 2011), 28.
6. See T. Herbert Bindley, trans., *The Apology of Tertullian for the Christians* (London: Parker & Co., 1890), 147. The Latin text is *semen est
sanguis Christianorum* ("the blood of Christians is seed"), which
Bindley translates as "the blood of the Christians is a source of new life."

Chapter 2: How to Get It Right

1. Saint Augustine, *Confessions* (New York: Penguin Books, 1961), 2.

2. These two aspects of justice are encompassed by the two main Hebrew words for "justice" in the Old Testament: *tzadeqah* (often translated "righteousness") and *mishpat* (often translated "justice"). *Tzadeqah* refers to "a life of right relationships," while *mishpat* refers to "giving people what they are due, whether punishment or protection." Timothy Keller, *Generous Justice: How God's Grace Makes Us Just* (New York: Riverhead Books, 2012), 3–4, 10.

Chapter 3: How to Persuade Others

1. George Washington, *Washington's Farewell Address* (New York: D. Appleton and Co., 1861), 16.

2. *Washington's Farewell Address,* 16.

3. James Madison, *Memorial and Remonstrance Against Religious Assessments* (1785), reprinted in Michael W. McConnell, John H. Garvey, and Thomas C. Berg, *Religion and the Constitution,* 3rd ed. (New York: Aspen, 2011), 53. Os Guinness called this "the golden triangle of freedom"—the idea that "freedom requires virtue, which requires faith, which requires freedom." Os Guinness, *A Free People's Suicide: Sustainable Freedom and the American Future* (Downers Grove, IL: InterVarsity, 2012), 99.

4. Martin Luther King Jr., *Strength to Love* (New York: Harper & Row, 1963), 47.

5. Of course, some used religion to justify slavery and oppose civil rights. But religion as a whole was a powerful force in efforts to abolish slavery and was indispensable to the success of the civil rights movement. See, e.g., Mark A. Noll, *God and Race in American Politics: A Short History* (Princeton, NJ: Princeton University Press, 2008), 105–6 ("The civil rights movement gained a measure of success for a number of reasons, but arguably the most important is that religious support for it was unusually strong while religious opposition to it was relatively weak."); David L. Chappell, *A Stone of Hope: Prophetic Religion and the Death of Jim Crow* (Chapel Hill, NC: University of North Carolina Press,

2004), 8 ("The civil rights movement succeeded for many reasons. This book isolates and magnifies one reason that has received insufficient attention: black southern activists got strength from old-time religion, and white supremacists failed, at the same moment, to muster the cultural strength that conservatives traditionally get from religion.").

6. Robert D. Putnam and David E. Campbell, *American Grace: How Religion Divides and Unites Us* (New York: Simon & Schuster, 2010), 456–72.

7. Brian J. Grim and Melissa E. Grim, "The Socio-economic Contribution of Religion to American Society: An Empirical Analysis," *Interdisciplinary Journal of Research on Religion* 12 (2016): 25, www.religjournal .com/pdf/ijrr12003.pdf [https://perma.cc/YZK6-A49H].

8. John Shinal, "The Ten Biggest US Tech Companies Will Top $1 Trillion in Sales This Year," *CNBC,* January 21, 2018, www .cnbc.com/2018/01/21/ten-largest-us-tech-firms-2018-revenue-seen -topping-1-trillion.html [https://perma.cc/EH82-LJWG].

9. John Stuart Mill, *On Liberty* (New York: Henry Holt and Co., 1895), 35.

10. Mill, *On Liberty,* 35.

11. Madison, *Memorial and Remonstrance,* 54.

12. Kevin Seamus Hasson, *The Right to Be Wrong: Ending the Culture War over Religion in America* (San Francisco: Encounter, 2005), 29–44.

13. Hasson, *Right to Be Wrong,* 45–52.

14. Madison, *Memorial and Remonstrance,* 51. On this point, Madison was quoting the 1776 Virginia Declaration of Rights.

15. John F. Kennedy, "Inaugural Address," January 20, 1961, John F. Kennedy Presidential Library and Museum, www.jfklibrary.org /asset-viewer/archives/USG/USG-17/USG-17 [https://perma.cc/MLB3 -94BP]; transcript of President John F. Kennedy's Inaugural Address (1961), www.ourdocuments.gov/doc.php?flash=false&doc=91&page =transcript [https://perma.cc/4FSJ-TM5J].

16. The words *under God* were first added to the pledge in 1954 by an act Congress signed by President Eisenhower.

17. Abraham Lincoln, "The Gettysburg Address" (November 19, 1863), emphasis added.

18. The Declaration of Independence, paragraph 2, emphasis added. The words *under God* hearken back even further to Henry of Bracton, who wrote in the 1200s that "the king must not be under man but under God and under the law." Henry of Bracton, *De legibus et consuetudinibus Angliae,* trans. Samuel E. Thorne, http://amesfoundation.law .harvard.edu/Bracton [https://perma.cc/U43G-D6WV]. A variation of this statement is carved into the pediment of the Harvard Law School Library: *"Non sub homine sed sub Deo et lege."*

19. Newdow v. Rio Linda Union Sch. Dist., 597 F.3d 1007 (9th Cir. 2010).

20. There is no better explication of this argument than Hasson, *Right to Be Wrong,* 115–30. I draw on that extensively here. Similarly helpful is Kevin J. Hasson, "Religious Liberty and Human Dignity: A Tale of Two Declarations," *Harvard Journal of Law and Public Policy* 27, no. 1 (2003): 81–92.

21. See Michael Hallett et al., *The Angola Prison Seminary: Effects of Faith-Based Ministry on Identity Transformation, Desistance, and Rehabilitation* (New York: Routledge, 2017), 199; Byron R. Johnson, *More God, Less Crime: Why Faith Matters and How It Could Matter More* (West Conshohocken, PA: Templeton, 2011), 101–13.

Chapter 4: Are Christians Under Attack?

1. Wisconsin v. Yoder, 406 U.S. 205 (1972).

2. Sherbert v. Verner, 374 U.S. 398 (1963).

3. Christian Legal Soc'y v. Martinez, 561 U.S. 661 (2010).

4. *Martinez,* 561 U.S. at 671.

5. Roe v. Wade, 410 U.S. 113 (1973); Planned Parenthood v. Casey, 505 U.S. 833 (1992).

6. *Casey,* 505 U.S. at 851.

7. Michael W. McConnell, "Roe v. Wade at 25: Still Illegitimate," *Wall Street Journal,* September 18, 2002, www.wsj.com/articles /SB122704335139038479 [https://perma.cc/PP5X-BA5E]. Prominent scholars and jurists on the left have also criticized *Roe* on various

grounds. See, e.g., John Hart Ely, "The Wages of Crying Wolf: A Comment on *Roe v. Wade*," *Yale Law Journal* 82 (1973): 947 (*Roe* is "a very bad decision . . . because it is not constitutional law and gives almost no sense of an obligation to try to be."); Laurence H. Tribe, "Foreword: Toward a Model of Roles in the Due Process of Life and Law," *Harvard Law Review* 87, no. 1 (1973): 7 ("One of the most curious things about *Roe* is that, behind its own verbal smokescreen, the substantive judgment on which it rests is nowhere to be found.").

8. *Casey,* 505 U.S. at 850.
9. NARAL Pro-Choice America, *Refusal Laws: Dangerous for Women's Health,* January 1, 2017, 2, 6, www.prochoiceamerica.org/wp-content/uploads/2017/01/1.-Refusal-Laws-Dangerous-for-Womens-Health.pdf [https://perma.cc/KLW4-N6ML]; Planned Parenthood, " 'Religious Refusal' Rules and Reproductive Health Care," www.plannedparenthoodaction.org/issues/birth-control/religious-refusal-and-reproductive-health [https://perma.cc/ELJ9-GCRW].
10. NARAL Pro-Choice America, *Refusal Laws,* 5.
11. NARAL Pro-Choice America, *Refusal Laws,* 6.
12. Planned Parenthood, " 'Religious Refusal' Rules."
13. Christina Brandt-Young and Jenny Lee, "Religion Isn't a Free Pass to Discriminate Against Employees," ACLU, September 17, 2012, www.aclu.org/blog/speakeasy/religion-isnt-free-pass-discriminate-against-employees?redirect=blog/womens-rights-religion-belief/religion-isnt-free-pass-discriminate-against-employees [https://perma.cc/SXH9-LJYD]. Louise Melling of the ACLU argued that protecting the right of conscientious objection to abortion is "discrimination based on gender," which "stigmatiz[es] women who get abortions." Louise Melling, "Religious Refusals to Public Accommodations Laws: Four Reasons to Say No," *Harvard Journal of Law and Gender* 38, no. 1 (2015): 191–92. She said her goal is to "normalize [abortion]." Louise Melling, "Lift the Scarlet Letter from Abortion," *Cardozo Law Review* 35, no. 5 (2014): 1726.
14. Church v. Rouillard, No. 215CV02165KJMEFB, 2017 WL 3839972 (E.D. Cal. Sept. 1, 2017).

15. Stormans, Inc. v. Wiesman, 794 F.3d 1064 (9th Cir. 2015). The Illinois regulation was struck down as a violation of a state conscience statute. Morr-Fitz, Inc. v. Quinn, 2012 IL App. (4th) 110398, 976 N.E.2d 1160 (Ill. App. Ct. Sept. 20, 2012).

16. Complaint, ACLU v. Trinity Health Corp., 2:15-cv-12611 (E.D. Mich. 2015) (arguing that declining to perform an abortion violates the Emergency Medical Treatment and Active Labor Act); Means v. United States Conference of Catholic Bishops, 1:15-cv-353 (W.D. Mich. 2015) (arguing that Catholic bishops are guilty of negligence by not allowing Catholic hospitals to perform abortions).

17. Some of those laws have been struck down in court. See, e.g., Nat'l Inst. of Family & Life Advocates v. Becerra, 138 S. Ct. 2361 (2018) (striking down a California law); Greater Baltimore Ctr. for Pregnancy Concerns, Inc. v. Mayor & City Council of Baltimore, 879 F.3d 101 (4th Cir. 2018), cert. denied, 138 S. Ct. 2710 (2018) (striking down a Baltimore law). Others have been upheld. See, e.g., First Resort, Inc. v. Herrera, 860 F.3d 1263 (9th Cir. 2017), cert. denied, 138 S. Ct. 2709 (2018) (upholding a San Francisco ordinance).

18. According to Pew, from 2008 to 2017, support for same-sex marriage rose among white evangelical Protestants from 16 percent to 35 percent, among white mainline Protestants from 44 percent to 68 percent, among black Protestants from 24 percent to 44 percent, and among Catholics from 43 percent to 67 percent. "Changing Attitudes on Gay Marriage," Pew Research Center, June 26, 2017, www.pewforum.org /fact-sheet/changing-attitudes-on-gay-marriage [https://perma.cc /NYB7-HHQN].

19. E.g., Elane Photography, LLC v. Willcock, 309 P.3d 53 (N.M. Aug. 22, 2013); Washington v. Arlene's Flowers, 389 P.3d 543 (Wash. Feb. 16, 2017); Klein v. Oregon Bureau of Labor & Indus., 410 P.3d 1051 (Or. Ct. App. Dec. 28, 2017).

20. Keeton v. Anderson-Wiley, 664 F.3d 865 (11th Cir. 2011); Ward v. Polite, 667 F.3d 727, 730 (6th Cir. 2012).

21. Patricia Wen, "'They Cared for the Children': Amid Shifting Social Winds, Catholic Charities Prepares to End Its 103 Years of Finding

Homes for Foster Children and Evolving Families," *Boston Globe,* June 25, 2006, http://archive.boston.com/news/local/massachusetts /articles/2006/06/25/they_cared_for_the_children [https://perma.cc /NPB3-QHSS] (Catholic Charities had to choose between following church beliefs and continuing to offer social services); Tom Roberts, "Catholic Services in Adoptions Ends in Illinois," *National Catholic Reporter,* November 22, 2011, www.ncronline.org/news/people /catholic-services-adoptions-ends-illinois [https://perma.cc /6YSA-MMKT]; "Same-Sex 'Marriage' Law Forces D.C. Catholic Charities to Close Adoption Program," *Catholic News Agency,* February 17, 2010, www.catholicnewsagency.com/news/same-sex_marriage_law _forces_d.c._catholic_charities_to_close_adoption_program [https:// perma.cc/M3GE-JT96].

22. Barrett v. Fontbonne Acad., No. NOCV2014-751, 2015 WL 10097972, at *11 (Mass. Super. Dec. 16, 2015) (ruling against a Catholic school that rescinded an employment offer after discovering the prospective employee was in a same-sex marriage); Amy Leigh Womack, "Mount de Sales, Fired Gay Band Director Settle Discrimination Lawsuit," *Macon Telegraph,* August 11, 2015, www.macon.com/news/local/education/article30704754 .html [https://perma.cc/V54Z-C8TU] (Catholic school was sued after firing a band director who planned to marry his same-sex partner).

23. E.g., Complaint, Conforti v. St. Joseph's Healthcare System, Inc., No. 2:17-cv-00050 (D.N.J. Jan. 5, 2017) (Catholic hospital sued for declining to perform a hysterectomy as part of a transition from female to male); First Amended Verified Complaint, Minton v. Dignity Health, No. CGC17558259, 2017 WL 7735084 (Cal. Super. Sept. 19, 2017) (same).

24. "America's Changing Religious Landscape," Pew Research Center, May 12, 2015, www.pewforum.org/2015/05/12/americas-changing-religious -landscape [https://perma.cc/7B2X-JV58].

25. "The 'Nones' Are Becoming Increasingly Secular," Pew Research Center, October 23, 2015, www.pewforum.org/2015/11/03/u-s-public -becoming-less-religious/pf_15-10-27_secondrls_overview_nonessecular 640px [https://perma.cc/ER2Z-VVNS].

26. "America's Changing Religious Landscape."

27. " 'Nones' Are Becoming Increasingly Secular."

28. For example, a Pew survey found that 63 percent of regular church attenders said business owners with religious objections should be able to refuse services for same-sex weddings. Among the religiously unaffiliated, that number dropped to 34 percent. "Where the Public Stands on Religious Liberty vs. Nondiscrimination," Pew Research Center, September 28, 2016, www.pewforum.org/2016/09/28/where-the -public-stands-on-religious-liberty-vs-nondiscrimination [https:// perma.cc/KQ88-N8P3].

29. Pew found that from 2007 to 2014 non-Christian faiths grew from 4.7 percent to 5.9 percent of the population. "America's Changing Religious Landscape." The study notes that it may underestimate the size of these groups because surveys were conducted only in English and Spanish— meaning religious groups that tend to speak a different language (such as Arabic, Hindi, or Cantonese) may be underrepresented.

30. Emp't Div. v. Smith, 494 U.S. 872, 888 (1990).

Chapter 5: Is Discrimination Evil?

1. Title VII of the Civil Rights Act of 1964, 42 U.S.C. section 2000e-1(a), U.S. Equal Employment Opportunity Commission, www.eeoc.gov /laws/statutes/titlevii.cfm [https://perma.cc/APP5-XUQX].

2. Corp. of the Presiding Bishop v. Amos, 483 U.S. 327 (1987).

3. *Amos,* 483 U.S. 327.

4. These commonsense intuitions are reflected in the law in various ways. For example, Title VII, the main federal law prohibiting employment discrimination, provides that it is *permissible* to hire on the basis of religion, sex, or national origin when "religion, sex, or national origin is a bona fide occupational qualification reasonably necessary to the normal operation of [the] particular business or enterprise." Title VII of the Civil Rights Act of 1964, 42 U.S.C. section 2000e-2(e). In the context of theater productions or television shows, some courts have also recognized a First Amendment right to make casting decisions without regard to antidiscrimination laws. See, e.g., Claybrooks v. Am. Broad.

Companies, Inc., 898 F. Supp. 2d 986, 1000 (M.D. Tenn. 2012) (concluding that a television network had a First Amendment right to choose contestants for *The Bachelor* and *The Bachelorette* "based on whatever considerations the producers wish to take into account," including race).

5. Perhaps we need another word for "necessary" or "good" discrimination. Perhaps it's not really discrimination at all, and the word *discrimination* should be reserved for *unnecessary* or *bad* distinctions based on race, age, religion, or sex. But our culture doesn't use the word *discrimination* that carefully. So it's helpful to recognize that sometimes discrimination is invidious and sometimes it's not. See Richard W. Garnett, "Confusion About Discrimination," *Public Discourse,* April 5, 2012, www .thepublicdiscourse.com/2012/04/5151 [https://perma.cc/HA88 -34XT?type=image].

6. E.g., The Universal Declaration of Human Rights, art. 18 (protecting the "freedom, either alone *or in community with others* and in public or private, to manifest his religion or belief in teaching, practice, worship and observance," emphasis added), www.un.org/en/universal-declaration -human-rights [https://perma.cc/AC48-KWMA]; International Covenant on Civil and Political Rights, art. 18.1 (same), www.ohchr.org/en /professionalinterest/pages/ccpr.aspx [https://perma.cc/3QUN-RJ43].

7. In Kedroff v. St. Nicholas Cathedral of the Russian Orthodox Church in North America, for example, the Supreme Court said that religious organizations have the right "to decide for themselves, free from state interference, matters of church government as well as those of faith and doctrine." 344 U.S. 94, 116 (1952).

8. *Amos,* 483 U.S. at 343.

9. *Kedroff,* 344 U.S. at 116.

10. Bouldin v. Alexander, 82 U.S. 131, 139–40 (1872).

11. Hosanna-Tabor Evangelical Lutheran Church & Sch. v. EEOC, 565 U.S. 171, 196 (2012).

12. *Hosanna-Tabor,* 565 U.S. at 179.

13. *Hosanna-Tabor,* 565 U.S. at 190.

14. *Hosanna-Tabor,* 565 U.S. at 192.

15. Fratello v. Roman Catholic Archdiocese of New York, 175 F. Supp. 3d 152 (S.D.N.Y. 2016).

16. Penn v. New York Methodist Hospital, No. 16-474-cv, 2018 WL 1177293 (2d Cir. 2018).

17. Alicea-Hernandez v. Catholic Bishop of Chi., 320 F.3d 698, 704 (7th Cir. 2003).

18. Shaliehsabou v. Hebrew Home of Greater Washington, Inc., 363 F.3d 299 (4th Cir. 2004).

19. EEOC v. Roman Catholic Diocese of Raleigh, 213 F.3d 795, 804 (4th Cir. 2000).

20. Cannata v. Catholic Diocese of Austin, 700 F.3d 169 (5th Cir. 2012).

21. Spencer v. World Vision, Inc., 633 F.3d 723 (9th Cir. 2011).

22. LeBoon v. Lancaster Jewish Cmty. Ctr. Ass'n, 503 F.3d 217 (3d Cir. 2007).

23. *Amos,* 483 U.S. at 327.

24. EEOC v. Townley Eng'g & Mfg. Co., 859 F.2d 610, 618 (9th Cir. 1988).

25. Fike v. United Methodist Children's Home of Va., Inc., 547 F. Supp. 286 (E.D. Va. 1982).

26. EEOC v. Kamehameha Sch./Bishop Estate, 990 F.2d 458 (9th Cir. 1993).

27. Some courts have focused primarily on whether an organization is for-profit or nonprofit. But many for-profit businesses pursue goals in addition to profit, such as environmental protection, community development, public health, or the advancement of religion. If a business holds itself out publicly as religious and publicly states that it has a religious preference in hiring, it should be treated as a religious organization under Title VII. There are plenty of market incentives for businesses *not* to do this. So if they do, it presumptively shows that they are religious.

28. This example was a real case: Geary v. Visitation of Blessed Virgin Mary Parish Sch., 7 F.3d 324, 329 (3d Cir. 1993).

29. EEOC v. Miss. College, 626 F.2d 477 (5th Cir. 1980); Curay-Cramer v. Ursuline Acad. of Wilmington, Inc., 450 F.3d 130, 138–42 (3d Cir.

2006); Leavy v. Congregation Beth Shalom, 490 F. Supp. 2d 1011 (N.D. Iowa 2007) (pretext inquiry "presses the civil court to become excessively entangled in internal church affairs and is prohibited by the First Amendment").

30. DeMarco v. Holy Cross High Sch., 4 F.3d 166, 171 (2d Cir. 1993); Boyd v. Harding Acad. of Memphis, Inc., 88 F.3d 410 (6th Cir. 1996); *Geary,* 7 F.3d 324; Hamilton v. Southland Christian Sch., Inc., 680 F.3d 1316 (11th Cir. 2012).

31. Title VII prohibits employment discrimination based on "sex," which is defined to include "pregnancy, childbirth, or related medical conditions." Title VII of the Civil Rights Act of 1964, 42 U.S.C. section 2000e(k). And courts have held that "the term 'related medical conditions' includes an abortion." Doe v. C.A.R.S. Prot. Plus, Inc., 527 F.3d 358, 364 (3d Cir. 2008).

32. Little v. Wuerl, 929 F.2d 944 (3d Cir. 1991) (Catholic schoolteacher was divorced and remarried in violation of church teaching).

33. Herx v. Diocese of Ft. Wayne-S. Bend, Inc., 48 F. Supp. 3d 1168 (N.D. Ind. 2014) (Catholic schoolteacher used in vitro fertilization in violation of church teaching).

34. Barrett v. Fontbonne Acad., No. NOCV2014-751, 2015 WL 10097972, at *11 (Mass. Super. Dec. 16, 2015) (ruling against a Catholic school that rescinded an employment offer after discovering the prospective employee was in a same-sex marriage); Amy Leigh Womack, "Mount de Sales, Fired Gay Band Director Settle Discrimination Lawsuit," *Macon Telegraph,* August 11, 2015, www.macon.com/news/local /education/article30704754.html [https://perma.cc/V54Z-C8TU] (Catholic school was sued after firing a band director who planned to marry his same-sex partner). Compare Hall v. Baptist Mem'l Health Care Corp., 215 F.3d 618, 627 (6th Cir. 2000) (Baptist college employee was ordained in a church that affirmed same-sex marriages contrary to Baptist teaching).

35. Boyd v. Harding Acad. of Memphis, Inc., 88 F.3d 410, 414 (6th Cir. 1996).

36. *Curay-Cramer,* 450 F.3d at 141.

37. These decisions are correct not only as a matter of principle but also as a matter of law. Title VII, which bans employment discrimination, says religious groups have a right to hire persons of a particular religion. Title VII of the Civil Rights Act of 1964, 42 U.S.C. section 2000e-2(e). Although that might be interpreted to mean merely "persons who hold particular religious beliefs," Title VII defines *religion* to include "all aspects of religious observance and practice, as well as belief." Title VII of the Civil Rights Act of 1964, 42 U.S.C. section 2000e(j). In other words, religious groups have a right to hire people based not only on their belief, but also on their observance and practice—i.e., their religious conduct.

38. Dias v. Archdiocese of Cincinnati, No. 1:11-cv-00251, 2013 WL 360355, at *1 (S.D. Ohio Jan. 30, 2013); Bob Driehaus, "Ohio Teacher Awarded $171,000 After Firing over Artificial Insemination," *Reuters,* June 3, 2013, www.reuters.com/article/us-usa-catholic-court/ohio -teacher-awarded-171000-after-firing-over-artificial-insemination -idUSBRE95302920130604 [https://perma.cc/32NV-FDJ7].

39. *Herx,* 48 F. Supp. 3d 1168; Rebecca S. Green, "Herx, Church File Motion to Dismiss After Case Settled," *Fort Wayne Journal Gazette,* March 15, 2016, www.journalgazette.net/news/local/courts/Herx--church-file -motion-to-dismiss-after-case-settled-9842918 [https://perma.cc/G5D6 -G8QM]. The verdict was later reduced but remained significant.

40. In cases where the religious group has prevailed, such as *Boyd* and *Curay-Cramer,* the courts pointed out that there was no evidence the religious group was enforcing its standards of conduct inconsistently. In cases where the religious group has lost, such as *Dias* and *Herx,* the courts said the opposite.

Chapter 6: Will Abortion Have to Be Accepted?

1. This account of the Quakers is drawn from Kevin Seamus Hasson, *The Right to Be Wrong: Ending the Culture War over Religion in America* (San Francisco: Encounter, 2005), 49–52.

2. Hasson, *Right to Be Wrong,* 49.

3. Hasson, *Right to Be Wrong,* 50.

4. Lillian Schlissel, ed., *Conscience in America: A Documentary History of Conscientious Objection in America, 1757–1967* (New York: E. P. Dutton, 1968), 28; Louis Fisher, *Congressional Protection of Religious Liberty* (Hauppauge, NY: Novinka Books, 2003), 11.

5. Paul F. Boller Jr., "George Washington and the Quakers," *Bulletin of Friends Historical Association* 49, no. 2 (Autumn 1960): 73, www .jstor.org/stable/41944729?seq=1#page_scan_tab_contents [https:// perma.cc/58AD-NLLM]; George Washington, "George Washington to Pennsylvania Safety Council, January 19, 1777," Library of Congress, www.loc.gov/resource/mgw3c.001/?sp=394 [https://perma .cc/Q92J-4UYC].

6. Pennsylvania (1776), Vermont (1777), New Hampshire (1784), and Maine (1819) wrote protections for conscientious objectors into their new constitutions. Fisher, *Congressional Protection,* 12. Similar protections were enacted in states that entered the Union after the Revolutionary War period, including Illinois (1818), Alabama (1819), Iowa (1846), Kentucky (1850), Indiana (1851), Kansas (1855), and Texas (1859), among others. Lillian Schlissel, ed., *Conscience in America,* 57.

7. J. G. Randall and Richard N. Current, *Lincoln the President: Last Full Measure* (Urbana, IL: University of Illinois Press, 2000), 174.

8. United States v. Seeger, 380 U.S. 163, 171 (1965).

9. Mark L. Rienzi, "The Constitutional Right Not to Kill," *Emory Law Journal* 62, no. 1 (2012): 133–34, http://law.emory.edu/elj/_documents /volumes/62/1/articles/rienzi.pdf [https://perma.cc/C973-38N4].

10. *Seeger,* 380 U.S. at 163.

11. Doe v. Bolton, 410 U.S. 179, 197–98 (1973).

12. Church Amendment, 42 U.S.C. section 300a-7(b)-(c)(1) (enacted 1973).

13. Rienzi, "Constitutional Right," 148–50 (collecting laws).

14. Rienzi, "Constitutional Right," 152.

15. Louise Melling, "Religious Refusals to Public Accommodations Laws: Four Reasons to Say No," *Harvard Journal of Law and Gender* 38, no. 1 (2015): 192 (arguing that protecting conscientious objection to abortion "has fostered the cultural norm of stigmatizing women who get abortions").

16. Although abortion-rights activists sometimes claim that the morning-after pill works only by preventing ovulation or fertilization, the FDA warns that it may also work by "inhibit[ing] implantation" of an embryo in the wall of the uterus. FDA, *Highlights of Prescribing Information,* July 2009, 4, www.accessdata.fda.gov/drugsatfda_docs /label/2009/021998lbl.pdf [https://perma.cc/6AAF-PTPU]. For many conscientious objectors, that possibility is enough to make it morally problematic to participate. In their view, it is like someone is handing them a revolver, telling them it probably isn't loaded, and then asking them to point it at someone and pull the trigger.

17. Petition for Writ of Certiorari, Stormans, Inc. v. Wiesman, No. 15-862, 2016 WL 94218, at *11 (2016).

18. Stormans, Inc. v. Selecky, 854 F. Supp. 2d 925, 946 (W.D. Wash. 2012).

19. Stormans, Inc. v. Selecky, 844 F. Supp. 2d 1172, 1179 (W.D. Wash. 2012).

20. Stormans, Inc. v. Wiesman, 136 S. Ct. 2433 (2016).

21. I address these arguments at greater length in Luke W. Goodrich, "The Health Care and Conscience Debate," *Engage* 12, no. 1 (2011), https://s3.amazonaws.com/fedsoc-cms-public/library/doclib/20110603 _GoodrichEngage12.1.pdf [https://perma.cc/BS7F-R827], and I quote portions of that discussion here.

22. The state also suggested that there might be pharmacies in rural areas where customers had no other options. But again the state pointed to no examples of this. The morning-after pill is widely available from multiple sources, including home delivery via the internet. It is also available on grocery store shelves without a prescription. In today's economy, it is extremely rare, if it happens at all, that the only way to get a particular drug or health-care service is from a conscientious objector.

23. Goodrich, "Health Care," 126 (citing report on eleven Alabama nurses forced to resign).

24. Melling, "Religious Refusals," 192.

25. Petition for Writ of Certiorari, Stormans, Inc. v. Wiesman, No. 15-862, 2016 WL 94218, at *11 (2016).

26. "Moralists at the Pharmacy," *New York Times,* April 3, 2005, www
.nytimes.com/2005/04/03/opinion/03sun2.html [https://perma
.cc/79HV-F7UF]; Julie D. Cantor, "Conscientious Objection Gone
Awry—Restoring Selfless Professionalism in Medicine," *New England
Journal of Medicine* 360, no. 15 (2009): 1485 ("Physicians and other
health care providers have an obligation to choose specialties that are
not moral minefields for them. Qualms about abortion, sterilization,
and birth control? Do not practice women's health.").

27. Melling, "Religious Refusals," 192. She said her goal is to "normalize
[abortion]." Louise Melling, "Lift the Scarlet Letter from Abortion,"
Cardozo Law Review 35, no. 5 (2014): 1726.

28. "Our Story," Hobby Lobby, www.hobbylobby.com/about-us/our-story
[https://perma.cc/3QNL-3QTB].

29. Burwell v. Hobby Lobby Stores, Inc., 134 S. Ct. 2751, 2757 (2014).

30. Specifically, in *Hobby Lobby,* the court noted that the government had
created an accommodation for religious nonprofit organizations and
the government could at least extend that option to the Green family.
In *Little Sisters,* the court ordered the lower courts to provide the
government an opportunity "to arrive at an approach going forward
that accommodates the [Little Sisters'] religious exercise." Zubik v.
Burwell, 136 S. Ct. 1557, 1560 (2016). The government ultimately
admitted it had other ways to provide contraception and issued a new
rule protecting the Little Sisters. Religious Exemptions and Accommodations for Coverage of Certain Preventive Services Under the Affordable Care Act, 83 Fed. Reg. 57,536 (Nov. 15, 2018) (to be codified at
47 C.F.R. pt. 147).

31. *Hobby Lobby,* 134 S. Ct. at 2785.

32. Department of the Treasury, et al., "Religious Exemptions and Accom-
modations for Coverage of Certain Preventive Services Under the
Affordable Care Act," *Federal Register,* October 13, 2017, http://s3
.amazonaws.com/becketnewsite/2017-21851.pdf [https://perma.cc
/E9ES-S4UX]; "Statutes and Regulations: Title X Notice of Proposed
Rulemaking," HHS.gov, www.hhs.gov/opa/title-x-family-planning

/about-title-x-grants/statutes-and-regulations/index.html [https://perma
.cc/CW3W-J3PM].

33. RFRA originally applied to both the federal government and the states.
    But in City of Boerne v. Flores, 521 U.S. 507 (1997), the Supreme Court
    ruled that Congress lacked authority to apply RFRA to the states.

34. "Insurance Coverage of Contraceptives," Guttmacher Institute, last
    updated April 1, 2019, www.guttmacher.org/state-policy/explore
    /insurance-coverage-contraceptives [https://perma.cc/2B4Q-LTHM].

35. Laurie Sobel, Caroline Rosenzweig, and Alina Salganicoff, "Abortion
    Coverage in the Premium Relief Act of 2017 (HR 4666)," Henry J.
    Kaiser Family Foundation, March 19, 2018, www.kff.org/womens
    -health-policy/issue-brief/abortion-coverage-in-the-premium-relief-act
    -of-2017-hr-4666 [https://perma.cc/W5KQ-MQXT]; Katie Rogers,
    "Washington State Senate Passes Reproductive Parity Act Following
    Six Years of Debate," Planned Parenthood Votes Northwest and
    Hawaii, January 31, 2018, www.plannedparenthoodaction.org
    /planned-parenthood-votes-northwest-and-hawaii/press-releases
    /washington-state-senate-passes-reproductive-parity-act-following
    -six-years-of-debate [https://perma.cc/J6CP-96JF].

36. Complaint, ACLU v. Trinity Health Corp., 2:15-cv-12611 (E.D. Mich.
    2015) (arguing that declining to perform an abortion violates the
    Emergency Medical Treatment and Active Labor Act).

37. Amended Complaint, Chamorro v. Dignity Health, No. 15-549626
    (Cal. Super. 2016) (arguing that declining to perform a sterilization is
    sex discrimination); Complaint, Means v. United States Conference
    of Catholic Bishops, 1:15-cv-353 (W.D. Mich. 2015) (arguing that
    Catholic bishops are guilty of negligence by not allowing Catholic
    hospitals to perform abortions).

38. "Hospital Mergers: The Threat to Reproductive Health Services,"
    ACLU, www.aclu.org/other/hospital-mergers-threat-reproductive
    -health-services [https://perma.cc/6TK7-F38K].

39. First Resort, Inc. v. Herrera, 860 F.3d 1263 (9th Cir. 2017), cert.
    denied, 138 S. Ct. 2709 (2018).

40. Greater Baltimore Ctr. for Pregnancy Concerns, Inc. v. Mayor & City Council of Baltimore, 879 F.3d 101 (4th Cir. 2018), cert. denied, 138 S. Ct. 2710 (2018); Nat'l Inst. of Family & Life Advocates v. Becerra, 138 S. Ct. 2361 (2018).

41. 138 S. Ct. 2361.

42. The states are California, Colorado, Hawaii, Montana, Oregon, Vermont, and Washington.

43. Kimberly Callinan, letter to Health and Human Services Department, Office for Civil Rights, March 26, 2018, 5, www.regulations.gov /document?D=HHS-OCR-2018-0002-69480 [https://perma.cc /5K8D-FHAA?type=image].

44. Callinan, 5.

Chapter 7: Will Gay Rights Trump Religious Freedom? (The Problem)

1. Verified Petition, Odgaard v. Iowa Civil Rights Comm'n, No. CVCV046451 (Polk Cty. Dist. Ct. Oct. 7, 2013), https://s3 .amazonaws.com/becketpdf/Odgaard-Complaint.pdf [https:// perma.cc/TT5A-X26Y].

2. Grant Rodgers, "Grimes' Gortz Haus to Stop All Weddings in Wake of Discrimination Complaint," *Des Moines Register,* January 28, 2015, www.desmoinesregister.com/story/news/investigations/2015/01/28 /gortz-haus-owners-decide-stop-weddings/22492677 [https://perma .cc/3RWL-AXX8].

3. Grant Rodgers, "Struggling Gortz Haus to Close Without Wedding Business," *Des Moines Register,* June 22, 2015, www.desmoinesregister .com/story/news/2015/06/22/gortz-haus-owners-closing-business-sex -marriage/29114043 [https://perma.cc/Z62K-72WK].

4. Title II of the Civil Rights Act of 1964, 42 U.S.C. section 2000a(a), Department of Justice, www.justice.gov/crt/title-ii-civil-rights-act -public-accommodations [https://perma.cc/37WW-HKHL].

5. Boy Scouts of Am. v. Dale, 530 U.S. 640 (2000); Roberts v. U.S. Jaycees, 468 U.S. 609 (1984).

6. Hurley v. Irish-Am. Gay, Lesbian & Bisexual Grp. of Boston, 515 U.S. 557 (1995).

7. "State Public Accommodation Laws," National Conference of State Legislatures, July 13, 2016, www.ncsl.org/research/civil-and-criminal -justice/state-public-accommodation-laws.aspx [https://perma.cc/6H98 -8PNY] (listing twenty-two states that prohibit discrimination based on sexual orientation, and nineteen based on gender identity).

8. Verified Petition, Odgaard v. Iowa Civil Rights Comm'n, No. CVCV046451 (Polk Cty. Dist. Ct. Oct. 7, 2013), https://s3.amazonaws .com/becketpdf/Odgaard-Complaint.pdf [https://perma.cc/TT5A -X26Y]; Bernstein v. Ocean Grove Camp Meeting Ass'n, Num. DCR PN34XB-03008 (N.J. Off. of Att'y Gen., Div. on Civil Rts., Oct. 23, 2012) (Methodist organization violated public accommodations law by denying same-sex couples use of wedding pavilion while opening pavilion for other weddings); Sarah Pulliam Bailey, "Farm Owners Fined for Saying No to Lesbian Wedding," *Washington Post,* August 19, 2014, www.washingtonpost.com/national/religion/farm-owners-fined -for-saying-no-to-lesbian-wedding/2014/08/19/1cfe5ca2-27dd-11e4-8b10 -7db129976abb_story.html?utm_term=.a51a90721a9d [https://perma .cc/ZGD8-VLSE] ($13,000 fine).

9. Associated Press, "Court Upholds $80,000 Fine Against B&B over Refusal of Same-Sex Civil Union Ceremony," *Chicago Tribune,* August 17, 2017, www.chicagotribune.com/news/ct-bed-breakfast-civil-union -ruling-0818-20170817-story.html [https://perma.cc/M88W-GUDZ].

10. Curtis M. Wong, "This Bridal Shop Is Under Fire (Again) for Turning Away a Lesbian Couple," *Huffington Post,* July 24, 2017, www .huffingtonpost.com/entry/pennsylvania-bridal-shop-lesbian-brides _us_5976160ee4b00e4363e11237 [https://perma.cc/9J8W-Z6V3].

11. Curtis M. Wong, "Indiana Pizzeria That Refused to Cater Same-Sex Weddings Closes," *Huffington Post,* April 25, 2018, www .huffingtonpost.com/entry/indiana-memories-pizzeria-closed _us_5ae0ae4be4b04aa23f1e73a5 [https://perma.cc/4R2C-WALW].

12. Elane Photography, LLC v. Willock, 309 P.3d 53 (N.M. Aug. 22,

2013); Washington v. Arlene's Flowers, 389 P.3d 543 (Wash. Feb. 16, 2017); Klein v. Oregon Bureau of Labor & Indus., 410 P.3d 1051 (Or. Ct. App. Dec. 28, 2017).

13. Masterpiece Cakeshop v. Colorado Civil Rights Comm'n, 138 S. Ct. 1719 (2018).

14. Complaint, Holladay Investors, Inc. v. Holy Rosary Church of Portland, Oregon, Inc., No. 18CV20835 (May 22, 2018), https://media.oregonlive.com/portland_impact/other/holy-rosary-church-suit.pdf [https://perma.cc/KEV7-E7SR].

15. Memorandum in Support of Intervenors' Motion to Dismiss, Catholic Charities of the Diocese of Springfield-in-Illinois v. Illinois, No. 11-MR-254 (7th Cir. July 29, 2011), www.aclu-il.org/sites/default/files/field_documents/memo_in_support_of_mtd_for_sj.pdf [https://perma.cc/ACB3-4F74]; see also Butler v. Adoption Media, LLC, 486 F. Supp. 2d 1022 (N.D. Cal. 2007) (Arizona adoption facilitation website was public accommodation under California law).

16. E.g., Complaint, Conforti v. St. Joseph's Healthcare System, Inc., No. 2:17-cv-00050 (D.N.J. Jan. 5, 2017) (Catholic hospital sued for declining to perform a hysterectomy as part of a transition from female to male); First Amended Verified Complaint, Minton v. Dignity Health, No. CGC17558259, 2017 WL 7735084 (Cal. Super. Sep. 19, 2017) (same).

17. Just a few examples include Barrett v. Fontbonne Acad., No. NOCV2014-751, 2015 WL 10097972, at *11 (Mass. Super. Dec. 16, 2015) (ruling against a Catholic school that rescinded an employment offer after discovering the prospective employee was in a same-sex marriage); Amy Leigh Womack, "Mount de Sales, Fired Gay Band Director Settle Discrimination Lawsuit," Macon Telegraph, August 11, 2015, www.macon.com/news/local/education/article30704754.html [https://perma.cc/V54Z-C8TU] (Catholic school was sued after firing a band director who planned to marry his same-sex partner); Dias v. Archdiocese of Cincinnati, No. 1:11-cv-00251, 2013 WL 360355, at *1 (S.D. Ohio Jan. 30, 2013) (lesbian teacher sued Catholic school after

being fired for using artificial insemination); Montana Standard Staff, "Teacher Fired for Pregnancy Sues Butte Catholic Schools," *Montana Standard,* August 21, 2014, https://mtstandard.com/news/local /teacher-fired-for-pregnancy-sues-butte-catholic-schoolsarticle _9f3df7ce-29a7-11e4-805b-001a4bcf887a.html [https://perma.cc /V7NL-BCPH] (same); Mark Guarino, "Backlash at Catholic High School over Firing of Pregnant Gay Teacher," *Guardian* (US edition), September 26, 2014, www.theguardian.com/world/2014/sep/26 /detroit-catholic-school-morality-clause-gay-teacher-fired [https:// perma.cc/W36Z-9AE6] (highlighting protests for a lesbian teacher who was fired for using artificial insemination, and citing similar incidents involving gay teachers at Catholic schools in St. Louis, Los Angeles, and Bensalem, Pennsylvania, who were fired for entering same-sex marriages).

18. This was a significant issue in the 1990s when religious landlords declined to rent to unmarried, cohabiting couples. See, e.g., Thomas v. Anchorage Equal Rights Comm'n (9th Cir. 1999); Attorney General v. Desilets (Mass. 1994). It has not yet become a prominent issue with respect to same-sex couples.

19. Levin v. Yeshiva Univ., 754 N.E.2d 1099 (N.Y. 2001) (lesbian couple sued Jewish university over student housing).

20. Patricia Wen, " 'They Cared for the Children': Amid Shifting Social Winds, Catholic Charities Prepares to End Its 103 Years of Finding Homes for Foster Children and Evolving Families," *Boston Globe,* June 25, 2006, http://archive.boston.com/news/local/articles/2006/06/25 /they_cared_for_the_children [https://perma.cc/NPB3-QHSS]; Tom Roberts, "Catholic Services in Adoptions Ends in Illinois," *National Catholic Reporter,* November 22, 2011, www.ncronline.org/news /people/catholic-services-adoptions-ends-illinois [https://perma.cc /2NEZ-QPEN]; "Same-Sex 'Marriage' Law Forces D.C. Catholic Charities to Close Adoption Program," *Catholic News Agency,* February 17, 2010, www.catholicnewsagency.com/news/same-sex_marriage_law _forces_d.c._catholic_charities_to_close_adoption_program [https:// perma.cc/M3GE-JT96].

21. "New Responsibilities When Making Referrals," *Counseling Today,* October 2014, 24–25, www.counseling.org/docs/default-source/ethics /ethics-columns/ethics_october-2014_making-referrals.pdf?sfvrsn =8924522c_4 [https://perma.cc/8F72-PTRE].

22. Ward v. Polite, 667 F.3d 727, 730 (6th Cir. 2012); Keeton v. Anderson-Wiley, 664 F.3d 865 (11th Cir. 2011).

23. Laurie Meyers, "License to Deny Services," *Counseling Today,* June 27, 2016, https://ct.counseling.org/2016/06/license-deny-services [https:// perma.cc/8933-2QCM].

24. D. Smith, "Accreditation Committee Decides to Keep Religious Exemption," *Monitor on Psychology* 33, no. 1 (January 2002): 16, www.apa.org /monitor/jan02/exemption.aspx [https://perma.cc/BR39-SMQB].

25. Federal law currently requires accreditors to "respect the stated mission of [an] institution of higher education, including religious missions." 20 U.S.C. section 1099b(a)(4)(A). But this language is not crystal clear, and enforcement depends on the political will of the Department of Education.

26. Law Soc'y of British Columbia v. Trinity Western Univ., 2018 SCC 32, [2018] (Can.), https://scc-csc.lexum.com/scc-csc/scc-csc/en/item/17140 /index.do [https://perma.cc/2M6F-MMPV].

27. Joel C. Hunter et al., letter to Barack Obama, July 1, 2014, www .scribd.com/fullscreen/232375302?access_key=key -fjNWPPZDdP2A2KUPRuLb&allow_share=true&escape =false&view_mode=scroll [https://perma.cc/SX2P-WG3K].

28. Matt Rocheleau, "Salem Ends Gordon College's Use of Town Hall: Cites School's Policy on Gays," *Boston Globe,* July 10, 2014, www .bostonglobe.com/metro/2014/07/09/salem-cut-ties-with-gordon -college-over-school-request-for-religious-exemption-antigay -discrimination-rules/goy5ep3SGqAD0yqHWp77oO/story.html [https://perma.cc/343C-QCNE].

29. Defending the ban on Gordon students, Charles Gallo, the school committee member who sponsored the ban, said, "You have to draw the line somewhere. . . . If the Ku Klux Klan, for example, made the best school lunch in the world, we're not going to hire them to make the

school lunch in the Lynn Public Schools." Valerie Richardson, "Gay-Rights Advocates Accused of Discriminating Against Gordon College Students," *Washington Times,* April 8, 2015, www.washingtontimes.com/news/2015/apr/8/gordon-college-backlash-sparks-discrimination-accu [https://perma.cc/PK8U-XR9R].

30. Matt Rocheleau, "Accrediting Agency to Review Gordon College," *Boston Globe,* July 11, 2014, www.bostonglobe.com/metro/2014/07/11/agency-review-whether-gordon-college-antigay-stance-policies-violate-accrediting-standards/Cti63s3A4cEHLGMPRQ5NyJ/story.html [https://perma.cc/PTW8-NTPQ].

31. Grove City College v. Bell, 465 U.S. 555 (1984).

32. Liz Bowie, "Private School Loses State Voucher Money over Anti-LGBT Policy," *Baltimore Sun,* October 13, 2017, www.baltimoresun.com/news/maryland/education/bs-md-school-voucher-discrimination-20171012-story.html [https://perma.cc/L23W-6GFJ?type=image].

33. The proposal was dropped after intense lobbying by religious groups, but its sponsor promised to revisit the issue. Patrick McGreevy, "State Senator Drops Proposal That Angered Religious Universities in California," *Los Angeles Times,* August 10, 2016, www.latimes.com/politics/essential/la-pol-sac-essential-politics-updates-senator-drops-proposal-that-had-angered-1470853912-htmlstory.html [https://perma.cc/JZ48-GKMN].

34. Catholic Charities of Maine, Inc. v. City of Portland, 304 F. Supp. 2d 77 (D. Me. 2004).

35. Fulton v. City of Philadelphia, 320 F. Supp. 3d 661, 668 (E.D. Pa. 2018).

36. Equal Access in Accordance with an Individual's Gender Identity in Community Planning and Development Programs, 24 CFR Part 5 (2016), https://s3.amazonaws.com/public-inspection.federalregister.gov/2016-22589.pdf [https://perma.cc/JNA2-5TVR].

37. A federal court ruled that the regulation was likely unlawful and stopped the federal government from enforcing it. Franciscan All., Inc. v. Burwell, 227 F. Supp. 3d 660 (N.D. Tex. 2016). I represented the plaintiffs in the case.

38. Boy Scouts of Am. v. Till, 136 F. Supp. 2d 1295 (S.D. Fla. 2001).

39. Boy Scouts of Am. v. Wyman, 335 F.3d 80 (2d Cir. 2003).

40. Barnes-Wallace v. Boy Scouts of Am., 275 F. Supp. 2d 1259 (S.D. Cal. 2003).

41. Evans v. City of Berkeley, 129 P.3d 394 (Cal. 2006).

42. Cradle of Liberty Council, Inc. v. City of Philadelphia, 851 F. Supp. 2d 936, 939 (E.D. Pa. 2012).

43. In re Neely, 2017 WY 25, 390 P.3d 728 (Wyo. 2017), cert. denied sub nom. Neely v. Wyoming Comm'n on Judicial Conduct & Ethics, 138 S. Ct. 639, 199 L. Ed. 2d 527 (2018).

44. Derek Hawkins, "Kentucky Judge Who Refused to Hear Gay Adoption Cases Resigns Amid Ethics Probe," *Washington Post,* October 27, 2017, www.washingtonpost.com/news/morning-mix/wp/2017/10/27/kentucky-judge-who-refused-to-hear-gay-adoption-cases-resigns-amid-ethics-probe/?utm_term=.a5e2e9c76390 [https://perma.cc/TLL2-WS4G].

45. Robin Fretwell Wilson, "A Matter of Conviction: Moral Clashes over Same-Sex Adoption," *Brigham Young University Journal of Public Law* 22, no. 2 (2008): 480.

46. See Cochran v. City of Atlanta, Georgia, 289 F. Supp. 3d 1276 (N.D. Ga. 2017) (Atlanta fire chief was fired for publishing a men's devotional book that touched briefly on homosexuality); Dixon v. Univ. of Toledo, 702 F.3d 269, 271 (6th Cir. 2012) (university employee was fired for publishing an op-ed rejecting comparisons between the gay-rights movement and the civil rights movement).

47. Bob Jones Univ. v. United States, 461 U.S. 574 (1983).

48. Mark Oppenheimer, "Now's the Time to End Tax Exemptions for Religious Institutions," *Time,* June 28, 2015, http://time.com/3939143/nows-the-time-to-end-tax-exemptions-for-religious-institutions [https://perma.cc/W9K5-2KLD].

49. Transcript of Oral Argument at 38:6-15, Obergefell v. Hodges, 135 S. Ct. 2584 (2015) (No. 14-556), www.supremecourt.gov/oral_arguments/argument_transcripts/2014/14-556q1_l5gm.pdf [https://perma.cc/VV74-S45S].

50. Bill Analysis of SB 323 (Aug. 21, 2013), www.leginfo.ca.gov/pub/13-14
    /bill/sen/sb_0301-0350/sb_323_cfa_20130820_093735_asm_comm
    .html [https://perma.cc/32VZ-8V7U].

51. SB 323, 2013 Assemb. (Ca. 2013), http://leginfo.legislature.ca.gov/faces
    /billTextClient.xhtml?bill_id=201320140SB323 [https://perma.cc
    /9FSK-6Q3K]; Aaron Sankin, "Boy Scouts Nonprofit Stripped in
    California Legislation," *Huffington Post,* May 30, 2013, www
    .huffingtonpost.com/2013/05/30/boy-scouts-nonprofit-status_n
    _3362079.html [https://perma.cc/3XP4-X67C].

52. Jill P. Capuzzo, "Group Loses Tax Break over Gay Union Issue," *New
    York Times,* September 18, 2007, www.nytimes.com/2007/09/18
    /nyregion/18grove.html [https://perma.cc/W5HT-TL8F]; Bill Bowman,
    "$20G Due in Tax on Boardwalk Pavilion: Exemption Lifted in Rights
    Dispute," *Asbury Park Press,* February 23, 2008.

53. James Oleske, professor of law, Lewis & Clark Law School, posting to
    Law & Religion Issues for Law Academics listserv, religionlaw@lists
    .ucla.edu (April 30, 2015), on file with author.

54. Oleske.

55. E.g., Newman v. Piggie Park Enterprises, Inc., 390 U.S. 400, 402n5
    (1968); *Bob Jones Univ.* 461 U.S. 574.

56. Douglas Laycock, "Sex, Atheism, and the Free Exercise of Religion,"
    University of Detroit Mercy Law Review 88, no. 3 (2011): 418–19
    ("There will come a time when religious hostility to gays and to same-
    sex relationships will be as disreputable as religious hostility to blacks
    and to interracial relationships. The Catholic Church may or may not
    change its official teaching, but if it does not, American Catholics will
    pay no more attention than they pay to *Humanae Vitae.* The trend in
    the polling data is clear, and the age structure in that data is equally
    clear."); James M. Oleske Jr., "The Evolution of Accommodation:
    Comparing the Unequal Treatment of Religious Objections to Inter-
    racial and Same-Sex Marriages," *Harvard Civil Rights–Civil Liberties
    Law Review* 50, no. 1 (2015): 104–5 (same); Martin Lederman, visiting
    associate professor of law, Georgetown Law, posting to Law & Religion
    Issues for Law Academics listserv, religionlaw@lists.ucla.edu (April 29,

2015), on file with author (Within "a couple decades," the traditional view of human sexuality will become "anathema" to "all religions, the same way race discrimination had become by 1981," and almost all "of today's conservative Christian organizations . . . will have voluntarily ended their discriminatory practices.").

57. Laycock, "Sex, Atheism, and the Free Exercise of Religion," 419.

58. Harold Schindler, "War on Polygamy: Federal Vengeance Finally Wears Down Mormon Doctrine," *Salt Lake Tribune,* October 15, 1995, www .waughfamily.ca/Russell/EdmundsLaw.pdf [https://perma.cc/66A4 -8G85].

59. Sarah Barringer Gordon, "What We Owe Jehovah's Witnesses," *American History Magazine,* January 27, 2011, www.historynet.com /what-we-owe-jehovahs-witnesses.htm [https://perma.cc/MWB7 -ZV44].

60. There is, of course, another possibility: widespread conflict that leads to a split, dissolution, or collapse. The United States is a young polity, less than three hundred years old. It won't last forever. But I don't think religious freedom conflicts will be the sole cause of a split or collapse, and I don't presume to predict when it will occur.

Chapter 8: Will Gay Rights Trump Religious Freedom? (The Solution)

1. Ward v. Polite, 667 F.3d 727, 731–32 (6th Cir. 2012).

2. *Ward,* 667 F.3d at 727, 735.

3. *Ward,* 667 F.3d at 735.

4. Professor Douglas Laycock has made the same basic point: "In resisting legal and social pressures to conform to majoritarian norms, [religious minorities and sexual minorities] make essentially parallel and mutually reinforcing claims against the larger society. They claim that some aspects of human identity are so fundamental that they should be left to each individual, free of all nonessential regulation, even when manifested in conduct. No human being should be penalized because of his beliefs about religion, or because of his sexual orientation. And no human being should be penalized because of her religious practice, or because

of her choice of sexual partners, unless her conduct is actually inflicting significant and cognizable harm on some other person. Both religious and sexual minorities need space in which to live their lives according to their own beliefs, values, and identity." Douglas Laycock, afterword to *Same-Sex Marriage and Religious Liberty: Emerging Conflicts,* ed. Douglas Laycock, Anthony R. Picarello Jr., and Robin Fretwell Wilson (Lanham, MD: Rowman & Littlefield, 2008), 189.

5. Douglas Laycock, "Religious Liberty and the Culture Wars," *University of Illinois Law Review* 2014, no. 3 (2014): 872.

6. The court in Ward's case made the same point: "Allowing a referral would be in the best interest of Ward (who could counsel someone she is better able to assist) and the client (who would receive treatment from a counselor better suited to discuss his relationship issues)." *Ward,* 667 F.3d at 740.

7. Bob Jones Univ. v. United States, 461 U.S. 574 (1983).

8. *Bob Jones Univ.,* 461 U.S. at 604. Another oft-cited case is *Newman v. Piggie Park Enterprises.* There a Baptist restaurant owner claimed he wasn't required to serve African Americans because "his religious beliefs compel him to oppose any integration of the races whatever." 256 F. Supp. 941, 944 (D.S.C. 1966). The Supreme Court rejected this defense as "patently frivolous." Newman v. Piggie Park Enterprises, Inc., 390 U.S. 400, 403 n.5 (1968).

9. Jonathan Rauch, "Nondiscrimination for All," *National Affairs,* Summer 2017, www.nationalaffairs.com/publications/detail /nondiscrimination-for-all [https://perma.cc/QM3Z-8P5L]. Rauch is a gay atheist who supports both same-sex marriage and religious freedom, and this short article is well worth reading.

10. Loving v. Virginia, 388 U.S. 1, 11 (1967).

11. Obergefell v. Hodges, 135 S. Ct. 2584 (2015).

12. Andrew Koppelman, "Gay Rights, Religious Accommodations, and the Purposes of Antidiscrimination Law," *Southern California Law Review* 88, no. 3 (2015): 651, https://southerncalifornialawreview.com/2015 /03/05/gay-rights-religious-accommodations-and-the-purposes-of -antidiscrimination-law-article-by-andrew-koppelman [https://perma .cc/CTH6-YEXL].

13. Koppelman, "Gay Rights," 653.

14. Amy Leigh Womack, "Mount de Sales, Fired Gay Band Director Settle Discrimination Lawsuit," *Macon Telegraph,* August 11, 2015, www .macon.com/news/local/education/article30704754.html [https://perma .cc/V54Z-C8TU] (Catholic school was sued after firing a band director who planned to marry his same-sex partner); Barrett v. Fontbonne Acad., No. NOCV2014-751, 2015 WL 10097972, at *11 (Mass. Super. Dec. 16, 2015) (ruling against a Catholic school that rescinded an employment offer after discovering the prospective employee was in a same-sex marriage).

15. Employment Non-Discrimination Act of 2013, S. 815, 113th Cong., section 6 (incorporating 42 U.S.C. 2000e–1[a]), November 12, 2013, www.congress.gov/bill/113th-congress/senate-bill/815/text [https:// perma.cc/4DPN-RXH3].

16. Jennifer Bendery and Amanda Terkel, "Gay Rights Groups Pull Support for ENDA over Sweeping Religious Exemption," *Huffington Post,* July 8, 2014, www.huffingtonpost.com/2014/07/08/enda-religious -exemption_n_5568736.html [https://perma.cc/VL3E-7EAU].

17. Steven T. Dennis, "LGBT Executive Order Signed by Obama," *Roll Call,* July 21, 2014, www.rollcall.com/news/lgbt-executive-order-signed -by-obama [https://perma.cc/6MDN-PTPG].

18. Liz Bowie, "Private School Loses State Voucher Money over Anti-LGBT Policy," *Baltimore Sun,* October 13, 2017, www.baltimoresun.com/news /maryland/education/bs-md-school-voucher-discrimination-20171012 -story.html [https://perma.cc/L23W-6GFJ?type=image].

19. Fulton v. City of Philadelphia, 320 F. Supp. 3d 661, 668 (E.D. Pa. 2018); Patricia Wen, "'They Cared for the Children': Amid Shifting Social Winds, Catholic Charities Prepares to End Its 103 Years of Finding Homes for Foster Children and Evolving Families," *Boston Globe,* June 25, 2006, http://archive.boston.com/news/local/articles /2006/06/25/they_cared_for_the_children [https://perma.cc/NPB3 -QHSS] (Catholic Charities had to choose between following church beliefs and continuing to offer social services); Tom Roberts, "Catholic Services in Adoptions Ends in Illinois," *National Catholic Reporter,*

November 22, 2011, www.ncronline.org/news/people/catholic-services -adoptions-ends-illinois [https://perma.cc/58XM-J73V]; "Same-Sex 'Marriage' Law Forces D.C. Catholic Charities to Close Adoption Program," *Catholic News Agency,* February 17, 2010, www.catholic newsagency.com/news/same-sex_marriage_law_forces_d.c._catholic _charities_to_close_adoption_program [https://perma.cc/M3GE-JT96].

20. For example, in *Trinity Lutheran v. Comer,* 137 S. Ct. 2012 (2017), the Supreme Court held that the state of Missouri violated the Free Exercise Clause by denying a grant to a religious day care because of its religious status.

21. For example, in *Locke v. Davey,* 540 U.S. 712 (2004), the Supreme Court ruled that the state of Washington could deny a college scholar- ship to a student who wanted to study devotional theology. And in *Christian Legal Soc'y v. Martinez,* 561 U.S. 661 (2010), the Supreme Court ruled that a state university could deny recognition to a Christian student group that required its leaders to refrain from sex outside traditional marriage. These cases would have turned out differently if, instead of merely denying benefits, the government had imposed civil liability on students who studied theology or groups that required their leaders to refrain from extramarital sex.

22. John P. Elwood, "Application of the Religious Freedom Restoration Act to the Award of a Grant Pursuant to the Juvenile Justice and Delin- quency Prevention Act," Department of Justice, June 29, 2007, www .justice.gov/file/451561/download [https://perma.cc/KF26-ZAS9].

23. Elwood.

24. Elane Photography, LLC v. Willcock, 309 P.3d 53 (N.M. Aug. 22, 2013).

25. Washington v. Arlene's Flowers, 389 P.3d 543 (Wash. Feb. 16, 2017).

26. Masterpiece Cakeshop, Ltd. v. Colorado Civil Rights Comm'n, 138 S. Ct. 1719 (2018).

27. Koppelman, "Gay Rights," 644.

28. See Douglas NeJaime and Reva B. Siegel, "Conscience Wars: Complicity-Based Conscience Claims in Religion and Politics," *Yale Law Journal* 124, no. 7 (2015): 2574–78 (discussing dignitary harms).

29. Nat'l Socialist Party of Am. v. Vill. of Skokie, 432 U.S. 43 (1977).

30. Snyder v. Phelps, 562 U.S. 443, 458 (2011).

31. *Snyder,* 562 U.S. at 458. Similarly, in *Boy Scouts v. Dale,* it was no doubt painful for a gay scoutmaster to be expelled from the Boy Scouts after he had been a scout since childhood. 530 U.S. 640, 665 (2000). Yet the Supreme Court ruled that "public or judicial disapproval" of the organization's conduct "does not justify" compelling the Boy Scouts to violate its beliefs. *Boy Scouts,* 530 U.S. at 661.

32. Klein v. Oregon Bureau of Labor & Indus., 410 P.3d 1051 (Or. Ct. App. Dec. 28, 2017).

33. Koppelman, "Gay Rights," 652–53.

34. *Masterpiece Cakeshop,* 138 S. Ct. at 1719; *Arlene's Flowers,* 389 P.3d at 543.

35. Lee v. Ashers Baking Co., Ltd., 22 (UKSC Oct. 10, 2018).

Chapter 9: Will Muslims Take Over?

1. Douglas Laycock and Luke W. Goodrich, "RLUIPA: Necessary, Modest, and Under-Enforced," *Fordham Urban Law Journal* 39, no. 4 (2012): 1021.

2. Opening Brief at *3, Elijah Grp., Inc. v. City of Leon Valley, Tex., No. 10-50035, 2010 WL 3050290 (5th Cir. Apr. 7, 2010).

3. Response Brief, Rocky Mountain Christian Church v. Bd. of Cty. Comm'rs of Boulder Cty., No. 09-1188, 2009 WL 3866546 (10th Cir. Nov. 4, 2009).

4. For a summary of the facts, see Plaintiffs' Memorandum of Law in Support of Plaintiffs' Application for a Temporary Restraining Order or Preliminary Injunction, Islamic Center of Murfreesboro v. Rutherford Cty. Tenn., https://s3.amazonaws.com/becketpdf/Memo-in-Support-of-TRO-07.18.12.pdf.pdf [https://perma.cc/7H2M-5P6N].

5. 146 Cong. Rec. S7774 (daily ed. July 27, 2000) (joint statement of Sen. Hatch and Sen. Kennedy), www.gpo.gov/fdsys/pkg/CREC-2000-07-27/pdf/CREC-2000-07-27-pt1-PgS7774.pdf [https://perma.cc/SPH8-2RB9].

6. Haven Shores Community Church v. City of Grand Haven, Becket,

www.becketlaw.org/case/haven-shores-community-church-v-city-grand
-haven [https://perma.cc/ZHF5-SFT3].

7. Midrash Sephardi, Inc. v. Town of Surfside, 366 F.3d 1214 (11th Cir. 2004); see also Consent Decree, United States v. Vill. of Airmont, No. 05-cv-5520 (LAK) (PED) (S.D.N.Y. May 6, 2011), ECF No. 53, www .justice.gov/crt/about/hce/documents/airmontsettle.pdf [https://perma .cc/4873-XXT6].

8. Guru Nanak Sikh Soc'y of Yuba City v. Cty. of Sutter, 456 F.3d 978 (9th Cir. 2006).

9. Islamic Soc'y of Basking Ridge v. Twp. of Bernards, 226 F. Supp. 3d 320 (D.N.J. 2016).

10. *Midrash Sephardi*, 366 F.3d at 1214.

11. *Midrash Sephardi*, 366 F.3d at 1230–31.

12. Elijah Grp., Inc. v. City of Leon Valley, Tex., 643 F.3d 419, 424 (5th Cir. 2011).

13. Hobby Lobby Stores, Inc. v. Sebelius, 723 F.3d 1114, 1141 (10th Cir. 2013).

14. When the case reached the Supreme Court, the key cases became only more diverse, with the court relying on victories for Jews, Jehovah's Witnesses, Seventh-day Adventists, and a Brazilian spiritist sect, among others. Burwell v. Hobby Lobby Stores, Inc., 134 S. Ct. 2751 (2014) (citing *Crown Kosher, Braunfeld, Thomas, Sherbert,* and *O Centro*).

15. Tenafly Eruv Ass'n v. Borough of Tenafly, 309 F.3d 144 (3d Cir. 2002).

16. Church of the Lukumi Babalu Aye, Inc. v. City of Hialeah, 508 U.S. 520 (1993).

17. Fraternal Order of Police v. City of Newark, 170 F.3d 359 (3d Cir. 1999).

18. Martin Niemöller, "First They Came for the Socialists . . . ," Holocaust Encyclopedia, https://encyclopedia.ushmm.org/content/en/article /martin-niemoeller-first-they-came-for-the-socialists [https://perma .cc/RY23-SQRM].

19. The Becket Fund, open letter in support of Murfreesboro mosque, July 18, 2012, https://s3.amazonaws.com/becketpdf/MM-FINAL-LIST-v6 -1-2.docx.pdf [https://perma.cc/F9JN-XYSQ].

20. Declaration on Religious Freedom, *Dignitatis Humanae,* Vatican (December 7, 1965), www.vatican.va/archive/hist_councils/ii_vatican _council/documents/vat-ii_decl_19651207_dignitatis-humanae_en .html [https://perma.cc/4LEP-Y87N].

21. "The Baptist Faith and Message," Southern Baptist Convention ("The state owes to every church protection and full freedom in the pursuit of its spiritual ends. In providing for such freedom no ecclesiastical group or denomination should be favored by the state more than others."), www.imb.org/baptist-faith-and-message [https://perma.cc/2BMW -SC9E].

22. Roger Williams, *The Bloudy Tenent of Persecution for Cause of Conscience Discussed: and Mr. Cotton's Letter Examined and Answered,* ed. Edward Bean Underhill (London: J. Haddon, 1848), 2. I would have liked to use Williams's title for this book, but alas, the editors would not let me.

23. Mark Woods, "Southern Baptist Mission Trustee Resigns Rather Than 'Support False Religion,'" *Christian Today,* January 30, 2017, www .christiantoday.com/article/southern-baptist-mission-trustee-resigns -rather-than-support-false-religion/104253.htm [https://perma.cc/9CS5 -TGUW].

24. James Madison, *Memorial and Remonstrance Against Religious Assessments* (1785), reprinted in Michael W. McConnell, John H. Garvey, and Thomas C. Berg, *Religion and the Constitution,* 3rd ed. (New York: Aspen, 2011), 53.

25. James Palmer, "China's Muslims Brace for Attacks," *Foreign Policy,* January 5, 2019, https://foreignpolicy.com/2019/01/05/chinas-muslims -brace-for-attacks [https://perma.cc/RT7B-J5NU].

26. Asma T. Uddin, "The Latest Attack on Islam: It's Not a Religion," *New York Times,* September 26, 2018, www.nytimes.com/2018/09/26 /opinion/islamophobia-muslim-religion-politics.html [https://perma .cc/C3JQ-TGLF] (collecting examples).

27. Madison, *Memorial and Remonstrance,* 51. Madison drew this definition from the 1776 Virginia Declaration of Rights.

28. Catholic League for Religious & Civil Rights v. City & Cty. of San Francisco, 624 F.3d 1043, 1047 (9th Cir. 2010).

Chapter 10: *Will God Become a Dirty Word?*

1. Kondrat'yev v. City of Pensacola, Fla., No. 3:16CV195-RV/CJK, 2017 WL 4334248, at *3 (N.D. Fla. June 19, 2017), aff'd, 903 F.3d 1169 (11th Cir. 2018).
2. *Kondrat'yev,* 2017 WL 4334248 at *11.
3. American Legion v. American Humanist Association, No. 17-1717 (S. Ct.).
4. Michael W. McConnell, "Establishment and Disestablishment at the Founding, Part I: Establishment of Religion," *William & Mary Law Review* 44, no. 5 (2003): 2107. This article is one of the leading explanations of what an establishment of religion was at the time of the founding, and I draw on it heavily in this chapter.
5. McConnell, "Establishment and Disestablishment," 2107.
6. McConnell, "Establishment and Disestablishment," 2131.
7. McConnell, "Establishment and Disestablishment," 2118.
8. McConnell, "Establishment and Disestablishment," 2135, 2137–38.
9. McConnell, "Establishment and Disestablishment," 2144–45.
10. John Cotton and Roger Williams, *The Bloudy Tenet, Washed and Made White in the Bloud of the Lambe* (1647), quoted in McConnell, "Establishment and Disestablishment," 2181.
11. Thomas Hobbes, quoted in Michael W. McConnell, Thomas C. Berg, and Christopher C. Lund, *Religion and the Constitution,* 4th ed. (New York: Wolters Kluwer, 2016), *Leviathan* (1651), chapter 42.
12. Michael W. McConnell, "Establishment and Toleration in Edmund Burke's 'Constitution of Freedom,'" *Supreme Court Review* (1995): 393, 443.
13. McConnell, "Establishment and Disestablishment," 2187 (quoting Bishops and Clergy of Canterbury Constitutions and Canons Ecclesiastical, Canon 1, 1604).
14. McConnell, "Establishment and Disestablishment," 2188–89.

15. Massachusetts Constitution of 1780, art. III, quoted in McConnell, "Establishment and Disestablishment," 2197.

16. Kevin Seamus Hasson, *The Right to Be Wrong: Ending the Culture War over Religion in America* (San Francisco: Encounter, 2005), 29–44.

17. McConnell, "Establishment and Disestablishment," 2165–66.

18. McConnell, "Establishment and Disestablishment," 2164.

19. McConnell, "Establishment and Disestablishment," 2133.

20. McConnell, "Establishment and Disestablishment," 2206. Evangelicals also had a theological objection to an establishment of religion. They believed that true faith had to be a voluntary response to God. As Elisha Williams, a congregationalist minister inspired by the Great Awakening, wrote, "No action is a religious action without understanding and choice in the agent." Elisha Williams, *The Essential Rights and Liberties of Protestants* (1744), quoted in Michael W. McConnell, John H. Garvey, and Thomas C. Berg, *Religion and the Constitution*, 3rd ed. (New York: Aspen, 2011), 36. Thus, using the power of government to promote religion was inconsistent with the free exercise of religion. As a 1776 Baptist declaration put it, "Farewel to 'the free exercise of Religion,' if civil Rulers go so far out of their Sphere as to take the Care and Management of *religious Affairs* upon them!" Declaration of the Virginia Association of Baptists, Founders Online, December 25, 1776, https://founders.archives.gov/documents/Jefferson/01-01-02-0249 [https://perma.cc/56T7-7CHF].

21. David Hume, *The History of England from the Invasion of Julius Caesar to the Revolution in 1688,* vol. 3, (Indianapolis, IN: Liberty Fund, 1983), https://oll.libertyfund.org/titles/hume-the-history-of-england-vol-3 [https://perma.cc/3Z2R-24W3].

22. Hume, *History of England.*

23. "From James Madison to Robert Walsh Jr., 2 March 1819," Founders Online, https://founders.archives.gov/documents/Madison/04-01-02-0378 [https://perma.cc/S6YB-DUCK]. Similarly, Adam Smith argued in *The Wealth of Nations* that government-supported clergy "neglected to keep up the fervor of faith," "g[ave] themselves up to

indolence," and were "altogether incapable of making any vigorous exertion in defence even of their own establishment." Adam Smith, *The Wealth of Nations* (New York: Collier, 1902), 172. By contrast, Alexis de Tocqueville, a Frenchman who traveled extensively in America, "reported that religion was stronger in America than in any other country, and attributed this strength to the separation between church and state." McConnell, "Establishment and Disestablishment," 2206–7.

24. Dalia Fahmy, "Americans Are Far More Religious Than Adults in Other Wealthy Nations," Pew Research Center, July 31, 2018, www .pewresearch.org/fact-tank/2018/07/31/americans-are-far-more-religious -than-adults-in-other-wealthy-nations [https://perma.cc/EF64-UZ3P].

25. McConnell, "Establishment and Disestablishment," 2155.

26. McConnell, "Establishment and Disestablishment," 2155–56, 2195.

27. John Adams, quoted in William G. McLoughlin, *New England Dissent, 1630–1833: The Baptists and the Separation of Church and State,* vol. 1 (Cambridge, MA: Harvard University Press, 1971), 560.

28. Michael W. McConnell, "The Origins and Historical Understanding of Free Exercise of Religion," *Harvard Law Review* 103, no. 7 (1990): 1482.

29. Of course, not everyone agrees with this interpretation of the history. See Donald L. Drakeman, *Church, State, and Original Intent* (Cambridge: Cambridge University Press, 2010), 156–95 (surveying the scholarly debate).

30. McConnell, "Establishment and Disestablishment," 2119.

31. McConnell, "Establishment and Disestablishment," 2207.

32. Cf. Permoli v. Municipality, No. 1, New Orleans, 44 U.S. 589 (1845) (concluding that the Free Exercise Clause of the First Amendment does not restrain acts of state or local government).

33. McGowan v. Maryland, 366 U.S. 420 (1961); Walz v. Tax Comm'n, 397 U.S. 664 (1970); Marsh v. Chambers, 463 U.S. 783 (1983); Town of Greece v. Galloway, 572 U.S. 565 (2014).

34. Engel v. Vitale, 370 U.S. 421 (1962); Sch. Dist. of Abington Twp. v. Schempp, 374 U.S. 203 (1963); Lee v. Weisman, 505 U.S. 577 (1992); Santa Fe Indep. Sch. Dist. v. Doe, 530 U.S. 290 (2000).

35. Comm. for Public Educ. & Religious Liberty v. Nyquist, 413 U.S. 756 (1973).

36. Cty. of Allegheny v. ACLU Greater Pittsburgh Chapter, 492 U.S. 573 (1989); McCreary Cty. v. ACLU, 545 U.S. 844 (2005).

37. Zorach v. Clauson, 343 U.S. 306 (1952).

38. Mueller v. Allen, 463 U.S. 388 (1983).

39. Lynch v. Donnelly, 465 U.S. 668 (2002); Van Orden v. Perry, 545 U.S. 677 (2005).

40. *Lynch,* 465 U.S. 668; *Allegheny,* 492 U.S. 573.

41. Compare Bd. of Educ. v. Allen, 392 U.S. 236 (1968) (upholding loans of textbooks) with Wolman v. Walter, 433 U.S. 229 (1977) (striking down loans of maps); compare Everson v. Bd. of Educ., 330 U.S. 1, 17 (1947) (allowing the government to pay for bus rides to religious schools) with *Wolman,* 433 U.S. at 252–55 (forbidding the government to pay for bus rides from religious schools to field trips).

42. Lamb's Chapel v. Ctr. Moriches Union Free Sch. Dist., 508 U.S. 384, 399 (1993).

43. *Lamb's Chapel,* 508 U.S. at 398.

44. Elk Grove v. Newdow, 542 U.S. 1 (2004) (Thomas, J., concurring).

45. *Town of Greece,* 134 S. Ct. at 1819 (quoting *Allegheny,* 492 U.S. at 670).

46. *Town of Greece,* 134 S. Ct. at 1813.

47. Trunk v. City of San Diego, 629 F.3d 1099, 1101 (9th Cir. 2011).

48. Michael W. McConnell, "Religious Freedom at a Crossroads," *University of Chicago Law Review* 59, no. 1 (1992): 189.

49. McConnell, "Religious Freedom," 189.

50. McConnell, "Religious Freedom," 193.

51. McConnell, "Religious Freedom," 191–94.

52. *Engel,* 370 U.S. at 422.

53. Wallace v. Jaffree, 472 U.S. 38 (1985).

54. Santa Fe Indep. Sch. Dist. v. Doe, 530 U.S. 290 (2000).

55. *Engel,* 370 U.S. at 426.

56. *Engel,* 370 U.S. at 429.

57. Moss v. Spartanburg Cty. Sch. Dist., 683 F.3d 599 (4th Cir. 2012).

58. Similarly, if a college professor can discuss her personal opinions on various subjects with students outside class, she should be free to discuss her religious opinions too; if a high school valedictorian can address various controversial subjects in his graduation speech, he should be allowed to discuss religion too. McConnell, "Religious Freedom," 187.

59. *Nyquist,* 413 U.S. 756.

60. McConnell, "Religious Freedom," 183.

61. McConnell, "Religious Freedom," 183.

62. Liz Bowie, "Private School Loses State Voucher Money over Anti-LGBT Policy," *Baltimore Sun,* October 13, 2017, www.baltimoresun.com /news/maryland/education/bs-md-school-voucher-discrimination -20171012-story.html [https://perma.cc/L23W-6GFJ?type=image].

63. James Madison, *Memorial and Remonstrance Against Religious Assessments* (1785), reprinted in Michael W. McConnell, John H. Garvey, and Thomas C. Berg, *Religion and the Constitution,* 3rd ed. (New York: Aspen, 2011), 53.

64. *Zorach,* 343 U.S. at 313.

Chapter 11: Let Go of Winning

1. The baker in the *Masterpiece* case had yet another view: he believed he could sell a premade cake to any customer, including for a same-sex wedding, but he couldn't use his artistic abilities to design a custom-made cake for a same-sex wedding because he would then be celebrating the wedding. Masterpiece Cakeshop, Ltd. v. Colorado Civil Rights Comm'n, 138 S. Ct. 1719 (2018).

Chapter 12: Learn from Scripture

1. The Bible has earlier examples of people being persecuted for their faith—such as Abel being killed by Cain (Genesis 4), Lot being attacked by the men of Sodom (Genesis 19), and Joseph being sold by his brothers (Genesis 37). But this is the first conflict between the commands of God and the commands of civil government.

2. It is not clear in every passage that the deception is approved. But the midwives were blessed (Exodus 1:20), and Rahab was commended for her faith (Hebrews 11:31).

3. The prayers were not entirely bitter. Some parts reflected rejoicing: "Sing to the LORD; praise the LORD! For he has delivered the life of the needy from the hand of evildoers" (Jeremiah 20:13). Others declared faith: "The LORD is with me as a dread warrior; therefore my persecutors will stumble; they will not overcome me" (verse 11). But the overall tone was one of sincere pain.

4. Centuries later, Mordecai's refusal to bow to Haman was echoed by William Penn, a Quaker, who in the 1600s was famously jailed for refusing to remove his hat as a sign of respect for a British court. Penn's case prompted North Carolina and Maryland to enact religious accommodations for Quakers. Michael W. McConnell, "The Origins and Historical Understanding of Free Exercise of Religion," *Harvard Law Review* 103, no. 7 (1990): 1472.

Chapter 13: Prepare for the Future

1. Herx v. Diocese of Ft. Wayne-S. Bend, Inc., No. 1:12-cv-122 RLM, 2015 WL 1013783, at *1 (N.D. Ind. Mar. 9, 2015). The judge later reduced the award to $353,269.66.

2. Brief for Respondents at 8, Burwell v. Hobby Lobby Stores, Inc., 134 S. Ct. 2751 (2014) (No. 13-354), https://s3.amazonaws.com/becketpdf/13 -354-bs.pdf [https://perma.cc/DJ7W-MAPR].

3. Brief for Respondents at 8, *Hobby Lobby*.

4. Burwell v. Hobby Lobby Stores, Inc., 134 S. Ct. 2751 (2014).

5. In both *Hosanna-Tabor* and *Herx,* for example, the teachers emphasized that the schools hired non-Lutheran and non-Catholic teachers. See Brief for Respondent Cheryl Perich, Hosanna-Tabor Evangelical Lutheran Church & Sch. v. EEOC, No. 10-553, 2011 WL 3380507, at *5 (2011) ("Hosanna-Tabor . . . did not require its teachers . . . to be Lutheran"), www.americanbar.org/content/dam/aba/publishing /previewbriefs/Other_Brief_Updates/10-553_respondentcherylperich

.authcheckdam.pdf [https://perma.cc/38GS-FW7G]; Plaintiff's Response in Opposition to Defendants' Motion for Summary Judgment at 14, Herx v. Diocese of Ft. Wayne-S. Bend, Inc., No. 1:12-cv-122, 2014 WL 7692598 (N.D. Ind. June 12, 2014) ("Defendants permit the hiring of non-Catholic teachers.").

6. In *Amos,* for example, the LDS Church required all employees to have a temple recommend. Corp. of the Presiding Bishop v. Amos, 483 U.S. 327, 330 (1987). Calvin College requires all faculty to be "active members in good standing of a congregation in the Christian Reformed Church or a denomination in 'ecclesiastical fellowship' with the CRC as defined by the CRC Synod." "Faculty Membership Requirements: A Guide for Prospective Faculty," Calvin College, www.calvin.edu/admin /provost/facdocs/fac-requirements.htm [https://perma.cc/MF4H-GFF2].

7. E.g., Tomic v. Catholic Diocese of Peoria, 442 F.3d 1036, 1041–42 (7th Cir. 2006) (rejecting this argument).

8. *Herx,* 2015 WL 1013783 at *2.